THE NORBERT E

B

THE NORBERT ELIAS READER

A Biographical Selection

Edited by

Johan Goudsblom

and

Stephen Mennell

BLACKWELL
Publishers

First published 1998

2 4 6 8 10 9 7 5 3 1

Blackwell Publishers Ltd
108 Cowley Road
Oxford OX4 1JF
UK

Blackwell Publishers Inc.
350 Main Street
Malden, Massachusetts 02148
USA

British Library Cataloguing in Publication Data

A CIP catalogue record for this book is available from the British Library.

Library of Congress Cataloging-in-Publication Data

Elias, Norbert.
    The Norbert Elias reader : a biographical selection/edited by
Johan Goudsblom and Stephen Mennell.
        p.   cm.
    Includes bibliographical references and index.
    ISBN 0–631–19308–1. — ISBN 0–631–19309–X
    1. Elias, Norbert. 2. Sociology—Europe—History—20th century.
3. Sociology—Europe—Philosophy. 4. Civilization—Philosophy.
I. Goudsblom, Johan.   II. Mennell, Stephen.   III. Title.
HM22.E9E55   1998
301'.094—dc21   97–8619
                                                            CIP

Typeset in 10 on 12pt Ehrhardt by Grahame & Grahame Editorial, Brighton, East Sussex

Printed and bound in Great Britain by MPG Books Ltd, Bodmin, Cornwall

This book is printed on acid-free paper

CONTENTS

PART III: SOCIOLOGIST IN BRITAIN, 1950–1965

PART IV: A EUROPEAN SOCIOLOGIST, 1966–1990

SOURCES AND ACKNOWLEDGEMENTS

We would like to thank: Edmund Jephcott and Robert van Krieken for undertaking translations of essays included here; Eric Dunning, Hermann Korte, Barbara Mennell and Saskia Visser for their help and advice; and Anne Coogan for retyping 'Group Charisma and Group Disgrace'.

The selections from the writings of Norbert Elias are reprinted from the following sources. The editors and publishers wish to thank the copyright owners for permission to use the material.

1   'Idea and Individual', from *Idee und Individuum: Ein Beitrag zur Philosophie der Geschichte*, unpublished D.Phil. thesis, Universität Breslau, 1924, pp. 1–4. Translated by Johan Goudsblom and Stephen Mennell; published for the first time in this volume.
2   'On Primitive Art' from *Verhandlungen des Sechsten Deutschen Soziologentages vom 17. zu 19. September 1928 in Zürich*. Tübingen, J.C.B. Mohr, 1929, pp. 281–4. Translated by Johan Goudsblom and Stephen Mennell; published for the first time in this volume.
3   'Court Society as a Sociological Problem', from *The Court Society*. Oxford, Basil Blackwell, and New York, Pantheon Books, pp. 35–40. Translation from German by Edmund Jephcott. By permission of Blackwell Publishers and Random House, Inc.
4   'The Expulsion of the Huguenots from France': 'Die Vertreibung der

Hugenotten aus Frankreich.' *Der Ausweg* 1 (12) 1935: 369–76. Translation from German by Edmund Jephcott; published for the first time in this volume.

5 'The Kitsch Style and the Age of Kitsch': 'Kitschstil und Kitschzeitalter.' *Die Sammlung* 2 (5) 1935: 252–63. Translation from German by Edmund Jephcott; published for the first time in this volume.

6 An Outline of *The Civilizing Process*, from *The Civilizing Process*, one-volume edition. Oxford, Blackwell, 1994, pp. xi–xvii. Translation from German by Edmund Jephcott. By permission of Blackwell Publishers.

7 '*Kultur* and *civilisation*' from *The Civilizing Process*, one-volume edition. Oxford, Blackwell, 1994, pp. 39–41. Translation from German by Edmund Jephcott. By permission of Blackwell Publishers.

8 'The Rise of the Fork', from *The Civilizing Process*, one-volume edition. Oxford, Blackwell, 1994, pp. 103–5. Translation from German by Edmund Jephcott. By permission of Blackwell Publishers.

9 'The Sociogenesis of Courts', from *The Civilizing Process*, one-volume edition. Oxford, Basil Blackwell, 1994, pp. 330–4. Translation from German by Edmund Jephcott. By permission of Blackwell Publishers.

10 'Civilization and Rationalization', from *The Civilizing Process*, one-volume edition. Oxford, Blackwell, 1994, pp. 486–92. Translation from German by Edmund Jephcott. By permission of Blackwell Publishers.

11 'The Society of Individuals – I', from *The Society of Individuals*. Oxford, Basil Blackwell, 1991, pp. 20–7. Translation from German by Edmund Jephcott. By permission of Blackwell Publishers.

12 'Sociology and Psychiatry', from 'Sociology and Psychiatry', in S. H. Foulkes and G. Steward Prince (eds), *Psychiatry in a Changing Society*. London, Tavistock, pp. 122–5. By permission of Routledge.

13 'The Naval Profession' from 'Studies in the Genesis of the Naval Profession'. *British Journal of Sociology* 1 (4) 1950, pp. 308–9. By permission of Routledge.

14 'Involvement and Detachment', from *Involvement and Detachment*. Oxford, Basil Blackwell, 1987, pp. vii–xv. By permission of Blackwell Publishers.

15 'The Society of Individuals – II', from *The Society of Individuals*. Oxford, Basil Blackwell, 1991, pp. 93–6. Translation from German by Edmund Jephcott. By permission of Blackwell Publishers.

16 'The Quest for Excitement in Leisure', from Norbert Elias and Eric Dunning, *Quest for Excitement: Sport and Leisure in the Civilizing Process*. Oxford, Basil Blackwell, 1986, pp. 150–6. By permission of Blackwell Publishers.

17 'Group Charisma and Group Disgrace'. Paper presented at the Fifteenth German Sociological Congress, Heidelberg, in commemoration of the

centenary of the birth of Max Weber. The first two of the three sections of this paper are published for the first time in this volume.

18 'The Breakdown of Civilization', from *The Germans: Power Struggles and the Development of Habitus in the Nineteenth and Twentieth Centuries*. Oxford, Polity Press, and New York, Columbia University Press, 1996, pp. 308–16. Translation from German by Eric Dunning and Stephen Mennell. By permission of Polity Press and Columbia University Press.

19 '*The Civilizing Process* Revisited', from the Introduction to the second German edition of *Über den Prozess der Zivilisation*, 1969, reprinted here from *The Civilizing Process*, one-volume edition. Oxford, Basil Blackwell, 1994, pp. 183–7. Translation from German by Edmund Jephcott. By permission of Blackwell Publishers.

20 'The Concept of Figurations' from the Introduction to the second German edition of *Über den Prozess der Zivilisation*, 1969, reprinted here from *The Civilizing Process*, one-volume edition. Oxford, Basil Blackwell, 1994, pp. 214–15. Translation from German by Edmund Jephcott. By permission of Blackwell Publishers.

21 'African Art', from *African Art from the Collection of Professor Norbert Elias, April 24th–June 14th 1970, Leicester Museum and Art Gallery*. Leicester, Leicester Museums, 1970. By permission of Leicestershire Museums, Arts and Records Service.

22 'An Interview in Amsterdam', with Johan Goudsblom, *Sociologische Gids*, 17 (2) 1970: 133–40. (Original is in English).

23 'The Sciences', from 'The Sciences: Towards a Theory', in Richard Whitley (ed.), *Social Processes of Scientific Development*. London, Routledge & Kegan Paul, 1974, pp. 27–42. By permission of Routledge.

24 'On the Concept of Everyday Life': 'Zum Begriff des Alltags.' In: Kurt Hammerich and Michael Klein (eds), *Materialien zur Soziologie des Alltags (Kölner Zeitschrift für Soziologie und Sozialpsychologie*, Sonderheft 20), pp. 22–9. Köln, Westdeutscher Verlag, 1978. Translation from German by Edmund Jephcott; published for the first time in this volume.

25 'The Retreat of Sociologists into the Present', from *Theory, Culture and Society* 4 (2–3) 1987: 223–34. Translation from German by Stephen Kalberg and Volker Meja, revised and enlarged by the author. By permission of Sage Publications.

26 'Renate Rubinstein': 'Vorwort', in Renate Rubinstein, *Nichts zu verlieren und dennoch Angst. Notizen nach einer Trennung* (translated from Dutch), pp. 9–11. Frankfurt: Suhrkamp, 1978. Translation from German by Edmund Jephcott; published for the first time in this volume. By permission of J.M. Meulenhoff bv, Amsterdam.

27 'The Civilizing of Parents': 'Die Zivilisierung der Eltern', pp. 11–28 in Linde Burkhardt (ed.), *. . . und wie wohnst du?*, Berlin, Internationales

Design Zentrum, 1980. Translation Robert van Krieken; published for the first time in this volume. By permission of Internationales Design Zentrum and Robert van Krieken.

28 'Technization and Civilization', from 'Technization and Civilization', *Theory, Culture and Society*, 12 (3) 1995: 18–42, 34–41. Translation from German by Frank Pollock and Stephen Mennell. By permission of Sage Publications.

29 'The Society of Individuals – III', from *The Society of Individuals*. Oxford, Basil Blackwell, 1991, pp. 196–202. Translation from German by Edmund Jephcott. By permission of Blackwell Publishers.

30 'Informalization and the Civilizing Process', from *The Germans: Power Struggles and the Development of Habitus in the Nineteenth and Twentieth Centuries*. Oxford, Polity Press, and New York, Columbia University Press, 1996, pp. 31–43. Translation from German by Eric Dunning and Stephen Mennell. By permission of Polity Press and Columbia University Press.

31 'Mozart's Revolt', from *Mozart: Portrait of a Genius*. Oxford, Polity Press, and Berkeley, University of California Press, 1993, pp. 122–30. Translation from German by Edmund Jephcott. By permission of Polity Press and University of California Press.

32 'The Symbol Theory', from *The Symbol Theory*. London, Sage, 1991, pp. 134–47. By permission of Sage Publications.

Every effort has been made to trace all the copyright holders but if any have been inadvertently overlooked the publishers will be pleased to make the necessary arrangement at the first opportunity.

How strange these people are
How strange I am
How strange we are

Norbert Elias
Los der Menschen

INTRODUCTION

Norbert Elias is one of the great sociologists of our time. Born in 1897, he lived through most of the twentieth century, and found his life radically affected by some of that century's major events. Brought up as a Jewish boy in the German *Kaiserreich*, he served as a soldier in the First World War, became a sociologist in the short-lived Weimar Republic, had to flee his country from the National Socialists in 1933, suffered hard times as a refugee in Paris and London, and entered on a university career in England only in his late fifties. Having reached retirement age in 1962, he taught sociology in Ghana for two years, and, after his return to Europe, remained active for more than 25 years writing and teaching in various countries. He died in Amsterdam in 1990, at the age of 93. He never married; about his private affairs he was always discreet.

In this reader we present a selection from his work, in chronological order. Elias used to emphasize that we have to see the world, including the social world of which we form a part, as a process. His own work, while showing a striking continuity and consistency over the years, was also a process. In the writings we have selected, several developments may be observed: first of all, quite clearly, a move from philosophy to sociology; and then a gradual broadening of the scope of the sociological perspective, accompanied by an increasing facility in dealing with complicated subject matter at a high level of synthesis in relatively simple terms and phrases.

Our selection is intended to show how Elias's work is connected with his life experiences. It should not be regarded as a substitute for a biography, however. The emphasis is on the work, seen against the background of the life. For further biographical details the reader is referred, above all, to *Reflections on a Life* (Elias 1994b), Elias's own reminiscences, mainly about his years in Germany before 1933, preceded by a long and revealing interview about his life experiences. As long as there is no full biography, the *Reflections* are the best alternative. Further information may be found in Stephen Mennell's book on Elias (Mennell 1989), in a biographical introduction in German by Hermann Korte (1988, 1997), and in a recent study by Jörg Hackeschmidt (1997), also in German, about Elias's activities as a young man in Breslau in the Zionist youth movement Blau Weiss.*

The texts we have selected vary in length. They are all complete, however, in the sense that no passages have been deleted. In a few instances we have amended what seemed to us obvious typographical, grammatical or terminological errors. For the rest, however, we have made it a rule not to deviate from the original English text as written by Elias himself or an authorized translator. The only one exception we have made is clearly indicated in a note. Each text is preceded by a brief introduction, placing it within the larger context of Elias's life and work.

Along with the present volume, we have also edited a selection from Elias's work for the Heritage of Sociology Series of the University of Chicago Press. That book is formatted as a systematic overview of some of Elias's major contributions to sociology. With this biographical selection we hope to have succeeded in giving an impression of how, in a long process of research and reflection, Elias's ideas developed.

Our book is intended as a substitute neither for a biography nor for a fuller reading of Elias's multifaceted writings. On the contrary: while seeking extracts that were typical of Elias's work at certain stages in his life we often felt ourselves severely restricted by the limitations of space. We can only wish that our selections will whet our readers' appetites for more.

Johan Goudsblom *Amsterdam*
Stephen Mennell *Dublin*

* There are still several gaps in Elias's biography, and possibly even some in his bibliography. Just at the time when this book went to print, an article about anti-semitism in Germany came to light which Elias had published in 1929. We have included it in the Bibliography, but have been unable to comment on it, let alone include it in our selections.

PART I

THE EARLY YEARS, 1920–1935

1

IDEA AND INDIVIDUAL

Elias grew up in Breslau, which was then a German city, but has, since 1945, been within Poland and named Wrocław. Immediately after finishing secondary school in 1915 he became a soldier in the German army. After serving in a telegraph unit on both the Eastern and the Western fronts, he returned in 1917 to Breslau where he completed his military service as a medical orderly, while at the same taking up the study of medicine at the local university.

In his later life Elias often referred back to his early training as a physician. He found that it had made him familiar with the methods of the empirical natural sciences, and prepared him to be highly critical of the conventional dichotomy of 'body' and 'mind'. Although he never practised medicine, he retained a sense of the importance of anatomy and physiology for an understanding of how human beings, and therefore human societies, work.

Although his father had wanted him to become a doctor, Elias's heart lay in the more general study of human affairs. He switched to philosophy, and in July 1922 he handed in a dissertation, *Idea and Individual*, on the basis of which he received the title of Doctor of Philosophy in January 1924.

The long delay between the completion of the dissertation and the awarding of the degree was caused by a fierce conflict between Elias and his supervisor, the philosopher Richard Hönigswald. As Elias himself recalled it in his *Reflections on a Life*, the point at issue was a fundamental one – whether there are any grounds for postulating a notion of truth that is transcendental and independent of human experience and human history. According to his autobiography, while working on his dissertation Elias had come to the conclusion, 'in painful arguments with myself',

> that all that Kant regarded as timeless and as given prior to all experience, whether it be the idea of causal connections or of time or of natural and moral laws, together with the words that went with them, had to be learned from other people in order to be present in the consciousness of the individual human being. (1994b: 91)

In the dissertation itself Elias was not yet able to state his position as simply and clearly as he did in this passage. As he himself noted in retrospect, his arguments were still couched in a philosophical vocabulary pertaining to a one-dimensional world of 'the mind' rather than the world of 'five-dimensional people of flesh and blood' (Elias 1994b: 152). The idea of a 'fifth dimension' (of experience and consciousness) came to him only many years later (see below, pp. 252, 265).

The clash with Hönigswald seems to have tainted Elias's relationship with philosophy for the rest of his life. He continued to be fascinated by the problems of classical philosophy, but he found that they needed to be recast in sociological terms – a recasting which he himself undertook in, for example, his interpretation of Descartes' famous dictum 'I think therefore I am' (see below, p. 231).

The following section is a translation of the first pages of the dissertation. The young Elias here states a problem which was to occupy him throughout his life: the patterning of events in human history. All social facts are historical facts – they are positioned in and conditioned by historical time. How then are we to conceive of this particular order of facts?

The dissertation discusses this question in what Elias himself later was to call 'a frightful philosophical idiom' (1994b: 153). The characteristic features of any particular era are described as 'the idea' of that era. The development of society at large is thus reduced to a succession of mental structures. Yet, although in his later writings Elias worked out another approach and other concepts, we can already see in this early endeavour the search for a high level of synthesis that would remain characteristic of all his work.

> If one tries to form a clear picture of the task of the historical researcher, one arrives at more or less the following result: Before him lies as it were the material, waiting to be worked upon by him – the immense fullness of all that people have achieved. Well-considered principles must teach him to probe this material, to single out what is worthy of his work, to leave aside what is without significance. For this purpose he cannot, however, rely upon just any arbitrarily imposed precepts; the material itself must contain the inherent conditions which make a selection possible. Only then can he be certain that such probing is more than a technical and fundamentally inadequate tool of human reason. The object of historical investigation is not a structureless mass

of events which it would be futile to try to grasp in retrospect, but a sequence of facts which are arranged and linked to each other by the framework of a characteristic order. Even if the investigator aims at understanding the single object in its incomparable individuality, to the extent that he succeeds in singling out this and only this object from the fullness of the material, and in seemingly isolating it from everything that ever was or will be, he will actually be connecting it more closely with everything he is trying to exclude, and the sequence in which the object is located will emerge more graphically. For by the delineation of a single fact, other facts in its field – be it the field of art, law, science, or religion – will at once be thrown into sharper relief. The whole of this field, as distinguished from any other field, will be seen in another light. Eventually the clarification of that individual occurrence will put its entire era into a new perspective as a totality which comprises all these various fields. And anyone who looks again from this perspective at the single fact, will no longer perceive it as a seemingly isolated form, but will learn to understand it in a new sense as a constituent part of its era, contingent on the particular character of that era. This entire procedure in which the researcher typically directs his ideas to and fro between the singular and the whole and then back to the singular again, reflects more than a chance point of view – it reflects a particular order in history.

Even a historian who approaches his material with dogmatic prejudices about the laws of history will, once he immerses himself with complete honesty in his subject matter, be forced to return to a method which is implied in the order underlying the material itself. The more distinctly he perceives the meaning of a single historical occurrence, the more clearly will his research show him the concepts which people at the time of that occurrence had of God or truth, or morality or beauty, of the state or law – in brief, of the ideas of that time. And he will learn to understand a certain system of such ideas as the fundamental condition of that age. Learning to perceive, amidst the variety of expressions characteristic of one and the same era, the encompassing unity of the idea, will at the same time deepen the understanding which he has of each individual instance, of each single element of the era, because he is now able to view them all in the larger context of the full range of relationships which he can see arising out of the fundamental unity of that era.

But this is not all. For, as the particular chapter of history with which the historian is concerned, and the qualities which distinguish it from other chapters, gradually emerge for him with greater clarity, those other chapters become clearer as well. This means that the temporary forms which the idea takes in different periods are themselves joined together as 'single facts' within the whole of a system of ideas, and this system therefore, as an inner fabric, keeps the structure of history together as a unit, and order it. This system, then, also provides the point of view which is needed in order to select what is historically significant.

2

ON PRIMITIVE ART

The great inflation which hit Germany in 1923 made Elias's father's income practically worthless. Forced to support himself and his parents, Elias, without any previous commercial experience, accepted a job in a firm manufacturing iron goods. As he himself later remembered it, this contact with business life, together with his experiences as a soldier, may have strengthened his determination to turn away from philosophy towards sociology. When after a year the economic situation became less pressing, he returned to university. At Heidelberg, he took up postgraduate work in sociology with Alfred Weber, the younger brother of Max Weber (who had died in 1920). Here Elias also came into close contact with the promising young lecturer in sociology, Karl Mannheim.

In 1928, Alfred Weber, Mannheim, and Elias attended a conference of the German Sociological Association in Zürich. Mannheim gave one of the main lectures, on competition in the intellectual sphere (Mannheim 1928/1990). It was a brilliant presentation which elicited admiration and acclaim but also vehement criticism. His senior colleague, Alfred Weber, in particular, felt provoked by Mannheim's contention that a liberal world view, as espoused by most sociologists including Weber himself, was as much bound to a specific social situation as was Marxism – the *bête noire* of the German sociological establishment of the time. Weber protested that Mannheim failed to recognize the principles of individual creativity and spiritual freedom. When finally, in the hierarchical order of the discussion, it was the time for Elias to speak as a young PhD, he took the opportunity to point out that the audience had witnessed an encounter between two world views: an older view which adhered to the belief in an eternal truth, and a newer, revolutionary view which saw our lives and thoughts as enveloped in 'the immanent necessity of an endless stream'.[1]

In *Reflections on a Life* Elias commented at length on this episode. In retrospect, he suspected that at the time he may have attributed to Mannheim too much of his own emergent ideas about long-term processes (1994b: 118). How much these ideas were still 'in the making' may be gathered from the other contribution which Elias made to the discussions in Zürich: his remarks following a paper by the anthropologist Richard Thurnwald on the origins of art. A transcript of this intervention was recorded in the proceedings of the conference. These, and the comments on Weber and Mannheim, are the oldest sociological statements in print by Elias.

Ladies and Gentlemen. I don't intend to test your heroism much longer. Allow me to say just a few brief words. I should like first of all to connect today's debate with yesterday's debate. Here we have indeed one of those instances to which we must refer when we speak about 'understanding'. The question we have to consider is: have we actually *understood* the other person? Does what we have heard today help us to a better understanding of primitive people? Of course, every discipline has the right to behave as if it had already made a complete investigation of its subject-matter, and to believe at any moment that it can already grasp the whole of its subject. But it is perhaps not unnecessary for a critic once in a while to point out modestly what is still to be done. And I for one believe that, if one foregoes scientific terminology and thinks of the living primitive man, much still needs to be done before we can really say that we have understood him. Here lies one of the most decisive problems which has to be taken into account in a theory of understanding. The first thing we see when we encounter this strange person is that we do not understand him. In creating a theory of 'understanding', the task, therefore, is not just to show that man can understand man, but to show at the same time how it is possible that we do *not* understand each other. And this applies of course not only to our relation to the primitive, but also to our relations amongst ourselves. These very debates have shown that at times we do not understand each other amongst ourselves. So if one says that 'understanding' is based upon the fact that one mind recognizes the same in the other, it is necessary to explain – or at least to make intelligible – why we, who are all of the same mind, who are all people, are unable in a particular situation to understand each other. Please do not understand by this that I am advocating a particular metaphysic, that I wish to say with all this that it is definitely impossible to understand people from another culture, that they have a nature different from ours. On the contrary, I too believe that there is only *one* 'man'. But precisely when one believes in the unity of everything human, the question of how it is possible to understand everything human, and why it is that under certain conditions one does not understand, is still more difficult and still more important. How then does science in its practice cope with this?

Allow me to tell you a small anecdote about a French army commander who was fighting a war in North Africa with native troops when, one day, there was an eclipse of the sun which caused the troops to refuse advancing further toward the enemy. He called the headman to himself and said: 'I shall explain to you how the eclipse of the sun comes about. Then you will see that you need to have no fear.' So he explained: 'there is the sun, there is the earth, and there is the moon, and so on. Then, because the moon comes to stand between the earth and the sun, the eclipse of the sun comes about.' Then he asked the headman whether he had understood. 'Yes,' the headman replied, he had understood. So the general said: 'right, we can proceed.' 'No, we cannot,' the headman retorted. 'Why not?' 'Well, it is well known,' the headman answered, 'when the sun eclipses in this way, that is because a certain spirit holds his coat before the sun. Then one may not possibly move on.' The general shook his head and said: 'I have explained it to you exactly; you have not understood, and I will explain it once more.' And he told the same story again, of course with the same result. How is such non-understanding to be understood? Science, if it does not fully renounce any attempt at explaining this non-understanding, has a relatively simple way of coming to terms with this profound divergence, with this unbridged gulf between particular cultures: it describes the divergences the way one describes plants and animals, it gives them names, it says something like 'every native is entangled in magic or myth, and the European is not.' But I ask you: do we as yet understand this person when we say 'he is tied up in *magic*'? I believe that great advances have been made with this method – using concepts like myth, matriarchy, patriarchy. It offers a way of putting these things in some sort of order. But in dealing with something human, does all this not amount more to describing from the outside than to understanding from the inside? Regarding the possibility of understanding there are two opinions. One can say, 'we are definitely incapable of understanding and we must resign ourselves to that'; or one can say, 'we are able to go much further along the road of understanding'. I too believe that we only stand at the beginning of a real understanding of the primitive; I believe that the method followed thus far is a necessary and useful stage – but it does not yet allow us to understand those others, primitive people.

Allow me in this context to touch briefly upon the central question raised by the speaker, the question of the origins of art. This is certainly a very necessary and legitimate question. I believe myself to be in full agreement with the speaker, however, when I say that, just like concepts such as family, marriage and similar concepts which correspond to our own way of thinking, our concept of 'art' can evidently not be applied in any direct way to the creations of primitive people, simply because – and that is one of the decisive points – because it implies a degree of differentiation which is not yet even present to the consciousness of the primitive people themselves. The task of understanding seems to me to be to raise the question of how the primitive himself experiences the world. Why is he *forced* to experience the world thus and not differently, and why are we *forced* – we have no choice – to experience the world thus and not differently, although both of us apparently share the same human nature? From where does this constraint come, this inner necessity which makes the primitive experience a tree thus and not differently – as a spirit! – and makes it impossible for us to experience the tree as a spirit? We who live today have not ourselves brought about the transition from a view of the world as a world of spirits to a view of the world as 'nature', but we are forced to realize in ourselves this way of experiencing the world – as an inheritance to which we are bound. But none of these differentiations, such as art, nature, economy, and law, which we are compelled to experience as something self-evident, have yet come about for the primitive. For in his consciousness all such differentiations, in which the world has become diversified for us, are still held together undeveloped as in an embryo. So we cannot say about the creations of primitive people that something is either a piece of art or an economic or a religious object; rather every single object belongs to all these spheres simultaneously – it contains these spheres in itself in the way the seed contains in itself undeveloped the future organs of the plant. And this is our task, in trying to understand the primitive, to detach ourselves a little from the stage of differentiation we have reached, and to place ourselves in that other stage of differentiation in which all those spheres remain together undeveloped.

Finally it is necessary to raise the question of why it is that the primitive is nowadays increasingly arousing our interest. I shall not go into the most interesting problem of progress raised by the speaker. Can one say that we represent progress with regard to the primitive? If all that is meant by this is the mere observation that the primitive consciousness holds in itself undeveloped that which has developed for us, one may perhaps answer this question in the affirmative; but I will not go further into that. It seems to me possible, however, to give a brief answer to the question of why the primitive arouses our interest to such an extent nowadays. In earlier times the horizon of the researcher – the philosopher as well as any other researcher into human affairs – was usually limited by the caesura made by the first spurt of enlightenment in antiquity; today we have gradually reached the insight that the human becomes understandable only when it is comprehended it in its entirety. That does not precisely mean from its beginnings, for there are no absolute beginnings; but one realizes that it is necessary, in order to understand *oneself* to go back as far as at all possible in the study of man. In this sense I believe I can say that not only is every period in human history, as has been said, directly given to God, but that – if one wishes to understand man, if one wishes to understand oneself – every period in human history is equally relevant to us.

3

COURT SOCIETY AS A SOCIOLOGICAL PROBLEM

In 1930 Karl Mannheim, at the age of 37, was appointed Professor of Sociology at the University of Frankfurt. He asked Elias to join him as an assistant.

The University of Frankfurt was a recently founded university, with a faculty which included many scholars and scientists who had recently reached or were about to reach prominence in their fields, such as the neurologist Kurt Goldstein, the psychologist Max Wertheimer, the economist Adolf Löwe, and the psychoanalyst S. H. Fuchs (who was to change his name to Foulkes after his emigration to England). All these men, each in his own way, contributed ideas which Elias assimilated into his own thinking. Goldstein's neurology and Wertheimer's Gestalt psychology strengthened his conviction that thorough empirical research could bring us closer to understanding mental activities – and thereby to come to grips with problems that were traditionally treated as belonging to the philosophy of knowledge or epistemology. Löwe's work in institutional economics and Fuchs's ventures in psychoanalysis offered him clues for bringing seemingly disparate areas of human life within the range of a comprehensive sociological perspective.

In the same year 1930 when Mannheim was called to Frankfurt, Max Horkheimer became professor of Social Philosophy and director of the independently endowed Institute of Social Research. The Institute employed a number of leftish young intellectuals such as Theodor Adorno, Erich Fromm, and Franz Borkenau. Although the Sociology Department was housed in the same building as the Institute, relations between Horkheimer and his group, and Mannheim and Elias were tenuous at best, mainly for political reasons: Mannheim was considered too much of a liberal, and Elias refused to commit himself to any political creed.

At Frankfurt Elias supervised several students in research for their masters or doctoral theses. Among them were Gisèle Freund, who later became a famous photographer and wrote a sociological study of photography, and Hans Gerth and Kurt Wolff who became well-known sociologists in the United States. The auspices for sociology at the University of Frankfurt would have been highly favourable, had it not been for the advent of National Socialism.

The atmosphere in the Weimar Republic in the early 1930s was grim, with increasing political intimidation and street violence. Several German sociologists who lived through that period have remarked in retrospect how naïve they were and how grossly they underestimated the imminent catastrophe. When in 1933 the Nazis seized power, sociology at Frankfurt virtually came to an end. Mannheim, Horkheimer, and practically all of their younger associates and students were expelled from the university; within a year, most of them, including Elias, had fled the country.

For Elias this was a blow to his career at a most critical moment. He had just finished his *Habilitation*, the second 'grand' dissertation required in Germany if one wanted to qualify for a professorship. He now had to go into exile as a former university assistant, with no published *Habilitationsschrift* to his credit.

The subject of his 'grand' dissertation was life at the French royal court in the seventeenth and eighteenth centuries – a topic seemingly far removed from the political turmoil of those days. Yet in that monograph there was more at stake than the mere reconstruction of an historical scene. The book was a penetrating study of power, in the era of so-called absolute kingship, and of the constraints which the exercise of power put on all those concerned: on the king himself as well as on his entourage. Because Elias had to go into exile immediately after finishing this study, the typescript remained unpublished for more than thirty-five years. When eventually in 1969 it was published, Elias changed the text considerably – revising many passages and adding some entirely new sections. The text which follows is – as far as we can judge – the original introduction to the book. Although Elias may have made some amendments in it for the 1969 edition, the basic argument appears to have remained unchanged, as evinced by the quotations and other references.

What we find particularly striking in this chapter is, first of all, the clarity with which Elias states the problems he intends to discuss. He raises a series of questions, each requiring empirical historical investigation. Secondly, these questions are phrased in such a way as to make them relevant for a more general sociological theory.

1   The princely court of the *ancien régime* sets the sociologist no fewer problems than any other social formation – such as feudal society or the city – which has already been accorded detailed sociological investigation. At such a 'court' hundreds and often thousands of people were bound together in one place by peculiar restraints which they and outsiders applied to each other and to themselves, as servants, advisers and companions of kings who believed

they ruled their countries with absolute power and on whose will the fate of all these people, their rank, their financial support, their rise and fall, depended within certain limits. A more or less fixed hierarchy, a precise etiquette bound them together. The necessity of asserting themselves within such a figuration gave them all a special stamp, that of court people. What was the structure of the social field at the centre of which such a figuration could form? What distribution of power, which socially instilled needs, which relationships of dependence brought it about that people in this social field constantly converged over generations in this figuration, as a court, as court society? What demands were transmitted from the structure of court society to those who wished to rise or merely to survive within it? These, roughly sketched, are some of the questions which the social formation of the court and court society in the *ancien régime* pose for the sociologist.

2 It was not simply the free will of the court people that held them together at court and which, after their fathers and mothers, united the sons and daughters in this manner. Nor was it the brilliant inspiration of a single person, for example the king, which gave this form to the human community. From the Renaissance on the courts gained increasing importance in almost every European country, and even if the French court, above all that of Louis XIV, was exemplary of the detailed arrangements of the European courts of the seventeenth and eighteenth centuries, the 'court' of this period was itself the expression of a very specific social constellation and no more planned or intended by any single person or group than – to name other typical figurations at random – the Church, the city, the factory or bureaucracy. No more than we can understand the structure of our own Western society and the national social units composing it without studying the process whereby more and more people crystallized out of the social field in the form of 'cities', no more can we understand the preceding epoch without explaining from the social structure characteristic of it what produced the 'court', what, in other words, constantly brought and held together people of this social field in the figuration of the court and court society.

3 Within every social field there are representative and less representative, central and less central organs. The town, for example, and above all the large city, is one of the most representative organs of our own society. In our social field it represents the matrix with by far the most far-reaching influence; even the inhabitants of country districts cannot escape its effects however hard they try. The most influential human types in our society either come from the city or at least have received its stamp. In this sense, therefore, urban people are representative of our society. The 'princely court' as a special organ within the city – as far as it still exists – no doubt still has, in Western Europe, above all in England, some influence in modifying the imprint of the city, but is hardly representative, like the city itself, of the social field of the West today. It is precisely this representative and central significance that

the court had for most Western European countries in the seventeenth and eighteenth centuries. In this period it was not the 'city' but the 'court' and court society which were the centre with by far the most widespread influence. The town, as was said in the *ancien régime*, merely 'aped' the court.[1] This is particularly true of the French court.[2] An after-effect of the bourgeois opposition to the court, as was mentioned in the Introduction, frequently obstructs our view of the representativeness of the courts and court society in the preceding centuries, and prevents a study of its structure that is free of irritation and resentment, an observation of its functioning which is as free of emotional reactions as 'village', 'factory', 'horde', 'guild' or any other figuration formed by people.

Characteristic of this rather emotional approach to the court is the view of Franz Oppenheimer, which will be quoted here because it contains in very definite form a widespread and typical judgement on the court of the *ancien régime*:

The pre-capitalist, very opulent and very extravagant courts, above all those of the English Stuarts and the French Bourbons, but to a lesser extent the German and Slavonic dynasties too, were over-abundantly endowed, thanks to their extensive domanial possessions and the tributes from their 'crown peasants' flowing from them, with all the means of crude enjoyment. But they desired the means of satisfying refined tastes and perverse luxury, and were therefore interested firstly in fostering a flourishing trade within the country, and secondly in obtaining the cash needed to maintain the court in its refined splendour, to feed the noble parasites who had no other source of income than their pensions, and not least to conduct the endless wars in which the need for glory, dynastic family interests and confessional superstitions entangled with empires.[3]

This is the essence of what Oppenheimer sees of the 'court' as a social formation in his work that aspires to embrace the whole wealth of social forms. In this judgement, as far as it refers to France, there is nothing in the facts presented, apart from seeing the tributes from crown peasants as the primary basis of the Bourbon royal court,[4] that is actually wrong. But the perspective from which the judgement and evaluation of these facts are made completely obscures the context which produced them and in which alone they can be understood.

Max Weber saw somewhat further when he said: '"Luxury" in the sense of a rejection of the purposive-rational orientation of consumption is, to the feudal ruling class, not something "superfluous", but one of the means of its social self-assertion.'[5]

But in this brief remark Max Weber has merely indicated one of the problems of the court. To test the correctness of this view and to bring the problem posed in it some steps towards a conclusion is one of the objectives of this study.

4   We tend to assign importance to the functional aspects of earlier epochs which play a particular part in the present. In this way we often ask first of all about the economic views and arrangements of the court epoch; from this perspective it is called the epoch of mercantilism. We ask about its state structure, and from this perspective we call it the epoch of absolutism. We ask about its system of rule and its bureaucracy and from this standpoint we call it an epoch of patrimonialism. These are all categories which are of particular importance in our own society. But would a section cut through our society really touch on the decisive structural lines of the past epoch? Is it not rather the case that there are rising and falling planes of integration, so that a plane which is not especially relevant to us was once perhaps central, and, conversely, a stratum central today was once peripheral?

Max Weber makes his section through the *ancien régime* primarily at the level of the bureaucracy, so that for him the phenomenon of the bureaucracy, and the mode of rule expressed in the different types of bureaucracy, always overshadow the phenomenon of the court. In this way he contributes many illuminating facts and details on the structure of court rule and court society; but the 'court' itself is not among the types of social formations that he expressly discusses.[6]

5   Where the court is directly viewed as a social phenomenon, it is one aspect above all that interests researchers of our society: its luxury. This is a phenomenon which is important and characteristic, but which highlights only a particularly conspicuous difference between the behaviour of court people and that normal today, and tends to distract from the social structure of the court as a whole, which alone can make the isolated phenomenon of luxury comprehensible.

In other words, while it is sometimes possible today to investigate the structure of a simple tribe, for example, as an autonomous figuration of people, and largely to exclude one's own value-judgements in doing so, such detachment is much more difficult in the case of formations closer to us and classified as 'historical', the more so because the prevalent form of historical research leaves the prestige of heteronomous valuations unquestioned.

This observation should not be misunderstood. It is not meant as a 'reproach' but seeks only to lay bare the immanent structure of the process of research, which reveals the autonomy of its subject matter only very slowly and against inevitable resistances.

Moreover, the heteronomous view is not necessarily unfruitful. Sombart, for example, for whom the phenomenon of the court is relevant in connection with the rise of modern capitalism precisely through its quality as a 'centre of luxury', formulates the general problem of the court very trenchantly. The section he devotes to the courts, headed: 'The princely courts as centres of the spread of luxury', begins with the following ideas:

An important consequence and, in its turn, a decisive cause of the transformations undergone by the state constitution and army at the end of the Middle Ages, is the emergence of large princely courts in the sense in which we use the word today. The predecessors and models of these later developments are here, as in so many areas, the high dignitaries of the Church. Perhaps Avignon was the first modern 'court' because it was here that two groups of people first came together continuously and set the tone who were in the succeeding centuries to form what was called court society: noblemen without any other calling than to serve the court, and beautiful women 'souvent distinguées par les manières et l'esprit' who really set their stamp on life at the court.

With the courts of the Popes the other princes of Italy competed. But of decisive importance for the history of the court was the emergence of a modern court in the much larger and more powerful France, which from the end of the sixteenth century and throughout the next two centuries became the undisputed teacher in all matters concerning court life.[7]

This short survey, very useful for the purposes of this study, gives at least an indication of what the social formation of the court signified and of the problems it poses: at a certain stage in the development of European societies individuals are bound together in the form of courts and thereby given a specific stamp. What held them together and what stamped them in just this way?

This human stamp was one of the most important ancestors of the one prevalent today. As a central figuration of that stage of development, which after a long struggle gave way abruptly or gradually to a professional-bourgeois-urban-industrial stage, this aristocratic court society developed a civilizing and cultural physiognomy which was taken over by professional-bourgeois society partly as a heritage and partly as an antithesis and, preserved in this way, was further developed. By studying the structure of court society and seeking to understand one of the last great non-bourgeois figurations of the West, therefore, we indirectly gain increased understanding of our own professional-bourgeois, urban–industrial society.

4

THE EXPULSION OF THE
HUGUENOTS FROM FRANCE

After his flight from the National Socialist regime Elias first settled in Paris where, with two fellow refugees, he tried to set up a small business manufacturing and selling toys. The venture failed, and Elias lost the little money he had.

A few years later, in London, he wrote a long essay on the problem of how we are to conceive of the relationship between 'individuals' and 'society'. He evoked the picture of the bustle in the streets of a large city.

> Each individual person in this turmoil belongs in a particular place. He has a table at which he eats, a bed in which he sleeps; even the hungry and the homeless are both products and parts of the hidden order underlying the *mêlée*. Each of the people who pass has somewhere, at some time, a specific function, property or work, a task of some kind for others, or a lost function, lost possessions and lost work. (1991b: 13)

It is not difficult to perceive an autobiographical allusion in this scene. Elias himself had suffered these losses, and he was to suffer even greater losses in the years to come. Some of his grief found expression in poems. For many years, however, he did not explicitly address the current political problems of the day in his work as a sociologist. In that respect he took a very different course from Karl Mannheim.

Having been unable to find a foothold in Paris, Elias, with the aid of friends from Heidelberg who had preceded him, emigrated to England. In October 1935 he published an article, as Dr. Norbert Elias of Cambridge, in a German-language refugee journal, published in Paris. The article gave a brief exposé of the expulsion of the Huguenots from France in the seventeenth century. It did not contain a single reference to the current expulsion of the Jews from Germany; yet readers of Elias's account could hardly have failed to be impressed by the structural analogies he suggested. From the point of view of Elias's later work, it is striking how his interpretation of the fate of the Huguenots anticipated his theory of the relations between established and outsider groups.

Towards the end of the sixteenth century, the Protestants in France had been more or less assured of equal rights with the Catholics by the famous Edict of Nantes. In the penultimate decade of the seventeenth century these rights were taken from them and the majority of Protestants were expelled from France.

Why? What had happened?

When he came to the throne, Louis XIV had expressly confirmed to the Huguenots – or to the adherents of the RPR, the *Religion Prétendue Réformée*, as they were officially called – freedom of worship and all the rights they had been granted under the Edict of Nantes. This certainly did not put an end to the tensions between French Catholics and Protestants. But these tensions only became a threat to the weaker party when poverty increased in France.

The Protestants may not have been economically weaker than the Catholics. On the contrary. The wealth-owning stratum in France, the great French merchants and financiers, were mainly Protestant, whereas very few of the noble families who had converted to Protestantism during the religious wars remained true to the reformed faith. But taken as a whole, the Protestants did constitute only a minority. Those making up, above all, the administration, the judiciary and the army, the whole apparatus of royal rule were, leaving aside a few exceptions, Catholics. For in practice access to the bureaucracy and the court – the chief means of advancement in this society – was difficult for Protestants. For just this reason their energies were constantly channelled into activities in commerce, industry and finance. These provided a new opportunity to rise, the only one left open to them by the ruling Catholic society.

A French historian[1] sums up this situation as follows: 'Persecution engendered in the Huguenots the very capacity to enrich themselves for which the descendants of their persecutors censure them today. By the seventeenth century the jealousy of the poor for the rich, of the petty trader for the great merchant, of the weak industrialist for the strong, of land for money, can be seen contributing to the Catholics' hatred of Protestants.'

That the Catholic clergy fought with all their might against the emergence of another church hierarchy alongside their own, was a matter of course. And Louis XIV, who was accustomed to looking on France as a head of a household looks on his house – that is, as a piece of property subject to his sole will – Louis XIV took it as a personal affront that some of his subjects should reject the religion which he held to be right. He wished, and stated this wish often enough, that within the unified kingdom everyone should profess the same religion, his own. It is no accident, however, that he became seriously preoccupied with the question of the Protestants only decades after his accession to power. We can understand fairly readily when and why this became a critical issue. It was at the time when France's external expansion was meeting with ever greater difficulties, while social pressures within the country were increasing.

At that time France was the most densely populated country in Europe. What in Germany are called 'Louis XIV's predatory wars' were to a very substantial extent the consequence of the pressure which appears everywhere to be exerted, under certain circumstances, by more densely populated regions on less densely populated ones. This pressure is less detectable at times of economic prosperity, but it grows, it strains towards relief, it becomes what we are in the habit of calling 'overpopulation', when the bulk of the population find it harder and harder to meet their basic needs. There are a number of ways in which release can be obtained for such relative overpopulation – relative, that is, in respect to a particular economic and political system, for measured by its current population density, France, at the time of Louis XIV was by no means a heavily populated country. One form of release is war, another is peaceful emigration, a third is the more or less forcible expulsion of certain population groups, while a fourth is revolution, a violent change of the existing system of rule and economic organization.

Louis XIV's expansionist wars, initially successful, ended only by increasing the level of poverty in France. They exhausted the country. In his own consciousness, the king was driven by the desire to increase his own power and fame, by the wish to be the greatest ruler in Europe; but in fact he was driven also by the need for conspicuous outward successes in order to justify, and to reduce to a somewhat bearable level, the pressure of the immense burden which he and his governmental apparatus imposed on his subjects. Initially, the specific economic development of his country provided him with the necessary instruments. While it impoverished the rural masses, it favoured certain intermediate strata of the urban, commercial population. While the former flocked to join the army, the wealth of the middle class flowed, forcibly, into the king's coffers. Voluntary and involuntary contributions, a level of taxation which accounted for 35 per cent – or, according to Taine's estimate, as much as 50 per cent of the income of the taxable strata, financed the wars. Population growth also benefited the army. Between 1672 and 1678 the number of regular troops rose from 180,000 to 400,000.

Within this overall development, the Treaties of Nijmegen in 1678–79 formed a kind of turning point. They brought many benefits. They made the king appear to be, indeed, the mightiest ruler in Europe. But, measured by the dreams and wishes of the king and the needs of the country, they brought very little. While, in the short term, the outward glory of France was enhanced, in the long term the Treaties brought inward poverty. Holland, the main adversary, was not defeated, still less overrun and destroyed. And yet the king had thought it best to lay down his arms. The trade agreement demanded by the Dutch was more favourable to them than to France. Louis XIV had come up against the limits of his power. The internal pressure in the country had not been alleviated by the military success; poverty and tensions had been only increased. And at such a moment, when the external foe, despite all the apparent successes, has put up stronger resistance than had been expected, there is an increasing inclination to seek and find the enemy within the country itself. Rulers and peoples seldom take upon themselves the guilt for failures and unfulfilled dreams. The ageing king, turning more and more towards God after his Pyrrhic victories, needed a scapegoat in order to vindicate himself and do pleasing works in the eyes of his people. They, exhausted and wretched, needed a guilty party, a devil, someone to represent the root of all evil. Both found what they sought in the Protestants. As if following a recurrent law of social pressure, the hatred of the Catholic population and the punitive actions of the government were now directed more and more against these people, the group within their own country which seemed to them the most relatively alien.

Ideology and language, including official language, became increasingly violent. The king should do something for God, was the first demand; he should protect the injured Mother Church, bind up the festering sore; later this was simplified to: 'France needs to be purged of all these monsters.' There was no ill that was not to be laid at the Protestants' door. It began with the destruction of Protestant houses of prayer, and with the social demotion of Protestants so that others could fill their places. It ended with their actual expulsion.

Huguenot clergy were forbidden to call themselves 'pastor'; there were bureaucratic torments of every kind. As early as 1664 it had been decreed that only membership of the Catholic Church could be stated in licences granted to craftsmen. But this decree had been somewhat neglected over time. Now its observance began to be strictly enforced. In 1679 a decree was published whereby Protestants were excluded from all offices in the service of large landowners; a decree of 1680 removed them from offices in the service of tax farmers; in the same year a ban on marriages between Catholics and Protestants was promulgated; in 1682 Protestants were denied entry to the profession of notary, and to any official activity at court. This was followed by an influx of members of the reformed church to the so-called liberal professions. In Pau, for example, there were at that time 200 Protestant lawyers as compared to fifty Catholic. The result was a ban on the admission of

Protestants to the legal profession. In 1685 they were denied admission to the medical profession, and involvement in all branches of the publishing, printing and bookselling trades.

In the first phase of the intensifying persecution of Protestants, it was still possible to believe the assertion that what was at issue was religion, and there is no doubt that some of the persecutors really believed that they were fighting to uphold the old true faith, and for purity of doctrine. Their aim, so they declared, was to force those of the RPR to abjure their errors. Rewards for conversion were promised. And, indeed, under the growing pressure more and more of them were converted. But this was not enough to meet the social objectives of the movement. The people needed guilty parties, scapegoats, human devils, to discharge their fury and assuage their distress. They wanted to be rid of competitors, to attain better social functions, to exploit the attendant opportunities for wealth and prestige; and when too many were converted, seemingly or otherwise, for this purpose, finally no distinction was made between Protestant and recent convert. In terms of its social function, this religious persecution was a struggle of the majority against a minority which was economically and intellectually powerful but militarily weak, socially degraded and excluded from the apparatus of government. At a time when the population was increasing and the chances of satisfying the traditional standard of needs were growing fewer, this social function emerged in its nakedness.

This overt persecutory struggle was lent an especial intensity by the influx of soldiers returning after the Treaties of Nijmegen. An army of 400,000 men, which up to then had been fed at least in part by war, returned to France. And if some of them soon found employment in new wars, the flow of old soldiers and officers nevertheless accelerated the process of expelling the Protestants; and the involvement in this process of those accustomed to pillaging, plundering and tormenting their fellow humans in every way set its special, characteristic stamp on the religious persecution.

It is, of course, hardly more than a coincidence that the 400,000 returning from the wars were matched by 300,000 Protestants who left the country. What is certain, however, is that the influx of these hundreds of thousands immensely increased the population pressure, and that old soldiers played a quite specific role in the persecution of Protestants. The historical symbol of the meeting between the mercenaries flooding back and the Protestants condemned to emigration are the infamous dragonades. The horror of this technique of persecution has tarnished for ever the reputation of the reign of Louis XIV.

The wars of the seventeenth century were cruel in a somewhat different sense to those of today. The army had, as far as possible, to feed itself when on foreign soil. Plunder and rapine were not merely permitted, but were demanded by military technique. To torment the subjugated inhabitants of occupied territories and to set fire to their houses – all this was, as well as a means of satisfying lust, a deliberate means of collecting war contributions and bringing to light concealed treasure. Soldiers were supposed to behave like robbers. It was a banditry exacted and organized by the army commanders.

Grown accustomed to this life, the French mercenaries continued to behave in their own country, after the peace treaty, much as they had done previously on foreign soil. The Venetian ambassador wrote to his government at that time: 'I have with my own eyes seen small towns which previously had 700 or 800 dwellings but now, after the troops have passed through, have only thirty.' It was one of Louis XIV's provincial intendants who deliberately made use of this habit of the soldiery in the struggle against the Protestants. That was in 1680, one year after the Treaties had been concluded. Accompanied by monks and dragoons, he travelled through his province. The dragoons were billeted with Protestants. And they were allowed and obliged to abuse and beat their hosts as long as they refused to listen to the monks' sermons. What this meant is clear: women were dragged across the room by their hair, or with ropes; old people were tied to their beds and their children were mistreated before their eyes; people were made to sit on heated stoves; they were not allowed to sleep for days; the old soldiers were versed in torture of all kinds, indulging gladly in these practices in the name of the king and the affronted religion. An edict was issued: the billeted soldiers were to be copiously fed. In practice, this gave them the right to do and demand whatever they liked. To torture, rape and robbery were added economic ruin. The soldiers were ordered to create as much havoc as possible. The 'infernal legions' were allowed to commit any act short of direct murder; they could beat people, smoke them out, roast them, pour water into their mouths, make them dance till they fell, hang them by the nose or the toes – in a word: anything. Naturally, the king and his council had not directly and expressly ordered all this. 'It is possible', a historian writes, 'that they knew little of this; it is probable that they wished to know nothing.'

The first dragonades of 1680 had resulted immediately in 30,000 converts in one province. The great mass of Protestants still preferred to live in their own country, even at the price of returning to the Catholic Church, rather than flee to a foreign land. The mass emigration of members of the reformed church began only when there was really no other possibility, no other protection for life and property. To begin with, only a trickle of Protestants, the especially fervent and obstinate ones, made their way secretly across the border.

But the more Protestants were converted in order to stay at home, the less value their conversion had. Just because it was a mass conversion, the new converts formed a social group of their own. The Catholic Church was not able to digest them, clearly in part because at that time in France the Protestant clergy were superior to the Catholic in religious zeal, knowledge and power of conviction. For this very reason the Church urged the king to take a decisive step. The intendants, the judicial and administrative officials, and large sections of the Catholic population were also pushing, directly and indirectly, with various pretexts and for diverse practical reasons, in the same direction. In 1685 the king, inspired by his growing religious ardour and above all, by a desire for absolute unity among his subjects, bowed to the universal pressure and repealed the Edict of Nantes, thereby revoking in practice the equal rights of Protestants and of Protestant worship.

Central to the edict of revocation was the expulsion of all Protestant priests from France, the destruction of the houses of prayer and a ban on Protestant worship and schools. Forced labour in the galleys was the penalty imposed for any infringement. But if the wording of the Revocation was directed primarily against clergy, worship and schools, in reality it intensified the terrible pressure already being exerted on *all* Protestants. It became a signal for a mass exodus.

The Revocation itself, of course, had prohibited emigration. For the king and his ministers, people as such counted as a piece of national wealth – which the energetic and commercially competent Protestants actually and especially were. But the social constellation which from all sides strove for the expulsion of this section of society, was stronger than the will and intentions of the government. Illegally, using a thousand disguises and stratagems, Protestant men, women and children migrated in huge numbers across the strictly guarded frontiers. Special organizations grew up to help the refugees and, if possible, their wealth, to leave the country. The king or his counsellors yielded in one of the decrees which followed: 'We do not wish', it stated, 'to prevent the Protestants from emigrating, but their wealth must stay in the country.' None of this made much difference to the secret border-crossing. Legally or illegally, about 200,000 French Protestants had left their homeland by 1685.

Their fate as emigrants would be the subject of another chapter. At that time, the world was, economically, less interconnected than it is today. People of whom the economically overpopulated or – which comes to the same thing – the increasingly impoverished body politic of France had rid itself were, as we know, welcomed in other countries, especially Holland, Prussia, England, America and Switzerland. Louis XIV, who had hoped to annihilate Protestantism not only in France but in the whole of Europe, helped to spread and strengthen it.

The French who remained behind, however, suffered continuing poverty, at least in their great majority. These people who, unconsciously or half-consciously, had expected the extirpation of the Protestants to alleviate their misery, found themselves in no way better off. The king's financial policies, centrally determined by the desire for military power, for successful wars and for *gloire*, continued to burden the country. The state finances fell into increasing disorder. Poverty increased.

The connections between these phenomena can be discerned. The emigration of the Protestants from France is only an especially visible part of the wider social and economic process which the French social organism was undergoing at that time. In addition to the more or less consciously enforced Protestant emigration, there had already been a less visible Catholic one, as a simple consequence of the impoverishment of the country and of economic mismangement. And by 1720 a total of one million people, Catholic and Protestant, had emigrated from France.

But in France itself the ruinous financial policies led, after the king's death, to inflation and the concealed bankruptcy of the state. Moreover, as we know, the Protestants were never expelled entirely from France. Today, and for long past, they have again played a not inconsiderable role. All the same, from the time of the Protestant emigration onwards, Catholicism has shaped the national character of France more clearly than before.

5

THE KITSCH STYLE AND THE AGE OF KITSCH

Just as the article on the Huguenots adumbrated themes that were to recur in Elias's later writings, so did another article, on kitsch, in the émigré journal, *Die Sammlung*. The two articles were very different in tone, however. The piece on the Huguenots seemed to be 'under-theorized' – written as if it were nothing but a straight historical account. The essay about kitsch, on the other hand, was rather 'over-theorized', in a style reminiscent of the philosophies of culture of such men as Theodor Adorno and Walter Benjamin. Yet, unlike the work of those writers, it aimed primarily at giving a diagnosis rather than a critique. It was highly original, and, in our opinion, strikingly perceptive of cultural developments not just in the first but even in the second half of the twentieth century, with its leanings towards 'postmodernism'. Elias's arguments for designating the cultural style of our era as 'kitsch' appear to us as pertinent as when he propounded them in 1935.

In memory of Wolfgang Hellmert

I

That bourgeois strata fought their way to supremacy in the West in the course of the nineteenth century is well known; and the importance of bourgeois dominance for the social and political fate of nations has been discussed and evaluated often enough.

The profound transformation of aesthetic forms which took place in this period – the changes in architectural style or clothing, for example – has also been frequently mentioned and described.

But the connection between these two sets of changes, in society and aesthetics, has hardly ever been thoroughly investigated or made visible. One feels that there is a deeper division between the styles of the eighteenth and nineteenth centuries than between what we call the Baroque and the Rococo. But this difference in the nature of the aesthetic change only becomes clear if it is understood in terms of the situation of the society concerned. The change from the 'Baroque' to the 'Rococo', from the 'Louis Quatorze' to the 'Régence' style, is a change within the framework of the *same* social stratum. The deeper division which exists between the characteristic forms of the eighteenth and nineteenth centuries is an expression of the rise to power of a new social stratum, the capitalist-industrial bourgeoisie. Court style and taste were replaced by those of the capitalist bourgeoisie.

It has sometimes been said that the eighteenth century was the last to have a 'style' at all. And indeed, hardly has one dared to entertain the idea of a capitalist style than the doubts set in: Can one still speak of a 'style' in this context? It seems clear that the rise of bourgeois professional and industrial society was marked not only by the replacement of one aesthetic, one 'style' by another, but by the collapse of a coherent set of typical expressive forms. The aesthetic productions of capitalist society therefore tend to be described, far more than earlier ones, in relation to the single creative individual, or at most to various schools and tendencies. The existence of a unified development of forms and of common, typical basic structures, in short, of a 'style' of artworks in the capitalist world, remains more or less obscure. Names have been found, at most, for episodes in this development, for example, the so-called *Jugendstil*. A more comprehensive name is lacking, and the problem itself has hardly yet emerged into our consciousness.

If the term 'kitsch style' is used here to fill this gap, that may seem like a piece of eccentricity or even a malicious depreciation of the art of our time. In reality, the choice of this term is anything but a tendentious whim. For if we look beyond the general terms 'capitalist' or 'liberal' for underlying concepts expressing what is uniform in capitalist aesthetic idiom, after much sifting of terms which are either colourless or imply a positive evaluation, one comes across this term as one of the very few which express a pervasive feature of capitalist aesthetic products. To be sure, the term 'kitsch' is unclear enough in common usage. But if it can and should mean anything more than a random hotchpotch of tasteless abominations, if it is to be condensed from its vague generality to embrace the concrete phenomenon which underlies its topicality in our day, then its content and boundaries must be sought in the evolution of aesthetic form within bourgeois society. That the peculiarity of an age first becomes visible from a negative aspect is certainly not without precedent in history. Originally, terms such as 'Baroque' or 'Gothic' did not have a much more positive ring than 'kitsch' has today. Their value-content changed only in the course of social development, and – without giving undue weight to historical parallels – the term 'kitsch style' is sent on its way here with the same likelihood and expectation that its value may change, and to help prepare for such a change. It is used, first of all, to designate the stylistic character of the pre-war period. But no one is able to say whether we ourselves are not still 'pre-war' – that is, more closely tied to the pre-1914 period, when seen in a historical perspective – than appears to us today from our close, fore-shortening viewpoint.

What the term 'kitsch style' is intended to express first of all is an aesthetic quality of a very peculiar kind, namely the greater formal uncertainty inherent in all artistic production within industrial society. This can already be seen in the very early stages of the bourgeois-capitalist era. For to begin with liberal-bourgeois society certainly did not express itself in entirely new forms. Ornamentation persisted, and *Empire* and *Biedermeier* were clearly descend-ants of the old court style. What was lost, above all, was the certainty of taste and of the creative imagination, the solidity of the formal tradition which was discernible earlier in even the clumsiest products. Outbursts of feeling of unprecedented intensity shattered the old forms; groping for new ones, artists produced some well-formed works but, to an unprecedented degree, others marked by an extreme want of clarity and taste. In this groping, this co-existence of high standards with a total lack of standards, not only in different artists but often in one and the same individual, the change structure of the artistic process found especially vivid expression. For even the most capable artist the lapse into formlessness now became an acute and constant threat. Every successful, fully-formed work was now wrested from the abyss to a quite different extent than had been the case earlier, when a firm social tra-dition both fettered and sustained the creative urge. The formal tendencies of the works of great artists, whether they were called Heine or Victor Hugo, Wagner or Verdi, Rodin or Rilke, were intimately connected to those revealed by the mediocre works, which we dismiss as aberrations, as products of dis-integration and decadence, as 'kitsch'; one merges easily and imperceptibly into the other. Kitsch in the negative sense, therefore, is never only something antagonistic existing outside the true creators, but is also a basic situation within them, a part of themselves. This incessant interpenetration of struc-ture and disintegration is a feature of the lasting regularity to be observed in industrial society. It could be demonstrated no less in the works of the nine-teenth than of the twentieth century in the West, in Balzac as in Gide, in Ingres as in Picasso. And it is felt most strongly in precisely those works of this era in which form is most highly developed. The powerful accentuation, the peculiarly artificial and sometimes almost convulsive intensity of form characteristic of some of the greatest modern artists, expresses, funda-mentally, nothing other than this insecurity, this unabating struggle against formlessness and disintegration which even the most accomplished artists have to wage today. Think of Stefan George or Paul Valéry, of Proust or Thomas Mann, whose urbanely ironic speech rhythm is nothing but such a rampart. So much, in our age, has dilapidation become a constitutive element, decisively affecting even the positive aspect of artistic works. And, as we can see, the re-evaluation of kitsch as a positive concept begins already at this point.

II

There were gifted artists who created their works within the clear channel of a firm formal tradition, supported and restrained by the bearer of this tradition, a non-capitalist 'good society'. They were followed by others who had to make their way without such support, relying far more on themselves. But, certainly, the boundary-line between the two types can be only approximately drawn. The transition between them is made most vividly, if outwardly, visible by the destruction of the Parisian court society in the French Revolution. But this event was only a symptom of a comprehensive social regrouping which took place very gradually. Even the *pre*-revolutionary Greuze and the *pre*-revolutionary David were representatives of the new bourgeois style and belonged, to an extent, to the age of kitsch. Between them on one side, and the representatives of the court idiom such as Watteau, Fragonard and Boucher on the other, art slowly changed it direction.

The same is true of literature. In this sphere, too, at somewhat different times in each country, depending on its stage of social development, the same turning point is discernible. In France it is to be found roughly between Voltaire and Balzac, in Germany between Goethe and Heine. But even Goethe and Voltaire were no longer *ancien régime* in the strict sense, but more or less transitional figures on the periphery of court society.

Voltaire's style and sense of form were schooled and polished directly within the circles of the court nobility. Throughout his life he remained strongly attached to the traditions of this society with regard to form and taste. His deep understanding, his assurance in matters of form and taste were entirely of that society. But that he, the son of bourgeois parents, turned partly against the conservative maxims of court circles where reason and religion were concerned, that he *was able* to turn against them, already expresses the transitional situation of that society. He was exposed to the influences both of the high court society, which was already very decentralized, and of the bourgeois capitalist one which was gradually coming into being and emancipating itself.

In a different sense, corresponding to the different structure of the German countries, Goethe, too, was such a marginal figure, on the periphery of the court era and facing towards the bourgeois age. However, we should never forget that the *ancien régime* survived in Prussia-Germany, in a bourgeoisified and industrial form, until 1918, whereas it had, by and large, been demolished in France in 1789. But in France, with its continuous tradition over many centuries, the form-creating power of court society was extraordinarily strong. Despite its eradication as a political system, therefore, the *ancien régime*, through its tradition with regard to taste, has continued to exert, in that country, a vigorous influence within the framework of the industrial age and the kitsch style, until the present. In the most influential German country, Prussia, by contrast, the form-creating, cultural strength of court society, and thus the weight exerted on the kitsch style by the court tradition, was less. The uncertainty of taste was consequently greater, but so too was the willingness to try out new forms and directions.

Moreover, in this Germany of petty courts, the true culture-creating, or at least culture-consuming, stratum was formed, not by a nobility living on unearned income, but by a special form of the middle and upper civil service, which hardly existed in France and which included clergymen and university teachers no less than officers, court officials and the administrators of large estates. While this German bureaucracy, largely drawn from the bourgeoisie, always lived in a special dependence on court society proper, in secret it generally harboured a hopeless, almost unrealizable opposition to the court system, at least as long as it was largely denied access to the highest positions within court and government. German literature, from Lessing through the *Sturm und Drang* and the period of 'Sensibility' up to the Romanticism of the nineteenth and twentieth centuries, is full of testimonies to this impotent protest. And Goethe, too, must be understood within this context.

He, to be sure, belonged to the relatively small group of those who succeeded in rising from the burgeoisie to the top of an official hierarchy and a court society. And for this reason, too, he long remained a model and a wish-image for the German middle classes. He assimilated the attitudes and manners of court circles, but these were loose enough to allow him to manage and develop the court heritage in a highly independent way. In this fruitful situation of transition, this boundedness, the individual still had the firm support of tradition while enjoying much personal latitude. It is not least this situation which allows the direction in which Goethe's mighty talent expressed itself to be understood. He developed a greatness which was strictly bound to classicist forms, but at the same time had a very personal and individual coloration.

Of course, just like Voltaire or – in the field of music – Mozart (admittedly, a less marginal figure and a more direct representative of the *ancien régime*), he wrote works of very variable stature, shaped with greater or lesser power. But they are never formless; these men never ceased being guided by the accustomed good taste, which as demanded and monitored by society; their individual feeling never ruptured and destroyed the prescribed formal idiom. In this they differ fundamentally from the artists of the age of kitsch. They enlarged and loosened the traditional elements of style and expression, and undoubtedly felt their oppressive weight. But in the end they managed all this within the framework of the prevailing stylistic convention.

How much this changed in the following generations is well known. Beethoven, in whose hands the traditional formal and expressive idiom began to break up, was a far more marginal and transitional figure than Mozart or even Goethe. His inborn talent actually benefited from the fertility of the transitional situation. Later, however, in the succeeding generations, the break was complete. Here, in Schubert or Schumann, Heine or Balzac – to pick out a few of the many names – the sure guidance was lost. Side by side with highly successful works, fully-formed in a comparatively individual way, we find uncontrolled outbursts of feeling, aberrations and lapses of taste. The kitsch style, with its specifically new greatness and smallness, has arrived.

III

In the nineteenth century good taste was upheld by a different social stratum from previously. The position of the artist and the social function of art changed radically in bourgeois-industrial society. As the bourgeois influence spread through the whole of society, what had previously been handed down tacitly and almost automatically within the medium of the more stable 'good society' – *savoir vivre*, the correct attitude, assured taste – ceased to be imparted imperceptibly to each member of the social group concerned, and had to be taught to individuals by specialists. Napoleon consciously schooled himself, using actors as models. The dandy Beau Brummel, the archetypal specialist in taste, had to instruct English good society, the courtiers and even the Prince Regent himself, in poise and taste. An especially impressive example of this change is to be found in the history of painting. Up to Manet and the Impressionists, it had been 'good societies', ruling social groups, who had, if to an ever-diminishing extent, set their stamp on the prevailing style of painting as an important means of social self-projection. But with the Impressionists a specialist art asserted itself very clearly for the first time against the predominant social art and the prevailing taste, and from then on the peculiarity of great art and the existential situation of its creators cannot be fully understood unless this specialized individualization, the growing self-reliance of artists, the total change in their position within society, is seen constantly permeating the changing forms of their works and the figures depicted. The Impressionists were thoroughly bourgeois people and by no means revolutionaries in the social sense, or clear representatives of a class rising from below to challenge the ruling bourgeoisie. The initial incomprehension of professional society for impressionist art is symptomatic not of the social tension between different strata of workers, but of the rift and tension between the taste of the leading specialists, of great art of every kind on one side, and of mass society, of non-specialists, on the other.

Poussin and Watteau, Racine and even Voltaire, produced their works as servants, or at least as social inferiors, primarily for a court society which played an active part in shaping artistic taste. While Goethe rose to a position of equality, he was always contained and controlled by a rigid, socially powerful circle. Manet, Cézanne and Picasso, by contrast, or Valéry and George, were all roughly the social equals of their clientele. But now, as isolated individuals in the free market, using their own resources or with the support of patrons, they had to offer their wares to a more or less unknown public. Small circles of connoisseurs and collectors, specialists in their turn, found themselves and their lives expressed and heightened in this art. Around them a small coterie of snobs and imitators pretended to respond to this art since that conferred prestige. Beyond them the bulk of society stood puzzled and uncomprehending before these works which they were unable to see as representing, at least directly, their own psychological condition.

The term 'kitsch' is nothing other than an expression for this tension between the highly-formed taste of the specialists and the undeveloped, unsure taste of mass society. The word 'kitsch' probably originated in a specialist milieu of artists and art dealers in Munich in the early twentieth century, being first used to refer to certain 'sketches' which sold well among American tourists. The word 'kitsch' was thus derived from 'sketch'. Anything intended to be sold was said to be made for *Verkitschen*, for turning into kitsch. In this original meaning of the term 'kitsch' the whole contempt of the specialist for the uneducated taste of capitalist society is expressed, as well as the tragic aspect of this constellation, in which the specialists, whether artists, dealers or publishers, were obliged for economic reasons to produce and sell products which they themselves despised. The public, with all the economic and social power it wielded, necessarily had an impact on the specialists and their taste. Slowly, and often with a long time-lag, the specialists influenced the development of public taste. Despite all the tensions between the two, this interdependence gave rise to a certain linkage of expressive forms, as when the specialist forms of 'Expressionism' or 'Cubism' were adopted, after a time and in modified form, in advertising posters or coffeehouse architecture. But in addition, the two poles between which the kitsch style emerged, specialist taste and the taste of the multi-layered mass society, were linked by their common experiences and situation, the great destiny which swept all factions along together like an uncontrollable river – a destiny symbolized by wars or social conflicts, prosperity or crises. This encompassing regularity finally endowed the expressive forms of the fragmented society with a very specific uniformity, a 'style' which, admittedly, in keeping with the structure of the underyling society, was looser, more disparate and richer in contrasts than earlier styles.

IV

The particular formal problems raised by the kitsch style – which are highly revealing with regard to our own lives and those of our parents – still need to be resolved. In this context I must be content with a few pointers which at least show where the problems are to be found.

(1) *Leisure dreams of a working society*

If we leave aside obviously utilitarian forms, any aesthetic work has for the 'public', for the mass of the working population, the function of a leisure dream. This function gives our arts a very different face, compared to those of court, patrician or church hierarchies. The need of mass society for leisure pastimes, which the specialists have to satisfy, is supplementary to the primary needs for work and bread. It is never as vitally important as these, and the form it takes is determined by them – for example, by the constant strain of professional life, the desire to discharge feelings heavily suppressed in working life, or the tendency to seek in leisure substitute satisfactions for wishes not fulfilled by work. In face of the compulsive way in which professional life pushes the leisure activities of industrial man in a highly specific direction, the individual art specialist is powerless. He may poke fun at such activities as much as he likes, deriding the leisure dreams and the taste of souls deformed by work pressures as 'kitsch', and mocking the 'sentimental' manner in which feelings pent up and damaged under the constraint of work are expressed. *The need for that which is here called 'kitsch' is socially imposed*, while kitsch itself, in the negative sense of the word, is the faithful reflection of a state of the soul engendered by industrial society. This endows the problem of kitsch with a seriousness with which it is not normally credited.

(2) *The emancipation of individual feeling*

Almost all of the mediocre products of the kitsch era, and very many of the great ones, are distinguished from those of the past by a specific and especially powerful emotional charge. This manifests itself in the great works of music, for example, in which, from Beethoven, Schubert and Schumann, and through high points such as Verdi and Wagner, to Debussy, Ravel, Stravinsky and Weill, the permeation by feeling is carried forward through ever-new forms to ever-new strata of society. In painting, too – again disregarding certain countervailing tendencies – this phenomenon is no less clearly discernible. From at least the Impressionists onwards, despite the assertions of many artists themselves, what is presented again and again, and far more strongly than ever before, is not the so-called objective world but nature with its particular emotive value, as experienced and felt by the individual. This emotive charge manifests itself no less forcibly in what is called 'kitsch' in the negative sense, in kitsch postcards, for example, which are designed solely to touch the beholder's feelings, or in sentimental popular songs. It is characteristic of the problems posed by kitsch that the form of expression used in such songs seems so false and almost ridiculous, whereas the emotional need behind them, born of the impossibility of finding in scanty leisure time the relationships which working life precludes, is absolutely genuine.

(3) *Progressive and conservative tendencies of the kitsch style*

In industrial societies the disputes over the proper modes of expression of human life are hardly carried on any longer between the various social strata themselves, but between art specialists who act, consciously or unconsciously, as representatives of particular social groups and tendencies. Hence, peculiar tensions are to be found in the aesthetic sphere of industrial society which correspond fairly exactly to the existing social tensions. One pole is formed by tendencies which consciously or unconsciously take the artistic styles of earlier societies as their models. Its representatives want to admit only the great and the sublime, that is, an idealized and heavily censored version of existence, into the sanctuary of art. The other pole is formed by tendencies seeking to explode existing artistic forms and to find new forms for the new human and social situation, the changed relationships and experiences characteristic of industrial society. The former seek refuge from the uncertainty pressing in on them in the idealized world of beautiful forms. But whereas, for their models, this world was largely provided by the secure sense of form and the firmly established style of the society around them, their later emulators have to struggle to recreate it over and over again as isolated individuals.

The artists representing the other, progressive pole, such as Zola or Malraux, the early Gerhard Hauptmann or Brecht, want to wrest certain experiences from the mechanism of concealment. They no longer want to hide pettiness and confusion, shabbiness and helplessness behind the symmetry of well-rounded forms; in addition to joy and a masterful bearing they seek expression for threat, dirt and danger, deformity and excess. The problems inherent in their work are certainly different, but no less serious, than those facing the conservative artists. In the works of the latter, to put it briefly, a form which is at least still half-traditional too readily overwhelms the content; it excludes certain experiences, ideas and situations. The danger for the progressive artists is the converse, the overwhelming of form by content. For in their work it is on content, on the idea and what is to be represented, that the primary accent is placed.

In this antithesis, however, the social tension is exactly reflected. Within a given ruling class, as it distances itself from the stratum below, attitude and gesture, ostentation and the 'how' of self-projection, have always been of special importance. They are instruments of distancing. For the new, rising groups, by contrast, idea and content, precisely what the conservative classes would like to censor and leave unsaid, are incomparably more important than form. This helps to explain the preponderant role played by content and subject matter, whether it be feeling or purpose, in the artworks of the kitsch era – in all the inferior works and in many of the successful ones – as compared to the *form* of representation. It results not least from the characteristic constellation which makes it relatively easy to rise from the strata of the masses, but more and more difficult for a 'good society' to encapsulate and consolidate itself, to maintain a rigid tradition of social forms. Restlessness increases, families rise and fall more rapidly, there is a relative atomization of society, and aesthetic influence passes gradually from fixed social circles to isolated taste specialists and their schools. In conjunction with technological change and other factors which cannot be considered here, all this causes the mechanism of aesthetic production to operate very differently in industrial society than in those which preceded it. For this reason the chasm between the kitsch style and earlier styles is particularly deep.

The term 'kitsch' tends towards vagueness. I leave the argument about definitions to others. What has concerned me here are the conditions which gave rise, not to the term, but to 'kitsch' and the kitsch style itself. Did kitsch also exist at earlier times? That remains to be investigated. It will undoubtedly have existed if similar conditions of production were present earlier. Otherwise, to refer to earlier formal qualities as 'kitsch' is no more than an empty analogy.

Whether someone today perceives the paradoxical and antinomic connection between the great works of the artists–specialists and the works produced to satisfy mass taste, depends on the vision of the individual. The term 'kitsch style' has been used here to point to this connection. The difficult fertility, the problematic greatness of our social and artistic existence are encompassed by this term. But so, too, are the awareness of the radical transformation in which we are involved, and a presentiment of the immense new artistic possibilities which lie before us on the journey on which we have embarked.

PART II

THE CIVILIZING PROCESS, 1935–1940

6

AN OUTLINE OF *THE CIVILIZING PROCESS*[1]

When Elias arrived in England, the only people whom he knew there were a few fellow refugees from Germany. He had only a passive command of English, being able to read but not to speak it. He did not have a job; a Jewish refugee fund provided him with a small grant that enabled him to do research and to write a book. So he spent his days in the reading room of the library of the British Museum in Bloomsbury, where he wrote *The Civilizing Process*.

We can only marvel at the speed at which he must have worked, apparently in a continuous flurry of inspiration. He was able to draw both on historical material he had collected earlier, in Heidelberg, Frankfurt, and Paris, and on the powers of reasoning he had developed in his previous studies ranging from philosophy to physiology. According to his own testimony, in London the thought struck him that he could use successive editions of manners books as a source of evidence for long-term changes in conduct and sentiment. This enabled him to extend the empirical basis of cultural history as it had been written by such scholars as Johan Huizinga. He then proceeded to put his findings into a broad sociological perspective, in the tradition of Max Weber, and to connect them also with psychoanalytic theory as developed by Sigmund Freud.

Not surprisingly, the final result, *The Civilizing Process*, is a complex work – highly readable and easily accessible at first sight, but also replete with far-reaching and often subtle implications. It is a work of synthesis, in which many different strands of thought are woven together. By now it has reached the status of a 'classic' in several fields. Much has been written about it, by way of introduction, comment or critique. Yet in order to explain the general plan of the book – the problems it addresses and the way the argument unfolds – we cannot think of any text that would improve upon the original preface by Elias himself, dated September 1936.

Central to this study are modes of behaviour considered typical of people who are civilized in a Western way. The problem they pose is simple enough. Western people have not always behaved in the manner we are accustomed to regard as typical or as the hallmark of 'civilized' people. If a member of present-day Western civilized society were to find himself suddenly transported into a past epoch of his own society, such as the medieval-feudal period, he would find there much that he esteems 'uncivilized' in other societies today. His reaction would scarcely differ from that produced in him at present by the behaviour of people in feudal societies outside the Western world. He would, depending on his situation and inclinations, be either attracted by the wilder, more unrestrained and adventurous life of the upper classes in this society, or repulsed by the 'barbaric' customs, the squalour and coarseness that he encountered there. And whatever he understands by his own 'civilization', he would at any rate feel quite unequivocally that society in this past period of Western history was not 'civilized' in the same sense and to the same degree as Western society today.

This state of affairs may seem obvious to many people, and it might appear unnecessary to refer to it here. But it necessarily gives rise to questions which cannot with equal justice be said to be clearly present in the consciousness of living generations, although these questions are not without importance for an understanding of ourselves. How did this change, this 'civilizing' of the West, actually happen? Of what did it consist? And what were its causes or motive forces? It is to the solution of these main questions that this study attempts to contribute.

To facilitate understanding of this book, and thus as an introduction to the questions themselves, it seems necessary to examine the different meanings and evaluations assigned to the concept of 'civilization' in Germany and France. This inquiry makes up the first chapter. It may help the reader to see the concepts of *Kultur* and *civilisation* as somewhat less rigidly and self-evidently opposed. And it may also make a small contribution toward improving the German historical understanding of the behaviour of Frenchmen and Englishmen, and the French and English understanding of the behaviour of Germans. But in the end it will also serve to clarify certain typical features of the civilizing process.

To gain access to the main questions, it is necessary first to obtain a clearer picture of how the behaviour and affective life of Western peoples slowly changed after the Middle Ages. To show this is the task of the second chapter. It attempts as simply and clearly as possible to open the way to an understanding of the *psychical* process of civilization. It may be that the idea of a psychical process extending over many generations appears hazardous and dubious to present-day historical thinking. But it is not possible to decide in a purely theoretical, speculative way whether the changes in psychical makeup observable in the course of Western history took place in a particular order and direction. Only a scrutiny of documents of historical experience can show what is correct and what is incorrect in such theories. That is why it is not possible here, when knowledge of this documentary material cannot be presupposed, to give a brief preliminary sketch of the structure and central ideas of the whole book. They themselves take on a firmer form only gradually, in a continuous observation of historical facts and a constant checking and revision of what has been seen previously through what entered later into the field of observation. And thus the individual parts of this study, its structure and method, will probably be completely intelligible only when they are perceived in their entirety. It must suffice here, to facilitate the reader's understanding, to pick out a few problems.

The second chapter contains a number of series of examples. They serve to show development in an accelerated fashion. In a few pages we see how in the course of centuries the standard of human behaviour on the same occasion very gradually shifts in a specific direction. We see people at table, we see them going to bed or in hostile clashes. In these and other elementary activities the manner in which the individual behaves and feels slowly changes. This change is in the direction of a gradual 'civilization', but only historical experience makes clearer what this word actually means. It shows, for example, the decisive role played in this civilizing process by a very specific change in the feelings of shame and delicacy. The standard of what society demands and prohibits changes; in conjunction with this, the threshold of socially instilled displeasure and fear moves; and the question of sociogenic fears thus emerges as one of the central problems of the civilizing process.

Very closely related to this is a further range of questions. The distance in behaviour and whole psychical structure between children and adults increases in the course of the civilizing process. Here, for example, lies the key to the question of why some peoples or groups of peoples appear to us as 'younger' or 'more childlike', others as 'older' or 'more grown-up'. What we are trying to express in this way are differences in the kind and stage of the civilizing process that these societies have attained; but that is a separate question which cannot be included within the framework of this study. The series of examples and the interpretations of them in the second chapter show one thing very clearly: the specific process of psychological 'growing up' in Western societies, which frequently occupies the minds of psychologists and pedagogues today, is nothing other than the individual civilizing process to which each young person, as a result of the social civilizing process over many centuries, is automatically subjected from earliest childhood, to a greater or lesser degree and with greater or lesser success. The psychogenesis of the adult makeup in civilized society cannot, therefore, be understood if considered independently of the sociogenesis of our 'civilization'. By a kind of basic 'sociogenetic law'[1] the individual, in his short history, passes once more through some of the processes that his society has traversed in its long history.

It is the purpose of the third chapter, which constitutes the greater part of the second volume, to make certain processes in this long history of society more accessible to understanding. It attempts, within a number of precisely defined areas, to clarify how and why in the course of its history the structure of Western society continuously changes, and points at the same time to an answer to the question of why, in the same areas, the standard of behaviour and the psychical makeup of Western peoples change.

We see, for example, the social landscape of the early Middle Ages. There is a multitude of greater and smaller castles; even the town settlements of earlier times have become feudalized. Their centres too are formed by the castles and estates of lords from the warrior class. The question is: What are the sets of social relationships that press toward the development of what we call the 'feudal system'? The attempt is made to demonstrate some of these 'mechanisms of feudalization'. We see further how, from the castle landscape, together with a number of free, urban craft and commercial settlements, a number of larger and richer feudal estates slowly emerge. Within the warrior class itself a kind of upper stratum forms more and more distinctly; their dwelling places are the real centres of *Minnesang* and the lyrics of the troubadors, on the one hand, and of *courtois* forms of behaviour on the other. If earlier in the book the *courtois* standard of conduct is placed at the starting point of a number of sequences of examples giving a picture of the subsequent change of psychical makeup, here we gain access to the sociogenesis of these *courtois* forms of behaviour themselves.

Or we see, for example, how the early form of what we call a 'state' develops. In the age of absolutism, under the watchword of *civilité*, behaviour moves very perceptibly toward the standard that we denote today by a derivative of the word *civilité* as 'civilized' behaviour. It therefore seems necessary, in elucidating this civilizing process, to obtain a clearer picture of what gave rise to the absolutist regimes and therefore to the absolutist state. It is not only the observation of the past that points in this direction; a wealth of contemporary observations suggest strongly that the structure of civilized behaviour is closely interrelated with the organization of Western societies in the form of states. The question, in other words, is: How did the extremely decentralized society of the early Middle Ages, in which numerous greater and smaller warriors were the real rulers of Western territory, become one of the internally more or less pacified but outwardly embattled societies that we call states? Which dynamics of human interdependencies push toward the integration of ever larger areas under a relatively stable and centralized government apparatus?

It may perhaps seem at first sight an unnecessary complication to investigate the genesis of each historical formation. But since every historical phenomenon, human attitudes as much as social institutions, did actually once 'develop', how can modes of thought prove either simple or adequate in explaining these phenomena if, by a kind of artificial abstraction, they isolate the phenomena from their natural, historical flow, deprive them of their character as movement and process, and try to understand them as static formations without regard to the way in which they have come into being and change? It is not theoretical prejudice but experience itself which urges us to seek intellectual ways and means of steering a course between the Scylla of this 'statism', which tends to express all historical movement as something motionless and without evolution, and the Charybdis of the 'historical relativism' which sees in history only constant transformation, without penetrating to the order underlying this transformation and to the laws governing the formation of historical structures. That is what is attempted here. The sociogenetic and psychogenetic investigation sets out to reveal the *order* underlying historical *changes*, their mechanics and their concrete mechanisms; and it seems that in this way a large number of questions that appear complicated or even beyond understanding today can be given fairly simple and precise answers.

For this reason, this study also inquires into the sociogenesis of the state. There is, to take one aspect of the history of the state's formation and structure, the problem of the 'monopoly of force'. Max Weber pointed out, mainly for the sake of definition, that one of the constitutive institutions required by the social organization we call a state is a monopoly in the exercise of physical force. Here the attempt is made to reveal something of the concrete historical processes that, from the time when the exercise of force was the privilege of a host of rival warriors, gradually impelled society towards this centralization and monopolization of the use of physical violence and its instruments. It can be shown that the tendency to form such monopolies in this past epoch of our history is neither easier nor more difficult to understand than, for example, the strong tendency toward monopolization in our own epoch. And it is then not difficult to understand that with this monopolization of physical violence as the point of intersection of a multitude of social interconnections, the whole apparatus which shapes the individual, the mode of operation of the social demands and prohibitions which mould his social makeup, and above all the kinds of fear that play a part in his life are decisively changed.

Finally, the concluding 'Sketch of a Theory of Civilization' underlines once more the connections between changes in the structure of society and changes in the structure of behaviour and psychical makeup. Much of what could only be hinted at earlier, in depicting concrete historical processes, is now stated explicitly. We find here, for example, a short sketch of the structure of the fears experienced as shame and delicacy, as a kind of theoretical summing-up of what previously emerged of itself from the study of historical documents; we find an explanation of precisely why fears of this kind play an especially important role in the advance of the civilizing process; and at the same time, some light is shed on the formation of the 'superego' and on the relation of the conscious and unconscious impulses in the psyche of civilized people. Here an answer is given to the question of historical processes; the question of how all these processes, consisting of nothing but the actions of individual people, nevertheless give rise to institutions and formations which were neither intended nor planned by any single individual in the form they actually take. And finally, in a broad survey, these insights from the past are combined into a single picture with experiences from the present.

This study therefore poses and develops a very wide-ranging problem; it does not pretend to solve it.

It marks out a field of observation that has hitherto received relatively little attention, and undertakes the first steps toward an explanation. Others must follow.

Many questions and aspects which presented themselves in the course of this study I deliberately did not pursue. It was not so much my purpose to build a general theory of civilization in the air, and then afterward find out whether it agreed with experience; rather, it seemed the primary task to begin by regaining within a limited area the lost perception of the process in question, the peculiar transformation of human behaviour, then to seek a certain understanding of its causes, and finally to gather together such theoretical insights as have been encountered on the way. If I have succeeded in providing a tolerably secure foundation for further reflection and research in this direction, this study has achieved everything it set out to achieve. It will need the thought of many people and the cooperation of different branches of scholarship, which are often divided by artificial barriers today, gradually to answer the questions that have arisen in the course of this study. They concern psychology, philology, ethnology, and anthropology no less than sociology or the different special branches of historical research.

However, the issues raised by the book have their origin less in scholarly tradition, in the narrower sense of the word, than in the experiences in whose shadow we all live, experiences of the crisis and transformation of Western civilization as it had existed hitherto, and the simple need to understand what this 'civilization' really amounts to. But I have not been guided in this study by the idea that our civilized mode of behaviour is the most advanced of all humanly possible modes of behaviour, nor by the opinion that 'civilization' is the worst form of life and one that is doomed. All that can be seen today is that with gradual civilization a number of specific civilizational difficulties arise. But it cannot be said that we already understand why we actually torment ourselves in this way. We feel that we have got ourselves, through civilization, into certain entanglements unknown to less civilized peoples; but we also know that these less civilized peoples are for their part often plagued by difficulties and fears from which we no longer suffer, or at least not to the same degree. Perhaps all this can be seen somewhat more clearly if it is understood how such civilizing processes actually take place. At any rate, that was one of the wishes with which I set to work on this book. It may be that, through clearer understanding, we shall one day succeed in making accessible to more conscious control these processes which today take place in and around us not very differently from natural events, and which we confront as medieval people confronted the forces of nature.

7

KULTUR AND CIVILISATION

The Civilizing Process is a book with a complicated history. Elias wrote it in England, in his native language, German. When the text was finished, he sent it off to Breslau, where his parents still lived. There the book was printed, in two volumes. Since the author was Jewish, however, publication in Germany was forbidden, and plans were made to publish it in Prague. But then, in 1938, Czechoslovakia lost its independence, and publication in Prague also became impossible. Eventually the book appeared in Switzerland in 1939, under the imprint of a German publishing house in exile. The words 'printed in Germany' were obliterated in every copy sent out by the publisher.

The book appeared just in time for review copies to be dispatched to various countries which were not yet under German occupation. Some highly favourable reviews appeared, mostly written by men of Elias's own generation, several of whom belonged to his personal circle of acquaintances and were, like himself, living as refugees in England. There were about ten reviews altogether; they were written in no fewer than four European languages: English, German, Dutch, and French.

While these reviews helped to draw attention to Elias's work among the readers of some professional journals, they did not have much long-lasting effect. The reviewers, themselves in exile, were caught up in the concerns of their wartime lives, and they hardly ever saw occasion to refer again to Norbert Elias in writing – especially since for many years Elias himself did not bring out any new publication. The only country where some interest in his work continued to be expressed was the Netherlands (see below, pp. 141–2).

It took more than twenty years for the first edition of *The Civilizing Process* to be sold out. And it was not until 1969 that a Swiss–German academic publisher made the book available again, in an expensive new edition, consisting of a photographic two-volume reprint of the original book, supplemented by a new seventy-page introduction.

This reprint heralded a new, more propitious phase in the reception of Elias's work. In the 1970s and early 1980s *The Civilizing Process* was translated into several languages, including English. Unfortunately the English translation was published in a way that created unnecessary confusion. Volume One appeared in 1978, as a single book, with the fancy title *The History of Manners*. It was only in 1982 that Volume Two appeared, under two different titles: in the United States it was called *Power and Civility*, in England, more appropriately, *State Formation and Civilization*. In 1994 a one-volume edition was produced, with newly set type and continuous page numbers, but still containing two separate tables of contents, and reproducing all the typographic and other errors of the first edition.

As Elias's own Foreword (see above, pp. 39–45) made abundantly clear, *The Civilizing Process* is to be understood as a single monograph in its own right. He himself composed it in four successive parts. In our selections for this reader we have followed that four-part sequence.

Part One is the briefest part of the book. It discusses the social origins, or 'sociogenesis', of the concepts of civilization and culture in France and Germany. It shows how the divergent national careers of these concepts can be linked to the position of intellectuals in French and German society in the eighteenth century. Whereas in France at that time intellectuals already played a significant political role, in Germany they were confined to the 'cultural' sphere of philosophy and literature. For German intellectuals the main social base was the university, and their main vehicle of communication was writing. Their French counterparts, by contrast, had access to courtly circles, where they could discuss economic and political issues in serious conversation with people who held positions of power; some of them even attained very influential positions themselves.

It was in this context that the concept of *civilisation* was coined. The following excerpt, the concluding section of Part One, focuses on how the different *social* conditions of intellectual life in France and Germany gave rise to the particular meanings of *civilisation* and *Kultur* as expressions of different *national* identities.

Two ideas are fused in the concept of civilization. On the one hand, it constitutes a general counterconcept to another stage of society, barbarism. This feeling had long pervaded courtly society. It had found its courtly–aristocratic expression in terms such as *politesse* or *civilité*.

But peoples are not yet civilized enough, say the men of the courtly/middle-class reform movement. Civilization is not only a state, it is a process which must be taken further. That is the new element expressed in the term *civilisation*. It absorbs much of what has always made court society believe itself, as compared to those living in a simpler, more uncivilized or more barbaric way, a higher kind of society: the idea of a standard of morals and manners, i.e., social tact, consideration for others, and many related complexes. But in the hands of the rising middle class, in the mouth of the reform movement, the idea of what is needed to make a society civilized is extended. The civilizing of the state, the constitution, education, and there-fore of broader sections of the population, the liberation from all that was still barbaric or irrational in existing conditions, whether it be the legal penalties or the class restrictions on the bourgeoisie or the barriers impeding a freer development of trade – this civilizing must follow the refinement of manners and the internal pacification of the country by the kings.

'The king succeeded', Voltaire once said of the age of Louis XIV, 'in making of a hitherto turbulent nation a peaceful people dangerous only to its enemies. . . . Manners were softened. . . .'[33] It will be seen in more detail later how important this internal pacification was for the civilizing process. Condorcet, however, who was by comparison with Voltaire a reformist of the younger generation and already far more inclined to opposition, comments as follows on this reflection of Voltaire's: 'Despite the barbarity of some of the laws, despite the faults of the administrative principles, the increase in duties, their burdensome form, the harshness of fiscal laws, despite the pernicious maxims which direct the government's legislation on commerce and manu-facture, and finally despite the persecution of the Protestants, one may observe that the peoples within the realm lived in peace under the protection of law.'

This enumeration, itself not entirely without affirmation of the existing order, gives a picture of the many things thought in need of reform. Whether or not the term *civilisation* is here used explicitly, it relates to all this, every-thing which is still 'barbaric'.

This discussion makes very clear the divergence from developments in Germany and German concepts: it shows how members of the rising middle-class intelligentsia in France stand partly within the court circle, and so within the courtly-aristocratic tradition. They speak the language of this circle and develop it further. Their behaviour and affects are, with certain modifications, modelled on the pattern of this tradition. Their concepts and ideas are by no means mere antitheses of those of the courtly aristocracy. Around courtly-aristocratic concepts such as the idea of 'being civilized', they crystallize, in conformity with their social position within the court circle, further ideas from the area of their political and economic demands, ideas which, owing to the different social situation and range of experience of the German intelli-gentsia, were largely alien to it and at any rate far less relevant.

The French bourgeoisie – politically active, at least partly eager for reform, and even, for a short period, revolutionary – remained strongly bound to the courtly tradition in its behaviour and its affect-moulding even after the edifice of the old regime had been demolished. For through the close contact between aristocratic and middle-class circles, a great part of courtly manners had long before the revolution become middle-class manners. So it can be understood that the bourgeois revolution in France, though it destroyed the old political structure, did not disrupt the unity of traditional manners.

The German middle-class intelligentsia, politically entirely impotent but intellectually radical, forged a purely bourgeois tradition of its own, diverging widely from the courtly-aristocratic tradition and its models. The German national character which slowly emerged in the nineteenth century was not, to be sure, entirely lacking in aristocratic elements assimilated by the bourgeoisie. Nevertheless, for large areas of the German cultural tradition and German behaviour, the specifically middle-class characteristics were predominant, particularly as the sharper social division between bourgeois and aristocratic circles, and with it a relative heterogeneity of German manners, survived long after the eighteenth century.

The French concept of *civilisation* reflects the specific social fortunes of the French bourgeoisie to exactly the same degree that the concept of *Kultur* reflects the German. The concept of *civilisation* is first, like *Kultur*, an instrument of middle-class circles – above all, the middle-class intelligentsia – in the internal social conflict. With the rise of the bourgeoisie, it too comes to epitomize the nation, to express the national self-image. In the revolution itself *civilisation* (which, of course, refers essentially to a gradual process, an evolution, and has not yet discarded its original meaning as a watchword of reform) does not play any considerable part among the revolutionary slogans. As the revolution grows more moderate, shortly before the turn of the century, it starts on its journey as a rallying cry throughout the world. Even as early as this, it has a level of meaning justifying French aspirations to national expansion and colonization. In 1798, as Napoleon sets off for Egypt, he shouts to his troops: 'Soldiers, you are undertaking a conquest with incalculable consequences for civilization.' Unlike the situation when the concept was formed, from now on nations consider the *process* of civilization as completed within their own societies; they see themselves as bearers of an existing or finished civilization to others, as standard-bearers of expanding civilization. Of the whole preceding process of civilization nothing remains in their consciousness except a vague residue. Its outcome is taken simply as an expression of their own higher gifts; the fact that, and the question of how, in the course of many centuries, civilized behaviour has been attained is of no interest. And the consciousness of their own superiority, the consciousness of this 'civilization', from now on serves at least those nations which have become colonial conquerors, and therefore a kind of upper class to large sections of the non-European world, as a justification of their rule, to the same degree that earlier the ancestors of the concept of civilization, *politesse* and *civilité*, had served the courtly-aristocratic upper class as a justification of theirs.

Indeed, an essential phase of the civilizing process was concluded at exactly the time when the *consciousness* of civilization, the consciousness of the superiority of their own behaviour and its embodiments in science, technology, or art began to spread over whole nations of the West.

This earlier phase of the civilizing process, the phase in which the consciousness of the process scarcely existed and the concept of civilization did not exist at all, will be discussed in Part Two.

8

THE RISE OF THE FORK

Part Two has become the best known part of *The Civilizing Process*. It contains extensive excerpts from the successive editions of manner books, followed by Elias's own commentaries arguing how, out of the various fragments, a picture emerges of a long-term developmental change in the standards of conduct in a particular direction.

Medieval manner books were addressed primarily to young noblemen, who apparently needed to be taught how to behave when they came to live at a grand court. A great deal of attention was paid to the question of how to conduct yourself in company at table – typically a situation in which people would find themselves closely together, in a position to watch – and be watched by – others. The manners books urged their readers in such situations always to observe the proper hierarchy, and to show the respect due to one's table companions by abstaining from such uncouth acts as snorting, gobbling, and slurping.

From the sixteenth century onwards, the rules became increasingly more refined and elaborate. This tendency was clearly reflected in the recommendations about the use of the fork. It seems that forks were introduced to Western Europe in the eleventh century by a Byzantine princess married to a Venetian Doge. Although these eating utensils were at first regarded by many as an exotic luxury, useless and awkward, they gradually found their way – first to the tables of the courtly upper classes, and then to increasingly wider social circles.

As Elias made clear, the rise of the fork and the simultaneous increase of restrictions on the use of the knife were not isolated events. They were part of a much more general trend towards refinement of manners – a trend which, in turn, reflected an even more encompassing transformation of society at large. In Part Two, Elias was already hinting at the larger social and psychological dynamics at work here. He suggested that people, forced to live with one another in new ways, became more sensitive to the impulses of others, and therefore learned to subject their own conduct to more subtle and elaborate controls. The changes were gradual, and not always rectilinear. In the long run, however, they revealed a clear pattern. As Elias asserted, in spite of all its fluctuations 'a definite overall trend is nevertheless perceptible if all the varied voices from past centuries are heard together in context'.

Part Two sketched the developmental curve which Elias saw emerging. It remained for Parts Three and Four to explore in greater depth, respectively, the underlying social conditions and the psychological implications of this curve.

What is the real use of the fork? It serves to lift food that has been cut up to the mouth. Why do we need a fork for this? Why do we not use our fingers? Because it is 'cannibal', as the 'Man in the Club-Window', the anonymous author of *The Habits of Good Society* said in 1859. Why is it 'cannibal' to eat with one's fingers? That is not a question; it is self-evidently cannibal, barbaric, uncivilized, or whatever else it is called.

But that is precisely the question. Why is it more civilized to eat with a fork?

'Because it is unhygienic to eat with one's fingers'. That sounds convincing. To our sensibility it is unhygienic if different people put their fingers into the same dish, because there is a danger of contracting disease through contact with others. Each of us seems to fear that the others are diseased.

But this explanation is not entirely satisfactory. Nowadays we do not eat from common dishes. Everyone puts food into his mouth from his own plate. To pick it up from one's own plate with one's fingers cannot be more 'unhygienic' than to put cake, bread, chocolate, or anything else into one's mouth with one's own fingers.

So why does one really need a fork? Why is it 'barbaric' and 'uncivilized' to put food into one's mouth by hand from one's own plate? Because it is distasteful to dirty one's fingers, or at least to be seen in society with dirty fingers. The suppression of eating by hand from one's own plate has very little to do with the danger of illness, the so-called 'rational' explanation. In observing our feelings toward the fork ritual, we can see with particular clarity that the first authority in our decision between 'civilized' and 'uncivilized' behaviour at table is our feeling of distaste. The fork is nothing other than the embodiment of a specific standard of emotions and a specific level of revulsion. Behind the change in eating techniques between the Middle Ages and modern times appears the same process that emerged in the analysis of other incarnations of this kind: a change in the structure of drives and emotions.

Modes of behaviour which in the Middle Ages were not felt to be in the least distasteful are increasingly surrounded by unpleasurable feelings. The standard of delicacy finds expression in corresponding social prohibitions. These taboos, so far as can be ascertained, are nothing other than ritualized or institutionalized feelings of displeasure, distaste, disgust, fear, or shame, feelings which have been socially nurtured under quite specific conditions and which are constantly reproduced, not solely but mainly because they have become institutionally embedded in a particular ritual, in particular forms of conduct.

The examples show – certainly only in a narrow cross-section and in the relatively randomly selected statements of individuals – how, in a phase of development in which the use of the fork was not yet taken for granted, the feeling of distaste that first formed within a narrow circle is slowly extended. 'It is very impolite', says Courtin in 1672, 'to touch anything greasy, a sauce or syrup, etc., with your fingers, apart from the fact that it obliges you to commit two or three more improper acts. One is to wipe your hand frequently on your serviette and to soil it like a kitchen cloth, so that those who see you wipe your mouth with it feel nauseated. Another is to wipe your fingers on your bread, which again is very improper. [N.B. The French terms *propre* and *malpropre* used by Courtin and explained in one of his chapters coincide less with the German terms for clean and unclean (*sauber* and *unsauber*) than with the word frequently used earlier, *proper*.] The third is to lick them, which is the height of impropriety.'

The *Civilité* of 1729 by La Salle, which transmits the behaviour of the upper class to broader circles, says on one page: 'When the fingers are very greasy, wipe them first on a piece of bread.' This shows how far from general acceptance, even at this time, was the standard of delicacy that Courtin had already represented decades earlier. On the other hand, La Salle takes over fairly literally Courtin's precept that '*Bienséance* does not permit anything greasy, a sauce or a syrup, to be touched with the fingers.' And, exactly like Courtin, he mentions among the ensuing *incivilités* wiping the hands on bread and licking the fingers, as well as soiling the napkin.

It can be seen that manners are here still in the process of formation. The new standard does not appear suddenly. Certain forms of behaviour are placed under prohibition, not because they are unhealthy but because they lead to an offensive sight and disagreeable associations; shame at offering such a spectacle, originally absent, and fear of arousing such associations are gradually spread from the standard setting circles to larger circles by numerous authorities and institutions. However, once such feelings are aroused and firmly established in society by means of certain rituals like that involving the fork, they are constantly reproduced so long as the structure of human relations is not fundamentally altered. The older generation, for whom such a standard of conduct is accepted as a matter of course, urges the children, who do not come into the world already equipped with these feelings and this standard, to control themselves more or less rigorously in accordance with it, and to restrain their drives and inclinations. If a child tries to touch something sticky, wet, or greasy with his fingers, he is told. 'You must not do that, people do not do things like that.' And the displeasure toward such conduct which is thus aroused by the adult finally arises through habit, without being induced by another person.

To a large extent, however, the conduct and emotional life of the child are forced even without words into the same mould and in the same direction by the fact that a particular use of knife and fork, for example, if completely established in the adult world – that is, by the example of the environment. Since the pressure or coercion of individual adults is allied to the pressure and example of the whole surrounding world, most children, as they grow up, forget or repress relatively early the fact that their feelings of shame and embarrassment, of pleasure and displeasure, are moulded into conformity with a certain standard by external pressure and compulsion. All this appears to them as highly personal, something 'inward', implanted in them by nature. While it is still directly visible in the writings of Courtin and La Salle that adults, too, were at first dissuaded from eating with their fingers by consideration for each other, by 'politeness', to spare others a distasteful spectacle and themselves the shame of being seen with soiled hands, later it becomes more and more an inner automatism, the imprint of society on the inner self, the superego, that forbids the individual to eat in any other way than with a fork. The social standard to which the individual was first made to conform by external restraint is finally reproduced less smoothly within him, through a self-restraint which may operate even against his conscious wishes.

Thus the sociohistorical process of centuries, in the course of which the standard of what is felt to be shameful and offensive is slowly raised, is re-enacted in abbreviated form in the life of the individual human being. If one wished to express recurrent processes of this kind in the form of laws, one could speak, as a parallel to the laws of biogenesis, of a fundamental law of sociogenesis and psychogenesis.

9

THE SOCIOGENESIS OF COURTS

The study of long-term changes in standards of conduct, carried out in Part Two of *The Civilizing Process*, revealed a pattern, a direction. The standards prevailing among the secular upper strata of medieval society, known as the standards of *courtoisie*, gradually made way for more refined standards, known initially as *civilité*. Obviously, this overall change had not been planned in advance. What, then, had happened that could explain it?

Elias's solution to this problem was to view the changes in manners as an integral part of a general transformation of society. He followed the same strategy that psychologists had developed when they viewed the human personality as a *Gestalt* – a configuration of interdependent traits. Elias carried this approach one step further, by regarding the individual personalities as also constituting a configuration together. Such a social configuration is nothing but the way in which people are bonded to each other; changes in one part of it are bound to affect other parts as well.

In Part Three of *The Civilizing Process* Elias set out to analyse first of all the structure and dynamics of feudal society which was the social setting of the codes of *courtoisie* laid down in the manner books of medieval Europe. He showed how, for centuries, in feudal society all attempts to form larger political regimes always broke down ultimately because of the prevalence of countervailing centrifugal forces. The recurrent pull toward feudalization came to an end, however, when centripetal forces became stronger, setting the conditions for a process of state formation – that is, the establishment of more stable monopolies of taxation and organized force over larger areas.

A major theme in this part is 'the taming of the warriors': the process in the course of which a 'castle nobility' of knights with a strong sense of independence was transformed into a 'court nobility' of aristocrats, residing at the royal court in submission to the king. Whereas in the Middle Ages 'centrifugal' and 'centripetal' forces tended again and again to balance each other out, the sixteenth century marked a transition. In France in particular, a 'monopoly mechanism' now worked in favour of the central rulers, the kings, who managed to control a more extensive territory and, at the same time, to make their regime more stable than had been possible in the previous centuries. This regime rested, as Elias showed, on the dual monopoly of military and fiscal resources in the territory.

The following excerpt is the concluding section from the chapter on the dynamics of feudalization. It gives an impression of Elias's skill in applying a grand perspective. Thus, while viewing the *courtois* standards of conduct in the larger framework of late medieval society, he interspersed his historical analysis with some remarks on trends in the twentieth century which are still as pertinent as they were when they were first written down in 1936.

I

The sociogenesis of the great feudal courts is at the same time the sociogenesis of *courtois* conduct. *Courtoisie*, too, is a form of conduct that doubtless first developed among the more socially dependent members of this knightly-courtly upper class.[71] However that may be, one thing re-emerges here very clearly: this *courtois* standard of conduct is in no sense a beginning. It is not an example of how people behave when their affects have free, 'natural' play unfettered by society, that is to say, by the relations between people. Such a condition of totally uncontrolled drives, of an absolute 'beginning' simply does not exist. The relatively great licence for acting out emotional impulses characteristic of men in the *courtois* upper classes – great in comparison with the later secular upper classes in the West – corresponds exactly to the form of integration, the degree and kind of mutual dependence in which people live together here. The division of labour is less developed than in the phases when the stricter absolutist system of rule was developed; the trade network is smaller and so the number of people who can be sustained in one place is less. And whatever the form of individual dependencies may be, the social web of dependencies that intersect within the individual is here much coarser and less extensive than in societies with greater division of labour, where more people live continuously in close proximity in a more exactly ordered system. And, consequently, the control and restraint on the individual's drives and affects is here less strict, continuous and uniform. Nevertheless, it is already considerably greater at the larger feudal courts than at the small or in the warrior society at large, where the interdependence of people is much less extensive and complex, the network of individuals much more loosely woven, and where the strongest functional dependence between people is still that of war and violence. Compared to the behaviour and affective life to be found here, *courtoisie* already represents a refinement, a mark of distinction. And the polemics contained in fairly unchanging form in the many medieval precepts on manners – avoid this and refrain from that – refer more or less directly to the behaviour practised by the bulk of the knights, which changed as slowly and slightly between the ninth or tenth centuries and the sixteenth as did their conditions of life.

II

At the present stage of development we still lack linguistic instruments which do justice to the nature and direction of all these intertwining processes. It is an imprecise and provisional aid to understanding to say that the restraints imposed upon men and their drives became 'greater', integration 'closer', or interdependence 'stronger', just as it does not quite do justice to socio–historical reality to say that one thing belongs to a 'barter economy', and another to a 'money economy', or, to repeat the form of expression chosen here, that 'the money-sector of the economy grew'. By how much did it 'grow', degree by degree? In what way did the restraints become 'greater', integration 'closer', interdependence 'more pronounced'? Our concepts are too coarse; they adhere too much to the image of material substances. In all this we are not concerned merely with gradations, with 'more' or 'less'. Each 'increase' in restraints and interdependencies is an expression of the fact that the ties between people, the way they depend on one another, are changing, and changing qualitatively. This is what is meant by differences in social structure. And with the dynamic network of dependencies into which a human life is woven, the drives and behaviour of people take on a *different* form. This is what is meant by differences in personality structure and in social standards of conduct. The fact that such qualitative changes are sometimes, despite all the fluctuations within the movement, changes in one and the same direction over long periods, that is, continuous, directed processes rather than a random sequence, permits and indeed causes us to speak in comparative terms when discussing different phases. That is not to say that the direction in which these processes move is towards improvement, 'progress', or towards the opposite, 'retrogression'. But nor is it to say that they involve merely quantitative changes. Here, as so often in history, we are concerned with structural changes that are most easily, visibly, but perhaps most superficially grasped in their quantitative aspect.

We see the following movement: first one castle stands against another, then territory against territory, then state against state, and appearing on the historical horizon today are the first signs of struggles for an integration of regions and masses of people on a still larger scale. We may surmise that with continuing integration even larger units will gradually be assembled under a stable government and internally pacified, and that they in their turn will turn their weapons outwards against human aggregates of the same size until, with a further integration, a still greater reduction of distances, they too gradually grow together and world society is pacified. This may take centuries or millennia; however that may be, the growth of units of integration and rule is always at the same time an expression of structural changes in society, that is to say, in human relationships. Whenever the centre of gravity of society moves towards units of integration of a new order of magnitude – and in the shift that first favoured large feudal lords at the expense of small and middle-sized ones, then kings against the great feudal or territorial lords, a displacement in this direction is expressed – whenever such changes occur they do so in conjunction with social functions that have grown more differentiated, and with chains of organized social action, whether military or economic, that have lengthened. Each time, the network of dependencies intersecting in the individual has grown larger and changed in structure; and each time, in exact correspondence to this structure, the moulding of behaviour and of the whole emotional life, the personality structure, is also changed. The 'civilizing' process, seen from the aspects of standards of conduct and drive control, is the same trend which, when seen from the point of view of human relationships, appears as the process of advancing integration, increased differentiation of social functions and interdependence, and the formation of ever-larger units of integration on whose fortunes and movements the individual depends, whether he knows it or not.

It was attempted here to complement the general account of the earliest and least complicated phase of this movement with some illustrative factual evidence; next the further progress of this movement and the mechanisms driving it will be examined. It has been shown how and why, in the early phase of Western history which had a predominantly barter economy, integration and the establishment of stable governments over large empires had little chance. Conquering kings can, it is true, subjugate huge areas through battle and hold them together for a time by respect for their sword. But the structure of society does not yet permit the creation of an apparatus for ruling sufficiently stable to administrate and hold together the empire by relatively peaceful means over long periods of peacetime. It remains to be shown what social processes make possible the formation of such a more stable government and with it a quite different bonding of individuals.

In the ninth and tenth centuries when, at least in the western Frankish regions, the external threat was small – and when economic integration was slight – the disintegration of the ruler-function reaches extraordinary heights. Each small estate is under its own rule, a 'state' in itself, every small knight its independent lord and master. The social landscape comprises a chaotic multitude of governmental and economic units. Each of them is essentially autarkic with little dependence on others, with the exception of a few enclaves – foreign traders, for example, or monasteries and abbeys – which sometimes have links beyond the local level. In the secular ruling stratum integration through aggressive or defensive conflict is the fundamental form. There is not much to constrain members of this ruling stratum to control their affects in any continuous way. This is a 'society' in the broader sense of the word which refers to every possible form of human integration. It is not yet a 'society' in the narrower sense of a more continuous, relatively close and uniform integration of people with a greater constraint on violence, at least within its confines. The early form of such a 'society' in the narrower sense slowly emerges at the great feudal courts. Here, where there is a larger confluence of goods, owing to the amounts produced and the attachment of these courts to the trade network, and where more people congregate in search of service, a sizeable number of people is obliged to maintain a constantly peaceful intercourse. This demands, particularly towards women of higher rank, a certain control and restraint of behaviour, a more precise moulding of affects and manners.

III

This restraint may not always have been as great as it was in the relation of singer to lady in the *minnesang* convention. The *courtois* precepts on manners give a more accurate picture of the standard of behaviour demanded in everyday life. They also occasionally throw light on the conduct of knights towards women that is not confined to the relation of the minstrel to the lady of the court.

We read in a 'motto for men',[72] for example: 'Above all, take care to behave well towards women. . . . If a lady asks you to sit beside her, do not sit on her dress, or too near her, and if you wish to speak softly to her, never clutch her with your arms, whatever you have to say.'

Judging by the habitual standards of the lesser knights, this amount of consideration for women may have demanded considerable effort. But the restraint is slight, like that in other *courtois* precepts, in comparison to what became customary among courtiers at the court of Louis XIV, for example. This gives an idea of the different levels of interdependence and integration that shape the individual's habits in the two phases. But it also shows that *courtoisie* was indeed a step on the path that leads finally to our own affective and emotional mould, a step in the direction of 'civilization'.

On the one hand, a loosely integrated secular upper class of warriors, with its symbol, the castle on the autarkic estate; on the other, the more tightly integrated secular upper class of courtiers assembled at the absolutist court, the central organ of the kingdom: these are in a sense the two poles of the field of observation which has been isolated from the far longer and broader movement in order to gain initial access to the sociogenesis of civilizing change. The slow emergence from the castle landscape of the greater feudal courts, the centres of courtoisie, has been shown from a number of aspects. It remains to demonstrate the basic dynamics of the processes by which *one* of the great feudal or territorial lords, the king, gained preponderance over the others, and the opportunity to control a more stable government over a region embracing many territories, a 'state'. This is also the path that leads from the standard of conduct of *courtoisie* to that of *civilité*.

10

CIVILIZATION AND RATIONALIZATION

The fourth and final part of *The Civilizing Process*, called 'Towards a theory of civilizing processes', focuses upon the way in which the cultural and social trends examined in the preceding parts have affected the individual habitus or personality structure. As the relationships between people altered, so did each individual's behaviour, experience, and mentality. In order to interpret these changes at the level of mentality, Elias made use of the psychological insights of the day, drawing freely upon the work of such varied schools as behaviourism (for the concept of 'conditioning'), *Gestalt* psychology, and, especially, psychoanalysis.

In so doing, he did not enter into lengthy discussions with other authors. Still, at several points he took an outspoken position in ongoing debates – about questions of philosophy, history, and, most of all, psychoanalysis. The way he wrote down his arguments probably reflected not just his response to texts he had read, but even more the manner in which he had learned to define his position in oral discussions. His basic strategy always seemed to be to avoid becoming entangled in conventional dichotomies.

Already in the original preface to *The Civilizing Process* we can find several allusions to Freud's well-known essay *Civilization and Its Discontents*, first published in German in 1930. In a telling footnote to the text of Part Two, Elias expressed his great indebtedness to 'Freud and the psychoanalytic school'. Indeed, a particular passage written by Freud in 1933 can almost be read as an outline of the programme worked out in *The Civilizing Process*:

And finally we must not forget that the mass of human beings who are subjected to economic necessities also undergo the process of cultural development – of civilization as other people may say – which, though no doubt influenced by all the other factors, is certainly independent of them in its origin, being comparable to an organic process and very well able on its part to exercise an influence on the other factors. It displaces instinctual aims and brings it about that people become antagonistic to what they had previously tolerated. Moreover the progressive strengthening of the scientific spirit seems to form an essential part of it. If anyone were in a position to show in detail the way in which these different factors – the general inherited human disposition, its racial variations and its cultural transformations – inhibit and promote one another under conditions of social rank, profession and earning capacity – if anyone were able to do this, he would have supplemented Marxism so that it was made into a genuine social science. (Freud 1933/1964, p. 179)

While Elias may have drawn inspiration from these words, he would not have accepted them in every detail. He would certainly have objected to the civilizing process being regarded as 'comparable to an organic process'. On the whole his attitude to Freud and psychoanalysis was respectful but critical. As he was later to make more explicit, he found that adding a historical and sociological dimension to psychoanalysis necessitated a revision of some of its basic concepts and assumptions.

The following excerpt illustrates how Elias, while incorporating psychoanalytic insights into his own perspective, at the same time gave them a new twist.

The idea that the human 'psyche' consists of different zones functioning independently of each other and capable of being considered independently, has become deeply rooted in human consciousness over a long period. It is common, in thinking about the more differentiated personality structure, to sever one of its functional levels from the others as if this were really the 'essential' factor in the way men steer themselves in their encounter with their human fellows and with non-human nature. Thus the humanities and the sociology of knowledge stress above all the aspect of knowledge and thought. Thoughts and ideas appear in these studies as it were as that which is the most important and potent aspect of the way men steer themselves. And the unconscious impulses, the whole field of drive and affect structures, remains more or less in the dark.

But every investigation that considers only the consciousness of men, their 'reason' or 'ideas', while disregarding the structure of drives, the direction and form of human affects and passions, can be from the outset of only limited value. Much that is indispensable for an understanding of men escapes this approach. The rationalization of men's intellectual activity itself, and beyond that the whole structural changes of the ego and super-ego functions, all these interdependent levels of men's personality – as has been shown above and will be shown in more detail later – are only very imperfectly accessible to thought as long as enquiries are confined to changes in the intellectual aspects of men, to changes of ideas, and pay little regard to the changing balance and the changing pattern of the relationships between drives and affects on the one hand and drive- and affect-control on the other. A real understanding, even of the changes of ideas and forms of cognition, can be gained only if one takes into account too the changes of human interdependencies in conjunction with the structure of conduct and, in fact, the whole fabric of men's personality at a given stage of social development.

The inverse accentuation, with a corresponding limitation, is to be found often enough in a psycho-analytical research today. It frequently tends, in considering human beings, to extract something 'unconscious', conceived as an 'id' without history, as the most important thing in the whole psychological structure. Although recently this image may have undergone corrections in therapeutic practice, these corrections have not yet led to theoretical elaboration of the data supplied by practive into more adequate conceptual tools. On the theoretical level it still usually appears as if the steering of the individual by unconscious libidinal impulses has a form and structure of its own, independently of the figurational destiny of the individual, the changing fortunes of his relationships with others throughout his life, and independently too of the pattern and structure of the other self-steering functions of his personality, conscious and unconscious. No distinction is made between the natural raw material of drives, which indeed perhaps changes little throughout the whole history of mankind, and the increasingly more firmly wrought structures of control, and thus the paths into which the elementary energies are channelled in each person through his or her relations with other people from birth onward. But nowhere, except perhaps in the case of madmen, do men in their encounter with each other find themselves face to face with psychological functions in their pristine state, in a state of nature that is not patterned by social learning, by a person's experience of other persons who satisfy or frustrate his or her needs in accordance with a specific social setting. The libidinal energies which one encounters in any living human being are always already socially processed; they are, in other words, sociogenetically transformed in their function and structure, and can in no way be separated from the corresponding ego and super-ego structures. The more animalic and automatic levels of men's personality are neither more nor less significant for the understanding of human conduct than their controls. What matters, what determines conduct, are the balances and conflicts between men's malleable drives and the built-in drive-controls.

Decisive for a person as he appears before us is neither the 'id' alone, nor the 'ego' or 'super-ego' alone, but always *the relationship* between these various sets of psychological functions, partly conflicting and partly co-operating in the way an individual steers himself. It is they, these relationships *within* man between the drives and affects controlled and the built-in controlling agencies, whose structure changes in the course of a civilizing process, in accordance with the changing structure of the relationships *between* individual human beings, in society at large. In the course of this process, to put it briefly and all too simply, 'consciousness' becomes less permeable by drives, and drives become less permeable by 'consciousness'. In simpler societies elementary impulses, however transformed, have an easier access to men's reflections. In the course of a civilizing process the compartmentalization of these self-steering functions, though in no way absolute, becomes more pronounced.

In accordance with the sociogenetic ground rule (see *The History of Manners* p. xiii) one can observe processes in the same direction directly in every child. One can see that, in the course of human history and again and again in that of each individual civilizing process, the self-steering in the form of ego and super-ego functions on the one hand and that through drives on the other become more and more firmly differentiated. Hence it is only with the formation of conscious functions less accessible to drives that the drive automatisms take on more and more that specific character which one today commonly diagnoses as 'ahistoric', as a peculiarity of man throughout the ages which is purely natural, and independent of the developmental condition of human societies. However, the peculiarity of man discovered by Freud in men of our own time and conceptualized by him as a strict division between unconscious and conscious mental functions, far from being part of man's unchanged nature is a result of a long civilizing process in the course of which the wall of forgetfulness separating libidinal drives and 'consciousness' or 'reflection' has become harder and more impermeable.[1]

In the course of the same transformation, the conscious mental functions themselves develop in the direction of what one calls increasing 'rationalization' only with the sharper and firmer differentiation of the personality do the outward-directed psychological functions take on the character of a more rationally functioning consciousness less directly coloured by drive impulses and affective fantasies. Thus the form and structure of the more conscious and more unconscious psychological self-steering functions can never be grasped if they are imagined as something in any sense existing or functioning in isolation from one another. Both are equally fundamental to the existence of a human being; both together form a single great functional continuum. Nor can their structure and changes be understood if observation is confined to individual human beings. They can only be comprehended in connection with the structure of relationships *between* people, and with the long-term changes in that structure.

Therefore in order to understand and explain civilizing processes one needs to investigate – as has been attempted here – the transformation of both the personality structure and the entire social structure. This task demands, within a smaller radius, psychogenetic investigations aimed at grasping the whole field of individual psychological energies, the structure and form of the more elementary no less than of the more self-steering functions. Within a larger radius, the exploration of civilizing processes demands a long-range perspective, *sociogenetic* investigations of the overall structure, not only of a single state society but of the social field formed by a specific group of interdependent societies, and of the sequential order of its evolution.

But for an adequate enquiry into such social processes a similar correction of traditional habits of thinking is needed to the one that proved necessary earlier to obtain an adequate basis for psychogenetic enquiry. To understand social structures and processes, it is never enough to study a single functional stratum within a social field. To be really understood, these structures and processes demand a study of the *relationships between the different functional strata* which are bound together within a social field, and which, with the slower or more rapid shift of power-relationships arising from the specific structure of this field, are for a time reproduced over and over again. Just as in every psychogenetic enquiry it is necessary to take account not only of the 'unconscious' or the 'conscious' functions alone, but of the continuous circulation of impulses from the one to the other, it is equally important in every sociogenetic study to consider from the first the whole *figuration* of a social field which is more or less differentiated and charged with tensions.[2] It is only possible to do this because the social fabric and its historical change are not chaotic but possess, even in phases of greatest unrest and disorder, a clear pattern and structure. To investigate the totality of a social field does not mean to study each individual process within it. It means first of all to discover the basic structures which give all the individual processes within this field their direction and their specific stamp. It means asking oneself in what way the axes of tension, the chains of functions and the institutions of a society in the fifteenth century differ from those in the sixteenth or seventeenth centuries, and why the former change in the direction of the latter. To answer these questions knowledge of a wealth of particular facts is of course necessary. But beyond a certain point in the accumulation of material facts, historiography enters the phase when it ought no longer to be satisfied with the collection of further particulars and with the description of those already assembled, but should be concerned with those problems which facilitate penetration of the underlying regularities by which people in a certain society are bound over and over again to particular patterns of conduct and to very specific functional chains, for example as knights and bondsmen, kings and state officials, bourgeois and nobles, and by which these relationships and institutions change in a very specific direction. Beyond a certain point of factual knowledge, in a word, a more solid framework, a structural nexus can be perceived in the multitude of particular historical facts. And all further facts that can be discovered serve – apart from the enrichment of the historical panorama they may offer us – either to revise the insight already gained into these structures, or to extend and deepen it. The statement that every sociogenetic study should be aimed at the *totality* of a social field does not mean that it should be directed at the sum of all particulars, but at its structure within the entirety of its interdependencies. In the last resort the boundaries of such a study are determined by the boundaries of the interdependencies, or at least by the immanent articulation of the interdependencies.

It is in this light that what was said above about rationalization is to be understood. The gradual transition to more 'rational' behaviour and thought, like that to a more differentiated, a more comprehensive type of self-control, is usually associated today only with bourgeois functions. We often find firmly lodged in the minds of our contemporaries the idea that the bourgeoisie was the 'originator' or 'inventor' of more rational thought. Here, for the sake of contrast, certain rationalization processes in the aristocratic camp have been described. But one should not deduce from this that the courtly aristocracy was the social 'originator' of this spurt of rationalization. Just as the courtly aristocracy or the bourgeoisie in the age of manufacture did not have 'originators' in any other social class, so this rationalization equally lacked an originator. The very transformation of the whole social structure, in the course of which these figurations of bourgeois and nobles come into being, is itself, considered from a certain aspect, a process of rationalization. What becomes more rational is not just the individual products of men, nor, above all, merely the systems of thought set down in books. What is rationalized is, primarily, the modes of conduct of certain groups of people. 'Rationalization' is nothing other – think, for example, of the courtization of warriors – than an expression of the direction in which the moulding of people in specific social figurations is changed during this period. Changes of this kind, however, do not 'originate' in one class or another, but arise in conjunction with the tensions *between* different functional groups in a social field and *between* the competing people within them. Under the pressure of tensions of this kind which permeate the whole fabric of society, the latter's whole structure changes, during a particular phase, in the direction of an increasing centralization of particular dominions and a greater specialization, a tighter integration of the individual people within them. And with this transformation of the whole social field, the structure of social and psychological functions is also changed – first in small, then in larger and larger sectors – in the direction of rationalization.

The slow defunctionalization of the first estate and the corresponding diminution of its power potential, the pacification of the second estate and the gradual rise of the third, none of these can be understood independently of the others any more than, for example, the development of trade in this period is comprehensible independently of the formation of powerful monopolies of physical force and the rise of mighty courts. All these are levers in the comprehensive process of increasing differentiation and extension of all chains of action, which has played such a decisive role in the whole course of Western history. In this process – as was shown from particular aspects – the functions of the nobility are transformed, and with them bourgeois functions and the form of the central organs. And hand in hand with this gradual change in the totality of social functions and institutions, goes a transformation of individual self-steering – first in the leading groups of both the nobility and the bourgeoisie – in the direction of greater foresight and a stricter regulation of libidinal impulses.

In perusing the traditional accounts of the intellectual development of the West, one often has the impression of a vague conception in the minds of their authors that the rationalization of consciousness, the change from magical-traditional to rational forms of thinking in the history of the West, had its cause in the emergence of a number of geniuses and outstanding individuals. These enlightened individuals, such accounts appear to suggest, taught Western man how to use his innate reason properly.

Here, a different picture emerges. What the great thinkers of the West have achieved is certainly considerable. They gave to what their contemporaries experienced in their daily actions without being able to grasp it clearly in thought, comprehensive and exemplary expression. They tried to articulate the more reality-oriented or, in their own language, more rational forms of thinking which had gradually developed along with the overall changes in the structure of social interdependencies, and with their help to clarify the problems of human existence. They gave other people a clearer view of their world and themselves. And so they also acted as levers within the larger workings of society. They were to a greater or lesser degree, depending on their talent and personal situation, interpreters and spokesmen of a social chorus. But they were not on their own the originators of the type of thought prevalent in their society. They did not create what we call 'rational thought'.[3]

This expression itself evidently is somewhat too static and insufficiently differentiated for what it is intended to express. Too static, because the structure of psychological functions changes at the same rate as that of social functions. Insufficiently differentiated because the pattern of rationalization, the structure of more rational habits of thinking, was and is very different in different social classes – for instance, in the courtly nobility or the leading bourgeois strata – in accordance with their different social functions and their overall historical situation. And finally, the same is true of rationalization as was said above of changes of consciousness in general: in it only *one* side of a more comprehensive change in the whole social personality is manifested. It goes hand in hand with a corresponding transformation of drive structures. It is, in brief, *one* manifestation of civilization among others.

11

THE SOCIETY OF INDIVIDUALS – I

The Civilizing Process was a work of synthesis – of ideas current in various disciplines of the human sciences, but also of Elias's own thinking. It contained the results of many years of research and reflection.

A permanent theme in Elias's thought was his conviction that the concepts of 'individual' and 'society' were generally treated in a misleading manner, as if they referred to entities that could somehow be conceived of in separation. While working on the concluding part of *The Civilizing Process* he encountered this misconception again and again. He found that, on the one hand, the erroneous opposition of 'individual' and 'society' stood in the way of a proper understanding of the civilizing process while, on the other hand, the theory of the civilizing process could explain why that opposition had taken root so deeply in European culture.

The only way to break through the erroneous dichotomy of 'individual' and 'society' with its many misleading ramifications was, as Elias saw it, to regard the two concepts as inextricably linked. He found himself so deeply absorbed by this idea, and the commentaries he wrote on it became so extensive, that he decided to extract these from the main book, and to devote a small monograph to what could best be conceptualized as 'the society of individuals'. A monograph with that title was announced under two different imprints, one to appear in Uppsala, the other one in Basle. War broke out, however, and neither edition ever went into print.

Only in 1983 was a copy of the original German typescript discovered in Uppsala and circulated, with Elias's consent, as a photocopied working paper of the Department of the History of Ideas of the University of Stockholm. Many years before, however, in the 1950s, Elias himself had begun to translate the essay into English. Typically, in so doing he could not resist making revisions, and after a few pages he put the original text aside altogether, to write an entirely new essay on the theme of 'The Society of Individuals'. A quarter of a century later, the same thing happened again, as Elias sat down to prepare the two essays he now had for publication in German. Instead of editing, again he wrote a new text, so that when, in 1987, *The Society of Individuals* eventually came out in book form, it consisted of three parts, representing three successive stages in the formation and formulation of his ideas.

The following text is Section Two of the first essay, written in the late 1930s. Selections from the second and third essay are included later in this volume (pp. 92–5 and 230–4).

Half consciously, half unconsciously, most people carry about with them even today a peculiar myth of creation. They imagine that in the 'beginning' a single person first appeared on earth and was then joined afterwards by other people. That is how the Bible describes it. But echoes of this form of consciousness show themselves in various other versions today. The old Adam makes a secularized reappearance in talk about the 'primal man' or the 'original father'. It seems as if grown-up people, in thinking about their origins, involuntarily lose sight of the fact that they themselves and all adults came into the world as little children. Over and over again, in the scientific myths of origin no less than in the religious ones, they feel impelled to imagine: In the beginning was a single human being, who was an adult.

As long as we remain within the realm of experience, however, we are obliged to register that the single human being is engendered by and born of other human beings. Whatever the ancestors of humanity may have been, as far as we can see back into the past we see an unbroken chain of parents and children, who in turn become parents. And one cannot understand how and why individual people are bound together in a larger unity by and with each other if one conceals this perception from oneself. Each individual is born into a group of people who were there before him. Not only that: each individual is by nature so constituted that he needs other people who were there before him in order to be able to grow up. One of the basic conditions of human existence is the simultaneous presence of a number of interrelated people. And if, to symbolize one's own self-image, one needs a myth of origin, it seems time to revise the traditional myth: In the beginning, one might say, was not a single person, but several people who lived with each other, who caused each other joy and pain as we do, who came into being through each other and passed away into each other, as we do, a social unit large or small.

But there is no such leap out of nothingness, and no myth of origin is needed to make comprehensible the primal social relatedness of the individual, his natural dependence on a life with other people. The facts directly before us are enough.

At birth individual people may be very different through their natural constitutions. But it is only in society that the small child with its malleable and relatively undifferentiated mental functions is turned into a more complex being. Only in relation to other human beings does the wild, helpless creature which comes into the world become the psychologically developed person with the character of an individual and deserving the name of an adult human being. Cut off from such relations he grows at best into a semi-wild human animal. He may grow up bodily; in his psychological make-up he remains like a small child. Only if he grows up in a group does the small human being learn connected speech. Only in the society of other, older people does he gradually develop a specific kind of far-sightedness and instinct control. And which language he learns, which pattern of drive control and adult make-up develops in him, depends on the structure of the group in which he grows up, and finally on his position in this group and the formative process it entails.

Even within the same group the relationships allotted to two people, their individual histories, are never quite the same. Each person advances from a unique position within his network of relationships through a unique history to his death. But the differences between the paths followed by different individuals, between the positions and functions through which they pass in the course of their lives, are fewer in simpler societies than in complex ones. And the degree of individualization of adults in the latter societies is accordingly greater. Paradoxical as it may seem at the present stage in the development of mental habits, the individuality and the social relatedness of a person are not only not antithetical to each other, but the special shaping and differentiation of mental functions that we refer to as 'individuality' is only possible for a person who grows up in a group, a society.

Undoubtedly, people also differ in their natural constitutions. But the constitution a person brings with him into the world, and particularly the constitution of his or her psychical functions, is malleable. The new-born child is no more than a preliminary sketch of a person. His adult individuality does not grow necessarily and along a single path from what we perceive as his distinguishing features, his special constitution, as a plant of a particular species grows from its seed: the distinctive constitution of a new-born child allows scope for a great wealth of possible individualities. It shows no more than the limits and the position of the dispersion curve on which the individual form of the adult can lie. How this form actually develops, how the malleable features of the new-born child gradually harden into the adult's sharper contours, never depends solely on his constitution and always on the nature of the relations between him and other people.

These relationships, for example, between father, mother, child and siblings within a family, variable as they may be in details, are determined in their basic structure by the structure of the society into which the child is born and which existed *before* him. They are different in societies with different structures. For this reason the constitutional peculiarities with which a human being comes into the world have a very different significance for the relationships of the individual in different societies, and in different historical epochs of the same society. Similar natural constitutions in new-born babies lead to a very different development of consciousness and drives, depending on the pre-existing structure of relationships in which they grow up. Which individuality a human being finally evolves depends not only on his or her natural constitution but on the whole process of individualization. Undoubtedly, the person's distinctive constitution has an ineradicable influence on his or her entire fate. A sensitive child can expect a fate different from that of a less sensitive one in the same family or society. But this fate, and thus the individual shape which an individual slowly takes on in growing up, is not laid down from the first in the inborn nature of the baby. What comes of its distinctive constitution depends on the structure of the society in which it grows up. Its fate, however it may turn out in detail, is as a whole society-specific. Accordingly, the more sharply delineated figure of the grown-up, the individuality that gradually emerges from the less differentiated form of the small child as it interacts with its fate, is also society-specific. In keeping with the changing structure of western society, a child of the twelfth century develops a different structure of drives and consciousness from that of a twentieth-century child. It has emerged clearly enough from the study of the civilizing process to what extent the general modelling and thus the individual shaping of an individual person depends on the historical evolution of the social standard, on the structure of human relationships. Advances of individualization, as in the Renaissance, for example, are not the consequence of a sudden mutation within individual people or of the chance conception of a specially high number of gifted people; they are social events, consequences of a breaking up of old groupings or a change in the social position of the artist-craftsman, for example. In short, the consequences of a specific restructuring of human relationships.

From this side, too, it is easy to lose sight of the fundamental importance of the relations between people for the individual in their midst. And these difficulties too result, at least in part, from the type of thought-models that are used in thinking about these relationships. As so often, these models are derived from the simplest relationships between three-dimensional bodies. The effort of re-orientation needed to break free of these models is certainly no less than that which was necessary when physicists began thinking in terms of the relationships between bodies, rather than starting from individual bodies such as the sun or the moon. The relation between people is often imagined like that between billiards balls: they collide and roll apart. But the interactions between people and the social interweaving they engender are essentially different from the mechanical interactions of physical substances.

Think, for example, of a relatively simple form of human relationship, a conversation. One partner speaks, the other replies. The first responds and the second again replies. If one considers not only the individual remark and counter-remark but the course taken by the conversation as a whole, the sequence of interwoven ideas pushing each other along in continuous interdependence, one is dealing with a phenomenon that cannot be adequately represented either by the physical model of the action and reaction of balls, or by the physiological model of the relationship between stimulus and response. The ideas of either party may change in the course of the conversation. It may be, for example, that a certain agreement is arrived at by the partners in the course of the conversation. One might convince the other. Then something from one passes into the other. It is assimilated into his or her individual structure of ideas. It changes this structure, and is in its turn modified by being incorporated into a different system. The same applies if opposition arises in the conversation. Then the ideas of one party enter into the inner dialogue of the other as an adversary, and so drive on his thoughts. The special feature of this kind of process, that we might call a network-figure, is that in its course each of the partners forms ideas that were not there before, or pursues further ideas already present. But the direction and the order followed by this formation and transformation of ideas are not explained solely by the structure of one partner or the other but by the relation between the two. And precisely this fact that people change in relation to each other and through the relationship to each other, that they are continuously shaping and reshaping themselves in relation to each other, is characteristic of the phenomenon of social interweaving in general.

Suppose someone tried to view the sequence of answers given by one of the partners in such a conversation as a separate unity existing with its own order independently of the reciprocity of the conversation: that would be much as if one were to consider a person's individuality as something independent of the relations in which he finds himself, the constant weaving of threads through which he has become what he is. That people – unlike billiard balls – evolve and change in and through their relationships to each other may not be quite clear as long as one thinks exclusively of adults, whose characters, whose structures of consciousness and drives have become more or less fixed. They too are certainly never quite complete and finished. They too can change within their context of relationships, if with some difficulty and usually only in their more conscious self-control. But what we have called a process of 'interweaving' here to denote the whole relationship of individual and society, can never be understood as long as 'society' is imagined, as is so often the case, essentially as a society of individuals who were never children and who never die. One can only gain a clear understanding of the relation of individual and society if one includes in it the perpetual growing up of individuals within a society, if one includes the process of individualization in the theory of society.

The historicity of each individual, the phenomenon of growing up to adult-hood, is a key to an understanding of what 'society' is. The sociality integral to a human being only becomes apparent if one is aware what relations to other people mean for a small child.

The child is not only malleable or adaptable to a far greater degree than adults. It *needs* to be adapted by others, it *needs* society in order to become physically adult. In the child it is not only ideas, not only conscious behaviour that is constantly formed and transformed in and through its relations to others, but the very direction in which it learns to steer its basic drives. Of course, the dispositions which slowly evolve in the new-born child are never simply a copy of what is done to him by others. They are entirely his. They are *his* response to the way in which his drives and emotions, which are by nature orientated towards other people, are responded to and satisfied by these others. Only on the basis of this continuous affective dialogue with other people do the elementary, unformed impulses of the small child take on a more definite direction, a clearer structure. Only on the basis of such an affective dialogue does there develop in the child the complex psychical self-control by which human beings differ from all other creatures: a more or less individual character. In order to become psychically adult, a human individual, the child cannot do without the relation to older and more powerful beings. Without the assimilation of pre-formed social models, of parts and products of these more powerful beings, without the shaping of his psychical functions which they bring about, the child remains, to repeat the point, little more than an animal. And just because the helpless child needs social modelling in order to become a more individualized and complex being, the individuality of the adult can only be understood in terms of the relationships allotted to him or her by fate, only in connection with the structure of the society in which he or she has grown up. However certain it may be that each person is a complete entity in himself, an individual who controls himself and can be controlled or regulated by no one else if he does not do so himself, it is no less certain that the whole structure of his self-control, both conscious and unconscious, is a product of interweaving formed in a continuous interplay of relationships to other people, and that the individual form of the adult is a society-specific form.

The new-born, the small child – no less than the old man – has a socially appointed place shaped by the specific structure of the particular human network. If his function for his parents is unimportant or, through a shift in the social structure, less important than before, people either have fewer chil-dren or, in some cases, kill those already born. There is no zero-point of the social relatedness of the individual, no 'beginning' or sharp break when he steps into society as if from outside as a being untouched by the network and then begins to link up with other human beings. On the contrary, just as parents are needed to bring a child into the world, just as the mother feeds the child first with her blood and then with nourishment from her body, the individual always exists, on the most fundamental level, in relation to others, and this relation has a particular structure specific to his society. He takes on his individual stamp from the history of these relationships, these dependences, and so, in a broader context, from the history of the whole human network within which he grows up and lives. This history and this human network are present in him and are represented by him, whether he is actually in relationships to others or on his own, actively working in a big city or shipwrecked on an island a thousand miles from his society. Robinson Crusoe, too, bears the imprint of a particular society, a particular nation and class. Isolated from all relations to them as he is on his island, he behaves, wishes and plans by their standard, and thus exhibits behaviour, wishes and plans different from Friday, no matter how much the two adapt to each other by virtue of their new situation.

PART III

SOCIOLOGIST IN BRITAIN, 1950–1965

12

SOCIOLOGY AND PSYCHIATRY

After England had declared war on Germany in September 1939, Elias was evacuated from London to Cambridge with others from the London School of Economics, where he had been given a Research Fellowship. In 1940 he and many other German refugees were interned, first in a camp near Liverpool and then on the Isle of Man. After his release he went back to Cambridge, where he stayed till the end of the war. In 1945, he returned to London.

The post-war years were very difficult for Elias. His father had died in 1941, his mother was killed in Auschwitz. England offered him no opportunities for an academic career nor, consequently, for recognition of his qualities as a sociologist.

At that time there was only a very limited number of jobs in sociology at British universities. The closest Elias could come to an academic appointment was by teaching extension courses in adult education organized by the University of London. Another part-time occupation he found was work in group analysis, a new form of psychotherapy developed by his old friend and fellow refugee from Frankfurt, S. H. Foulkes.

Elias himself also underwent psychoanalysis during these years. He had chosen to do so partly because of troubles of his own, partly in order to gain credentials as a group analyst. At the same time, he continued to carry on intensive intellectual discussions about psychoanalysis, especially with Foulkes and with a former student from Frankfurt, Ilse Seglow, who had established a psychoanalytic practice in London.

In these discussions Elias always insisted on the impossibility of separating people's individual from their social experiences. When, in 1965, Foulkes chaired a meeting of the Psychotherapy and Social Psychiatry Section of the Royal Medico-Psychological Association in Britain, he invited Elias to contribute a paper on psychiatry and sociology. The following excerpt from that paper shows how Elias pleaded for individual psychoanalysis to be put into a larger social context.

All the various difficulties of communication between psychiatrists and sociologists, as between representatives of other human sciences, converge on a central difficulty. The specialists who are devoted to the scientific exploration of the human universe tend to build up from the limited segment of human beings under their care a unitary model of man on an all too narrow factual base. The best known of these parochial specialists' models of men is the *Homo economicus*. But one can observe in other social sciences equally parochial models of men. Thus psychiatrists make certain common assumptions about men in general, which reflect their circumscribed professional experiences. These permeate their procedures, their concepts, their whole mode of thinking about men. The same can be said of psychologists or of sociologists. One could speak of a *Homo psychiatricus*, a *Homo psychoanalyticus*, or a *Homo sociologicus*.

All of these groups are inclined to see their own province of the human universe as the most basic and the most central. As a result, those aspects with which they are professionally concerned stand out sharply and highly structured in the foreground of their image of people; other aspects that lie beyond their own field of studies and outside their own control are usually perceived as part of an unstructured background.

In the psychiatrist's perception, as I see it, the single individual – the single patient – stands out sharply in the foreground. All other people connected with him are perceived as a more or less unstructured background. The terms habitually used underline and reinforce this structure of the psychiatrist's perception and the picture of man that goes with it. It is not unusual to speak of a patient's 'social background'; one may speak of a child's 'bad background' if one means his family; or, worse still, one may speak of family, neighbourhood, community, and other similar social configurations as a person's 'environment'. In the eyes of many sociologists, by contrast, all these configurations are highly structured. One can study the structure of neighbourhoods and communities, and the structure of the families that live there. I myself have once undertaken such a study (see below pp. 104–5). Nor can I doubt that many psychiatrists are aware – if not with regard to neighbourhoods or occupations, at least with regard to families – that a person's relations with others are open to a fairly rigorous analysis. In point of fact, they often make attempts to determine the configuration of, say, husband, wife, elder son, and younger daughter in a particular case. But their training does not equip them too well for a systematic exploration of family structures. It expresses the implied evaluation of their concept of man that, by comparison with the individual with whom they are concerned, the network of relationships of which the individual forms part, all the social structures to which he belongs, come under the heading 'environmental factors'. The terminology itself implies the existence of a wall between the highly structured person in the foreground and the seemingly unstructured network of relations and communications in the background.

In discussions between psychiatrists and sociologists that is one of the sources of misunderstandings. Whereas sociologists, speaking of families or of groups and societies in general, may refer to what they perceive as configurations of people with structures, and often also with dynamics, of their own, psychiatrists may take up the sociologists' argument in terms of highly structured individuals with relatively unstructured 'backgrounds', without awareness of the difference. One can see at once the importance, for any collaborative effort in fields such as social psychiatry and group psychotherapy, of this confrontation between differences in the basic concepts, and of the evaluation of data that follow from them.

As a theoretical model, the *Homo psychiatricus* is based on the assumption of a fairly radical division between what goes on 'inside' and what goes on 'outside' the individual human being. The vocabulary of a psychiatric diagnosis, like that of a physical medical diagnosis, refers almost exclusively to the former; it refers to supposedly 'internal' processes of man, such as compulsion syndromes, object cathexis, perversion, and character disorders, which seem to run their course with almost complete autonomy in relation to the 'environment', to the network of relationships and communications of one human being with others.

The *Homo psychiatricus*, then, is a human being stripped of most attributes which one might call 'social', such as attributes connected with the standing of his family, with his educational attainments, his occupational training and work, or his national characteristics and identifications. The individual person is seen essentially as a closed system whose own internal processes have a high degree of independence in relation to what appear as 'external' or social factors. In general, the latter are evaluated as peripheral when a person is considered psychiatrically. They can be 'taken off', as it were, like a patient's clothes in a doctor's surgery.

The presentation of the psychiatrist's concept of man would be incomplete if one did not add that the *Homo psychiatricus* is in many respects a more sophisticated and refined version of the dominant concept of man of contemporary industrial societies as a *Homo clausus*. In these societies, terms such as 'group' or 'society' are very widely used as if they refer to something that lies outside of man, that surrounds or 'environs' the single individual. The image evoked by these conventions of speaking and thinking is that of a high wall surrounding the single individual, from which mysterious little dwarfs – the 'environmental influences' – throw small rubber balls at the individual, which leave on him some imprints. That is the way in which terms like 'social factors' and others of this kind are commonly employed.

It is, as one can see, the perspective of a human being who experiences himself alone at the centre of things, while everything else lies outside, separated from him by an invisible wall, and who imputes as a matter of course the same experience to all other individuals. From this basic experience of oneself as a somewhat lonely and isolated person, as the centre of all others, one arrives at the general concept of 'the individual' in the singular as the centre of the human world. This individual-centred perspective of the human universe is in many ways the contemporary counterpart of the former geocentric perspective of the natural universe.

13

THE NAVAL PROFESSION

After his arrival in England, Elias developed a lively interest in British society and culture. This had already become evident in *The Civilizing Process*, in which one of the main undercurrents of the argument was a comparison of the processes of state formation and civilization in France, Germany, and England.

Elias's first publication in English, after more than a decade's silence, was a contribution to the first volume of the *British Journal of Sociology* (1950a). The subject, the origin of the naval profession in seventeenth-century Britain, might seem rather off the beaten track for a sociologist. It gave Elias an opportunity, however, to delve deeply into a less well-known chapter in British history. He quoted at length from contemporary naval tracts and journals, revealing the difficulties that gentleman officers with an army background on the one hand, and experienced ship's captains on the other, had in sharing command in the naval hierarchy. Fierce individual conflicts, such as the fatal clash between the seaman captain Francis Drake and the gentleman officer Thomas Doughty during their voyage around the world, could be shown to be the outcome of the pressures emanating from the rival groups to which those men belonged.

An inquiry into those conflicts, and into the way they were finally resolved, yielded interesting historical insights. At the same time, as Elias remarked in the concluding section of his article reprinted here, it had a more general sociological significance.

In retrospect, one may find it difficult, at first, to visualize a profession in which people of different social rank and different professional training worked together as colleagues and, at the same time, struggled with each other as rivals.

However, the naval profession of the sixteenth and seventeenth centuries was certainly not the only profession in which two different social and professional groups, for a time, worked and struggled with each other. The personnel of the rudimentary airforce, for instance, was recruited early in the twentieth century, partly from men with the outlook of aviators and partly from military officers. In that case too it was necessary to co-ordinate the work of two sets of people of different mentality and, to some extent, of different social antecedents. But the dispute between them was short, and the rivalry restrained.

Nor are situations of this type confined to the history of military professions. Today, for instance, two groups with different social antecedents and different professional qualifications are sharing with each other the management of state industries. People in charge of these industries are recruited partly from the middle classes and partly from men of working class descent.

It would not be difficult to find other examples of this kind in past and present. In fact, a similar phase, an initial antagonism and struggle for position between rival groups, may be found in the early history not only of professions, but of almost every institution. If one attempted to work out a general theory of the genesis of institutions one would probably have to say that the initial conflict is one of the basic features of a nascent institution.

One can go still further; one can say that similar status-battles and struggles for position, longer or shorter, as the case may be, can be found whenever individuals, initially independent, are about to merge into a group, or smaller groups into a larger. In that sense, the tensions and conflicts between soldiers and mariners, between gentlemen and seamen in the history of the naval profession may serve as a simple model for other more complex conflicts and struggles in the history of mankind. They were group-tensions and institutional conflicts, that is, inherent in the group-situation of these men and caused by the institutional pattern of their relationships and functions, as distinct from primarily personal tensions and conflicts between people caused for instance by paranoic or sadistic tendencies or, more generally, by inner conflicts of individuals. For that reason, they reproduced themselves over many generations although the individuals changed.

The detailed account of this struggle and of the gradual emergence of a more unified profession must be left to separate studies. However, the study of the social characteristics of these two groups already gives some clues to the problems which had to be solved before this struggle could come to an end, and to the difficulties which stood in the way of a solution.

The problem made itself felt, as far as we know, first in the time of Elizabeth. As early as 1578, during his voyage of circumnavigation, Drake spoke of the quarrels between gentlemen and mariners and stressed how necessary it was for both groups to work together. More than a century later, in 1683, Pepys made a note on a discussion he had with Sir William Booth and others on the same subject and wrote[1] that they

do agree with me that gentlemen ought to be brought into the Navy as being men that are more sensible of honour than a man of meaner birth (though here may be room to examine whether as great actions in honour have not been done by plain seamen, and as mean by gentlemen, as any others and this is worth enquiring) but then they ought to be brought up by time at sea. . . . And then besides the good they would do for the King and Navy, by their friends at Court, they would themselves espouse the cause of the seamen and know what they deserve and love them as part of himself; and the seamen would be brought to love them rather more than one of themselves because of his quality, he being otherwise their fellow seaman and labourer.

And in 1694 the Marquis of Halifax again referred, in his *Rough Draught of a new Model at Sea*, to 'the present Controversie between the Gentlemen and the Tarpaulins'; he still discussed the question 'Out of what sort of Men the Officers of the Fleet are to be chosen . . .'[2] and gave it as his opinion that 'there must be a mixture in the Navy of Gentlemen and Tarpaulins'.[3]

From the time of Drake to that of Halifax, a compromise between the two groups and an integration of both appeared to many people as the ideal solution. However, as in many other cases, no one quite knew how this ideal was to be attained. Neither Drake, nor Pepys, nor Halifax produced a durable scheme by means of which it could be put into practice. For as the seamen were not gentlemen and the gentlemen not seamen, how was it possible to devise a unified scheme for the training and promotion of naval officers satisfactory to both groups?

14

Involvement and Detachment

In 1954 Elias obtained his first and only full-time academic appointment in England: he became a lecturer in the Department of Sociology at Leicester. Six years later, he was promoted to be a Reader – a post he held till 1962, when he reached retirement age. Throughout those eight years the Head of the Department was Ilya Neustadt, a refugee originally from Odessa, who after spells in Romania and Belgium had ended up living in England. Together, Neustadt and Elias set up a sociological curriculum with a strongly comparative and developmental emphasis.

At a time when sociology in Britain was expanding rapidly, the Department at Leicester became one of the largest and most prominent in the country. It counted among its students and junior lecturers many people who later played a prominent part in British academic life – including, for example, Keith Hopkins who became Professor of Ancient History at Cambridge, Earl Hopper who became a psychoanalyst, and sociologists such as Martin Albrow, Sheila Allen, Richard Brown, Percy Cohen, Eric Dunning, John Eldridge, Anthony Giddens, John H. Goldthorpe, Terence Johnson, Nicos Mouzelis, Bryan Wilson, and Sami Zubaida, who all developed in very different directions.

Some later testimonies suggest that at Leicester Elias was a highly-regarded and influential teacher and colleague (cf. Brown 1987; Eldridge 1990). Yet, at the time when he actually taught there his reputation in the Department was controversial, to say the least.[1] He did indeed command respect for his intelligence and erudition, but he was also considered a bit odd and old-fashioned, a typical pre-war continental scholar, learned and talkative, but not quite abreast of all the latest developments in the field.

His actual influence on the junior lecturers and students varied considerably. One of them, Eric Dunning, collaborated with him intensively, and never made a secret of his strong commitment to Elias's teachings. The work of several others also shows a great affinity with his sociological approach – as may be seen, for example, in Bryan Wilson's penetrating sketch of the emergence of charismatic leaders among the North American Indians in the eighteenth and nineteenth centuries (Wilson 1975: 38–58). Explicit references to Elias were virtually absent, however, even in Percy Cohen's book on 'modern social theory' (1968) in which the author, claiming to discuss some central problems of sociology from various angles, ignored Elias completely.

For Elias himself, the gap between his own ideas and those of most of his junior colleagues posed a stimulating challenge. He felt prompted to define as clearly as possible both his own position within sociology, and the place of sociology in the larger field of ideologies and sciences. In this context he wrote a great deal – much of which remained unpublished for a long time, including various papers which were later incorporated into his book *What is Sociology?* He prepared one long essay for publication, however. It was on 'Problems of Involvement and Detachment', and it appeared in the *British Journal of Sociology* in 1956.

In this essay Elias summed up his views on the current state of sociology – its task and promise as well as the formidable obstacles to the realization of its possibilities. Writing during the Cold War, he argued that the intellectual ability to perceive and handle the central problems of sociology was directly related to the ties by which the sociologists themselves were bound to their own society – in their capacity as members both of competing nation-states and of hierarchically ordered scientific establishments. The full text of this article was incorporated many years later, along with several equally long additions, in a book called *Involvement and Detachment* (Elias 1987d); here we present the first pages of the introduction Elias wrote in the early 1980s for that book, in which he clearly indicated the enormous challenges faced by sociology as well as the many difficulties that need to be overcome in order to meet those challenges.

1   The point of departure for the enquiries that follow was an enduring concern with the nature of sociological knowledge, with knowledge of human societies. Why are human societies more resistant than non-human nature to a successful exploration by human beings, and thus to a more adequate handling of their self-made dangers and possible catastrophes? And why is it that almost everybody seems to take it for granted that this must be so? Why do most people appear to consider it both impossible and undesirable that human beings might learn to rid themselves of the dangers they constitute for each other and for themselves, in the same way they learned to get rid of, or at least to contain, many of the dangers with which non-human nature threatened humans in former days? Those dangers were at least as uncontrollable as the human-made dangers that threaten them today. Is it not true that the threat of a new epidemic caused largely by non-human agents is today

immediately countered by the mobilization of scientists in many parts of the world? Everybody assumes as a matter of course that it is not beyond the power of human beings to find an explanation and then perhaps also a cure for the deadly menace. In the case of wars or revolutions, however, which are in no way smaller and often even greater human disasters than great floods or epidemics, few people would look to social scientists for help and advice; and if they did these scientists might come up with advice which few were ready to accept or even listen to.

To be sure, three or four centuries ago, in the case of natural catastrophes too, few would have turned to or listened to scientists for help and advice. In fact at that time many people might have spurned the very idea that human beings, thanks to their own capacity for producing reality-congruent knowledge, could have the power to prevent natural disasters from killing thousands of people. Not so long ago it might have seemed laughable and naïve to believe such a thing. Now, for the time being, the course of humanity in dealing with disasters brought about by humans themselves, appears to have been arrested in a condition not unlike that which, for thousands of years, also prevailed in the case of dangers resulting from non-human nature. Once upon a time there was nothing one could do but wail about the frequency with which women died in childbirth, or little children died in the first year of life. Now there is nothing one can do about social disasters, such as wars, revolutions and other forms of human violence which shorten further the already short life of great masses of people, and inflict crippling injuries on thousands of others.

As things are, one may even fail to recognize violent action between or within states as a human-made catastrophe. Social scientists have not yet succeeded in demonstrating convincingly that killing is no answer to killing, whether in a good or in a bad cause. Nor have they succeeded in making it more widely known and also better understood that cycles of violence, whether they are kept in motion by integration or by hegemonial struggles, by class conflicts or by interstate conflicts, have strong self-escalating tendencies. War processes, for example, are difficult to stop even if they are still in the preparatory state of reciprocal threats of violence creeping towards its use. They almost invariably breed professional killers of one kind or another, whether these killers have the social character of dictator or general, of freedom fighter or mercenary. Their impulses and their actions are geared to mutual suspicion, hatred and violence: as levers of human catastrophes they are to be feared no less than the plague which once seemed to humans equally uncontrollable.

2   There is another example which may help to illustrate the weakness of the social sciences in relation to their task. Quite a number of people are inclined to believe as a matter of course that the natural sciences in general, and physics in particular, are to blame for the danger of a nuclear or maybe a

chemical war which hangs over our heads on a very thin thread, like the infamous sword of Damocles. War processes, however, are closely linked to specific social institutions. Almost all governments, and certainly those of the more powerful nations, maintain as a matter of course military forces as large as they can afford and often larger. In their unending rivalry for power and status, they all try to secure for their own nation the highest position within their reach. Many of them, however, and particularly the most powerful states or blocks of states, by trying to maximize their own security, automatically optimize the insecurity of rival or enemy states and thus in fact their own.

The explanation of the danger of war cannot be found in the form of a stationary cause. It lies in an ongoing, self-perpetuating social process without absolute beginning, though – like cholera – possibly with an end. The institutional and the habitus tradition associated with this long-term process makes not only a country's security but also its prestige, and thus the pride and self-love of many of its citizens, dependent on the power potential of its military establishment. More often than not a large section of a nation's population rejoices in the strength and prowess of its military establishment. Hence, by continually threatening each other, militarily interdependent rival states drive each other in an endless spiral towards the development of even tougher and better-trained troops, of even more deadly weapons, and thus, in a world with more and more people, towards wars where mounting numbers can sacrifice their lives. The difficulty is that is cannot be of any help at all to change attitudes one-sidedly or to advocate such a change on behalf of either small or large sections of a country's population.

3   Whoever pays the piper calls the tune. Once upon a time armoured knights were the principal exponents of the age-old tradition which induced people to regard it not only as legitimate but also as praiseworthy to settle certain types of conflict by reciprocal attempts at killing or maiming. The smiths who, in a rising spiral improved, now the swords and other weapons of attack, now the armour and other means of defence, were not the reason why kings and their warriors went to war against each other. When at one stage a well-known spiral of violence resulted in the dominance of firearms, when even the heaviest knightly armour could be pierced and even the thickest fortress walls shattered, there was an outcry at the barbaric destructiveness of the new weapons. But the interstate rivalries and thus the war process continued. Knights and fortress walls disappeared, but the spiral of interstate violence went on, without halting in its unchecked – and so far uncheckable – course towards the invention and use of more and more destructive weapons and the employment of more and more resources for the preparation of war.

The arms race did not start yesterday. However, with or without a big bang, it may now be nearing the end of the road. Smiths were not the originators of endless wars between knights; nor are scientists and engineers who apply their professional knowledge to the improvement of weapons the reason why nations go to war. They are usually nothing more than servants or advisers of party politicians and other ruling groups who are the leading players in this game.

Nor is the reason for war to be found in weapons of one kind or another. It can only be found in groups of human beings themselves perceiving, and bound to, each other as rivals or enemies. These groups, nations among them, delight in their own superiority over each other, particularly their military superiority, past or present. They are deeply affected by its decline. They continue to live in the shadow of their greater military past and go into mourning for it, often generation after generation. The history books of nations, particularly those destined for children, are full of battles won and enemies defeated. Indeed, the handing on of this information from one generation to the other can hardly be avoided; for it forms an integral part of the knowledge that is needed for an understanding of the formative period in the development of nations and other survival units, and thus of their own identity. That some of the peoples of this world, in cases of conflict, try to coerce each other by violent means and that victories gained in the course of mutual woundings and killings are a source of collective pride and rejoicing has thus become part of a firmly entrenched tradition, with roots deep in the social habitus of individual members of these groups.

In our age, moreover, the concept of a just war, a kind of moral rehabilitation of the use of violence as a means of settling interstate conflicts, has been extended to the settling of conflicts within states. Partly thanks to the work of Marx and his followers, revolution has become a praise word. The reciprocal violence of groups of people in the course of a revolutionary process or any other kind of long-drawn-out civil war is as great a human disaster as a war between states. That revolutionary processes often start from a condition of one-sided violent oppression has often been mentioned. It is less often mentioned that they also quite frequently end with one-sided violent oppression. If one ceases to consider revolutions in an historical manner, that is, as short-term events, if one sees instead such violent explosions as phases of a long-term process, it becomes clearer that they too form part of a cycle and often a spiralling cycle of violence, which may go on smouldering for a long time after the overt revolutionary violence has died down.

The self-perpetuating propensity of long lasting cycles of violence can be observed as much in the processes of class revolutions or ethnic and other forms of civil war as in those of interstate war. In all these cases violence breeds violence, often generation after generation. It may take a long time before the impetus of such a process exhausts itself. As for the alternative, it requires a higher level of detachment, of self-restraint, and of patience, and a gradual toning down of mutual dislike, suspicion and hatred. The threat of war, in the last resort, has its roots in the relationship of groups of people with each other, in their attitudes towards and their feeling for each other. None of these can be changed at short notice. Yet people often act as if that were the case: their emotional make-up induces them to expect and to demand that their political aims and ideals be realized in their own lifetime. Perhaps it is necessary to say explicitly that work towards the fulfilment of many of these aims, and certainly that of outlawing the use of violence as a means of settling interstate conflicts, is likely to require the patient work of many generations united in their uncompromising adherence to the paramount goal and ready for many compromises on detail.

A rather neglected aspect of the dangers human groups constitute for each other deserves some attention here – their emotional aspect. Human groups seem to take a strange delight in asserting their superiority over others, particularly if it has been attained by violent means. The area one enters here has not been much explored. In referring to the pleasure people derive from the feeling that one of the groups to which they belong is superior to other groups, one touches on the emotional aspects of group relations and the dangers inherent in them. Part of the self-love of individuals, it seems, can attach itself to one of the groups with which they identify themselves, most of all to nations and other types of survival groups. The feeling of group superiority appears to provide members of that group with an immense narcissistic gratification. It is strange to observe that all over the world groups of people, great and small, huddle together as it were, and, with a gleam in their eyes and a nod of intimate understanding, assure each other how much greater, better, stronger they themselves are than some particular other groups or maybe even all other human groups. Secretly or not, they all have a self-praising vocabulary and a corresponding denigrating vocabulary directed against other groups. It depends on the balance of power between the groups concerned whether the denigrated groups can retaliate in stigmatizing terms of their own.

The unselfish aspects of people's attachment to groups, of their we-identity, have found some consideration. Praise words such as patriotism or national pride and self-esteem bear witness to the fact. The narcissistic component of these feelings, understandably, attracts less attention. Yet if one wants to know why the unrelenting drift in that direction continues with undiminished force – even now when another war threatens to destroy a large part of humanity, including the participant nations themselves – the lure of the narcissistic gratification of victory and group superiority, the hegemonial ecstasy associated with the prospect of continental or even global leadership and supremacy, provide at least part of the answer. People in power can usually count on a warm response of approval and often of affection or love from their compatriots whenever they praise or add to the glory of the social unit they all form with each other. The remarkable propensity of people for projecting part of their individual self-love into specific social units, to which they are linked by strong feelings of identity and of belonging, is one of the roots of the dangers which human groups constitute for each other.

It is not too difficult to recognize the ambivalent and the paradoxical character of the various types of group self-love. In many cases, people expect support, protection and help in distress, from their We-group, especially from a survival group, as well as the indispensable gratification of their self-esteem; and yet at the same time they may be ready to risk their lives for the sake of their group and its distinct values and beliefs. It is a remarkable blend of self-love and altruism, of narcissistic gratification and devotion to a collective, which one encounters here. The paradoxical situation is closely connected with the fact that the human self is an I-self as well as a We-self.

The vocabulary at one's disposal in this context is marred by its lack of detachment, by its emotional partisanship for the We-group. It shows clearly the black and white design of dominant involvement. According to this design, self love which leads to narcissism in human beings as individuals or as groups is bad, while love of others and even gratification of collective self-love are usually associated with strong positive evaluative undertones. The possibility that human beings may experience love for a group to which they themselves as well as others belong is one of many instances which show that a simple polarity between feelings of self-regard and of regard for others, of egotism and altruism, or even of good and bad, may not always fit the observable evidence. Moreover, the self-esteem of nations and other survival groups need not be undeserved: they may have achievements to their credit which are of great benefit to humanity. The praise people give to the affection they feel for themselves as a collective can be entirely realistic. But their self-praise may go far beyond their real merits. Often enough the virtues which such collectives attribute to themselves are dominated by communal fantasies. Nations feast on imaginary virtues, or on the virtues and merits of their forefathers which are no longer shared by themselves. In all these cases it is a question of balances, which requires exploration and recognition, rather than a black and white design, of a polarization of good and evil. Yet the pictures people have of themselves and each other are mostly of the latter type. They are often astonishingly simplistic. Their self-representation, characteristic of their cognitive involvement and their narcissism, is often uniformly good, while rivals or enemies tend to have no merits at all; they are bad all round.

A good example of the peculiar blend of reality-congruence and fantasy that one encounters in the self-images of survival units is the recurrent confusion of a higher power ratio with a higher human value in those endowed with more power and, correspondingly, the attribution of a lesser human value to those who are less powerful. I have alluded before to the profound traumatic effect on peoples' social habitus, to the wounding of their self-love which tends to follow a marked change for the worse in their nation's fortune. In just the same way, a decisive military victory, in present times as in past ages, has often been experienced by the victors as a reward from the gods for being more virtuous than their opponents, or, in human terms at any rate, superior to them. Thus the members of nations, even in our own time, experience the descent of their nation from the highest to a secondary position in the global power – and status – hierarchy of states as a fall from grace, as a lowering of their own human value. Their self love suffers. The loss of power is tacitly experienced as a loss of their value as human beings. As their pattern of self-restraint was formerly sustained and rewarded by the narcissistic enjoyment of their nation's power and pride, a decline in power can easily lead to a loosening of restraint. The lessening of a people's love for itself which before had a strong integrating function may turn into self-denigration if not self-hatred. For a while, a people's mourning for past greatness can thus have a de-civilizing effect.

I have shown in some detail a few of the reasons why human groups in so many cases constitute a threat and a danger for each other. It is not unusual to assume that the all-pervasive danger of violent action in the form of war or civil war, with which human groups threaten each other, has mainly what we call 'rational' reasons. However, violent struggles between human groups are a standing feature of the period we call history and presumably also of prehistory. It is in many cases hard to discover any reason for them that we might call rational today, any reason, that is, apart from an increment of wealth and power, from the gratification of collective self-love and the *Fata Morgana* of perfect security enforced by violence. Yet in spite of this age-old tradition and its visible perpetuation by the military institutions of our age – now grown on both sides of the great divide into powerful military industrial establishments – many people are inclined to assume that the day has dawned when this powerful tradition, with its roots deep in the feelings and attitudes of human groups towards each other, has come to an end. They tend to assume that realistic knowledge of the unprecedented destructiveness of warfare in our age, or in other words rational reasoning alone, is enough to break the impetus of the self-perpetuating tradition of war between survival groups, while the institutions and above all the collective feelings and attitudes of such groups retain their traditional character. This is quite a good example of people's involvement, in this case their wishful thinking, gaining the upper hand over a more detached view – of short term feelings displacing a long term diagnosis oriented towards facts, however unwelcome.

The stronger the hold of involved forms of thinking, and thus of the inability to distance oneself from traditional attitudes, the stronger the danger inherent in the situation created by peoples' traditional attitudes towards each other and towards themselves. The greater the danger the more difficult it is for people to look at themselves, at each other and at the whole situation with a measure of detachment.

15

THE SOCIETY OF INDIVIDUALS – II

Writing, in his years as a teacher at Leicester, about the basic problems of sociology, Elias also returned to his earlier essay on 'the society of individuals' (see above, pp. 68–74). He began by translating the German text prepared for publication in 1939, but soon found himself embarking upon an entirely new project. We are unable to date exactly when the following excerpt was written; it was not published until 1987. It clearly shows, in any case, Elias's effort to make sense of traditional problems of philosophy by turning them into objects of sociological inquiry. In an indirect way, the first part of the excerpt also evokes something of the loneliness that Elias must have felt as he stubbornly went his own way.

It may help to throw the strangeness of our own image of ourselves and of man into sharper relief if we see it retrospectively, in the mirror of the image of self and man that was again and again fundamental to the struggle to solve the problem of knowledge over the centuries.

Let us consider, for example, the man who first posed, in a paradigmatic way, the problem of knowledge and cognition in more or less the form it has kept to our day, Descartes. The dictum associated with his name, 'I think, therefore I am', has become a kind of slogan. But this dictum gives only a pale and misleading idea of the image of self and man underlying his meditations. To understand this basic conception we must recall at least the outlines of the process of thought, the period of doubt and uncertainty that he passed through before he found firm ground under his feet in the new certainty that the indubitable fact of one's own reflection also put the existence of one's own self beyond doubt.

He asked himself first whether there was anything of which one was absolutely certain, anything that could not be doubted under any circumstances. In social life, he realized, one had to accept many ideas as if they were the gospel, though they were anything but certain. Descartes therefore decided to set out in search of that which was absolutely certain, and to discard all conceptions on which there could be even the slightest doubt. 'Everything I have learned,' he said to himself, 'everything I know, I have learned through or from sense perceptions. But can one really trust one's senses? Can I be certain that I am sitting here beside my warm stove in my dressing-gown, holding this piece of paper in my hand? Can I be quite certain that these are my hands and my body? Of course, I see my hands; I feel my body. But,' said the dissenting voice of doubt, 'are there not people who believe they are kings while in reality they are paupers? Are there not people who are convinced that their heads are of stoneware and their bodies of glass? Is it not possible that God has so arranged things that I *believe* I see heaven and earth, and *believe* I have a three-dimensional body, while in reality nothing of the kind exists? Or, if God has not done so, is it not possible that an evil spirit may be deluding me into thinking that I feel, see and hear all these things which in reality do not exist? One cannot', he told himself, 'dismiss this possibility.' And as he felt compelled in this way to reject one by one all ideas of himself and the world as dubious and unreliable, he finally succumbed, like other people under the unremitting pressure of doubt, to the blackest despair. There was nothing certain in the world, so it seemed to him, nothing that could not be doubted.

'I must therefore', he wrote, 'take into account the possibility that heaven and earth, all forms in space, are nothing but illusions and fantasies used by an evil spirit to trap my credulity. I shall conceive that I myself have neither eyes nor hands, neither flesh, blood nor senses, but falsely believe I possess all of them.'

Only after he had spent some time wandering in the tunnel of uncertainty and subjecting all his experiences to the trial by fire of his radical doubt did he see a faint gleam of light at the end. However doubt may have gnawed at him and threatened to destroy all certainty, there was, he discovered, one fact that could not be doubted: 'Would it be possible', he asked, 'for me finally to convince myself that I myself do not exist? No. I myself exist. For I can convince myself that I am able to think something and to doubt it.'

Here we reach the core of this peculiar form of self-consciousness: sense perceptions and therefore the knowledge of physical objects including one's own body, all that may be doubtful and deceptive. But one cannot doubt, Descartes concludes, that one doubts. 'It is not possible for me to think that I do not think. And that I think is not possible unless I exist.'

The conception of the human self that we come across here and the questions it implies are far more than the mental games of a particular philosopher. They are highly characteristic of the transition from a conception of human beings and the world with strong religious underpinning to secularized conceptions, a transition which was making itself felt in Descartes's day. This secularization of human thought and action was certainly not the work of an individual or a number of individuals. It was connected to specific changes affecting all relationships of life and power in occidental societies. Descartes's deliberations represent a typical step in this direction in an original version. They indicate in a paradigmatic manner the peculiar problems with which people found themselves confronted in thinking about themselves and the certainty of their image of themselves when the religious picture of self and world became an open target of doubt and lost its self-evident status. This basic picture that dispensed certainty, the notion people had of themselves as part of a divinely created universe, did not thereby disappear, but it lost its central and dominant position in thought. As long as it held this position, that which could be perceived by the senses or confirmed by thought or observation played at most a secondary part in people's questions, thoughts and perceptions. The questions which mattered most to them concerned something that, in principle, could not be discovered by observation with the aid of the sense organs, or by thought supported by that which people ascertained by a methodical use of eyes and ears. They concerned, for example, the destination of the soul or the purpose of men and beasts in the framework of divine creation. To questions of this kind people could only find an answer with the help of recognized authorities of one kind or another, holy writings or favoured men – in short, through direct or indirect revelation. Individual observations were of very little help, individual reflection only helped in so far as it presented itself as an interpretation of one of the sources of revelation. And people accordingly felt themselves to be part of an invisible spiritual realm. They could feel themselves embedded in a hierarchy of beings the lowest rung of which was formed by the plants and animals, the highest by the angels, the pinnacle being God Himself. Or they may have experienced themselves as a kind of microcosm whose destiny was closely bound to that of the macrocosm of creation. Whatever the particular form, it was a basic feature of this picture of man and the world that what could be perceived by the senses took on its meaning from something that could be discovered and confirmed neither by individual reflection nor by individual observations.

One precondition of Descartes's thinking was a certain relaxation, a loss of power by the social institutions which had been the custodians of this intellectual tradition. His thought reflects the growing awareness of his time that people were able to decipher natural phenomena and put them to practical use simply on the basis of their own observation and thought, without invoking ecclesiastical or ancient authorities. Because of the prior work of thinkers of classical antiquity this discovery appeared to the people of the time like a rediscovery. It was a rediscovery of themselves as beings who could attain certainty about events by their own thought and observation, without recourse to authorities. And it moved their own mental activity – reified by the term 'reason' – and their own powers of perception into the foreground of their image of themselves.

16

THE QUEST FOR EXCITEMENT IN LEISURE

At Leicester Elias was once more able to play a role he had been forced to give up by the break in his career in 1933: supervising the research of advanced students. On the occasion of his eightieth birthday, several people who had been his students at Frankfurt testified how Elias had helped them to find a subject that suited their personal experience and interest, and how much time and care he used to spend in guiding and stimulating them in the actual research. The forced break in his academic career put an end to this form of supervision, which came close to actual collaboration in designing a research project and interpreting the findings.

His post at Leicester offered the opportunity to pick up that role again. Work with two students in particular turned out to be very productive. One was John Scotson, a schoolteacher interested in juvenile delinquency. For his master's thesis, he conducted a study of a local community, focusing initially on striking differences in delinquency rates in two working-class neighbourhoods. With Elias's help, the scope of the inquiry was soon extended to include power differentials and processes of stigmatization. Those latter themes, already central in the article on the Huguenots (see above, pp. 18–25), were now elaborated by Elias into a general model of established–outsider relations, for which the local investigation provided the material of a 'paradigmatic case study'.

Whereas the collaboration with John Scotson remained confined to a single project, a long-lasting cooperation grew up between Elias and Eric Dunning. Dunning came to Leicester in 1956 as a student of economics, but soon after hearing Elias lecture he became convinced that sociology was a more worthwhile subject. When Elias suggested that he undertake research on his favourite pastime, soccer, Dunning – after hesitating at first about whether this was really a promising field of study – soon became enthusiastic, as he began to realize that the development of football had occurred as part of a civilizing process. Out of that first initiative grew a series of articles and, eventually, a jointly written book on the sociology of sports and leisure called *Quest for Excitement* (1986a).

In the introduction to that book, Elias stressed the importance of the sociology of sport which, around 1960, was still stigmatized by the idea that physical pursuits and leisure activities were not quite worthy of serious intellectual attention. When viewed in a more detached manner, however, and especially from within a long-term perspective, the development of sport turned out to be a central aspect of the development of modern society, significant in its own right, and closely related to other long-term social processes. Thus, Elias was able to show a connection between the emergence of sport in England in the eighteenth century and a simultaneous spurt in the process of 'parliamentarization' – both tendencies representing a general 'calming down' of 'cycles of violence' (Elias and Dunning 1986a: 26).

The following excerpt – although revised for *Quest for Excitement* – was originally written in the 1960s. It is one more example of Elias's skill in developing a sociological argument by proceeding from a set of clearly posed questions.

I

A few centuries ago, the term 'sport' was used in England, together with the older version 'disport', for a variety of pastimes and entertainments. In *A Survey of London* written at the end of the sixteenth century,[1] we read about the 'show made by the citizens for the disport of the young Prince Richard', or of the 'sportess and passtimes yearly used, first in the Feaste of Christmass . . . There was in the Kinges house . . . a Lord of Misrule, or Maister of merry disports . . .'[2] In course of time, the term 'sport' became standardized as a technical term for specific forms of recreation in which physical exertion played a major part – specific forms of recreation of a type which first developed in England and which, from there, spread all over the world. Was the spread of these English spare-time occupations connected with the fact that the societies where people adopted them underwent structural changes similar to those which England had undergone before? Was it due to the fact that England was in advance of other countries with regard to 'industrialization'? The parallel pattern of these two processes, of the diffusion from England of industrial models of production, organization and work, and the diffusion of spare-time occupations of the type known as 'sport' and of the types of organization connected with it is certainly striking. As a first hypothesis, it does not seem unreasonable to assume that a transformation of the manner in which people used their spare-time went hand in hand with a transformation of the manner in which they worked. But what were the connections?

Much thought has been given to processes of industrialization and their conditions. To speak of processes of 'sportization' may jar upon the ear. The concept sounds alien. Yet it fits the observable facts quite well. In the course of the nineteenth century – and in some cases as early as the second half of the eighteenth century – with England as the model-setting country, some leisure activities demanding bodily exertion assumed the structural characteristics of 'sports' in other countries too. The framework of rules, including those providing for 'fairness', for equal chances to win for all contestants, became stricter. The rules became more precise, more explicit and more differentiated. Supervision of the observance of the rules became more efficient; hence, penalties for offences against the rules became less escapable. In the form of 'sports', in other words, game-contests involving muscular exertion attained a level of orderliness and of self-discipline on the part of participants not attained before. In the form of 'sports', moreover, game-contests came to embody a rule-set that ensures a balance between the possible attainment of a high combat-tension and a reasonable protection against physical injury. 'Sportization', in short, had the character of a civilizing spurt comparable in its overall direction to the 'courtization' of the warriors where the tightening rules of etiquette played a significant part and with which I have dealt elsewhere.[3]

The widespread tendency to explain almost everything that occurred in the nineteenth century as a result of the Industrial Revolution makes one a little wary of explanations in these terms. No doubt industrialization and urbanization played a part in the development and diffusion of spare-time occupations with the characteristics of 'sports', but it is also possible that both industrialization and sportization were symptomatic of a deeper-lying transformation of European societies which demanded of their individual members greater regularity and differentiation of conduct. The growing length and differentiation of chains of interdependence may have had something to do with it. This process found its expression in the submission of both people's feeling and acting to a minutely differentiated regulatory time-schedule and to an equally inescapable accountability in terms of money. It is possible to think that European societies, broadly speaking from the fifteenth century onwards, underwent a transformation which enforced among their members a slowly increasing regularity of conduct and sentiment. Maybe the ready acceptance of the sport type of pastimes in continental countries was a sign of the growing need for more orderly, more highly regulated and less physically violent recreational activities in society at large? Future research may help to give an answer to these questions. For the moment, it must be enough to clarify and to straighten some of the questions surrounding the early development of sports themselves. In the past the term 'sport' has often been used indiscriminately with regard to specific types of modern leisure activities and to the leisure activities of societies at an earlier stage of development as well, just as one often referred to modern 'industry' and, at the same time, to the 'industry' of Stone Age peoples. What I have said may be enough to bring out more clearly that sport is something relatively recent and new.

II

If one begins to work one's way further back from this brief vision of the spread of the sports movement beyond England to the preceding development of sport in England itself, one has to think about the best way to proceed. How does one find reliable evidence about processes of growth – about the development of games and other leisure activities into the form to which we now apply the term 'sport'? So much of these developments, one may think, has gone unrecorded. Are there enough records left for the reconstruction of the processes in which pastimes acquired the characteristics of sports and in which each sport in turn acquired its own distinguishing characteristics?

It is not evidence so much which is lacking. But, in looking for it, one is often prevented from taking note of such evidence as there is by preconceptions about history-writing in general and about writing the history of sports in particular. Thus, in studying the development of a sport, one is often guided by the wish to establish for it a long and respectable ancestry. And, in that case, one is apt to select as relevant for its history all data about games played in the past which bear some resemblance to the present form of the particular sport whose history one is writing. If one finds in a twelfth-century chronicle that, already at that time, the young people of London went on certain days into the fields in order to play with a ball, one is apt to conclude that these young people were already then playing the same game which, under the name of 'football', has now become one of the major games of England and which has, in that form, spread all over the world.[4] But, by thus treating the leisure activities of the fairly distant past as more or less identical with those of one's own time – the 'football' of the twelfth century with the football of the late nineteenth and twentieth centuries – one is prevented from placing at the centre of one's enquiry the questions of how and why playing with a large, leather ball grew into this particular form? One is prevented from asking how and why the particular rules and conventions developed which now determine the conduct of players when they play the game and without which the game would not be 'football' in our sense of the word. Or how and why the particular forms of organization developed which provided the most immediate framework for the growth of such rules and without which they could not be maintained and controlled.

In all these regards, the training, the study and the outlook to which we now apply the term 'sociological', directs attention to problems, and consequently to evidence, which are not always regarded as centrally relevant within the dominant tradition of history-writing. The sociologist's history is not the historian's history. Attention to the rules and norms which govern human behaviour at a given time, and to the organizations within which such rules are maintained and their observance controlled, has become a fairly normal task of sociological enquiries.

What is at present still rather unusual is attention to rules or norms in development. The problem as to how and why rules or norms have become what they are at a given time is not often systematically explored. Yet without exploration of such processes, a whole dimension of social reality remains beyond one's reach. The sociological study of sport-games, apart from its intrinsic interest, also has the function of a pilot scheme. One encounters here in a field which is relatively limited and accessible, problems of a type which are often encountered in other larger, more complex and less accessible areas. Studies in the development of sports provide experiences in many ways and sometimes lead to theoretical models which can be of help in the exploration of these other areas. The problem as to how and why rules develop is an example. The static study of rules or norms as something given has often led in the past, and still leads today, to an equivocal and somewhat unrealistic picture of society.

If one tests current theories of society, one discovers strong tendencies to regard norms and rules – in the succession of Durkheim – almost as if they had an existence independently of persons. One often speaks of norms or rules as if they were data which account by themselves for the integration of individual persons in the form of societies and for the particular type of integration, for the pattern or structure, of societies. In short, one is often given the impression that norms or rules, like Plato's ideas, have an existence of their own, that they exist, as it were, somehow by themselves and constitute, therefore, the point of departure for reflections on the way in which living persons form themselves into societies.

If one enquires into the way in which rules or norms develop, one is better able to see that the Durkheimian approach, which explains the cohesion, the interdependence and the integration of human beings and groups in terms of the rules or norms which they follow, still has a strong nominalistic ring about it. It lends itself to a misconception about the nature of society which is now fairly widespread. According to it, the sharp evaluating distinction between forms of human conduct and human grouping which agree with the set norms and others which run counter to them, is uncritically taken over into the conceptual apparatus of those whose task it is to study, and as far as possible to explain, problems of society. Sociological studies aimed at explaining the connection of events in society would fail in their task if they were to classify events in this way. For, in terms of explanation, activities and groupings which agree with the set norms, and others which deviate from them – 'integration' and 'disintegration', 'social order' and 'social disorder' – are interdependent and constitute exactly the same kind of events.[5]

If one enquires into the processes in which norms and rules develop, this factual interdependence of 'order' and 'disorder', of 'function' and 'dysfunction', becomes strikingly clear. For in the course of such processes, one can see again and again how specific rules or norms are set by human beings in order to remedy specific forms of malfunctioning, and how malfunctionings in turn lead to other changes in norms, in the codes of rules governing the conduct of people in groups.

One can see more clearly, too, the illusionary character of any conception of society which makes it appear that norms or rules have a power of their own, as if they were something outside and apart from the groups of people, and could serve as such as an explanation for the way in which people group themselves as societies. The study of the development of 'sport-games'[6] and, as one aspect of it, the development of their rules, enabled me to explore in a comparatively manageable field the technique of sociological research for which I use, as an appropriate name, the term 'figurational' analysis and synthesis, and to show how I think it should be used. More particularly, such a study shows very clearly one of the basic facts about the structure of societies generally, namely that – given unchanging non-human conditions – the specific forms in which people group themselves can only be explained in terms of other specific forms in which people group themselves. At the present stage, it still sounds rather odd if one says that what one studies as 'social patterns', 'social structures' or 'figurations' are patterns, structures or figurations formed by human beings. Linguistic usages and habits of thinking make us inclined to speak and to think of such patterns, structures, figurations almost as if they were something outside and apart from the people who form them with each other.

Many sociological standard terms, of course, have reached a high degree of appropriateness to observable structures. Among them is the term 'structure' itself. And yet I have some reservations with regard to standard expressions such as that which we use when we say a society or group *has* a structure. One can easily interpret this manner of speaking as if the group were something apart from the people who form it. What we call 'structure' is, in fact, nothing but the pattern or figuration of interdependent individual people who form the group or, in a wider sense, the society. What we term 'structures' when we look at people as societies, are 'figurations' when we look at them as individuals.

Figurations form the core of what one investigates if one studies sports. Every sport – whatever else it may be – is an organized group activity centred on a contest between at least two parties. It requires physical exertion of some kind. It is fought out according to known rules, including, if physical force can be used at all, rules which define the permitted limits of violence. The

rules determine the starting figuration of the players and its changing pattern
as the contest proceeds. But all kinds of sports have specific functions for the
participants, for spectators or for their countries at large. When the given form
of a sport fails to perform these functions adequately, the rules may be
changed.

Sports differ in accordance with their different rules and, therefore, the
different pattern of the contest or, in other words, of the different figurations
of individuals concerned as determined by their respective regulations and the
organizations controlling adherence to them. The problem is evidently what
distinguished the English type of 'playing the game' – the type of games
contest, of rules and organization, to which we now refer as 'sports' – from
other types of games contest. How did they come into being? How did the
distinguishing character of the rules, the organizations, the relationships, the
groups of players in action peculiar to 'sports' develop in the course of time?
Evidently this was one of those processes in the course of which specific
structures of group relations and activities developed over many generations
through the concourse of the actions and aims of many individuals even
though none of the participating people, as individuals or as groups, intended
or planned the long-term outcome of their actions. Thus it is not merely a
manner of speaking if one envisages the emergence of sports as a developmental and not merely as an historical problem. In history books, the history
of sports is often presented as a series of almost accidental activities and
decisions of a few people. What appears to lead up to the 'final', the 'mature'
form of the game is put into the limelight. What is different from or opposed
to the 'ultimate' pattern is often left as irrelevant in the shade. As one shall
see, the growth of the 'mature' form of a sport cannot be adequately presented
if it is envisaged largely as a haphazard medley of activities and decisions of a
few known individuals or groups. Nor can it be adequately presented in the
manner suggested by current sociological theories as a series of 'social
changes'. The changes which one can observe in the development of sports
such as cricket and football as well as fox-hunting and horse-racing, have both
a pattern and a direction of their own. That is the aspect of the history of sports
to which one refers if one speaks of it as a 'development'. But in using this
term, one has to dissociate oneself from its philosophical or metaphysical use.
What is meant by social development can only be found out with the help of
detailed empirical studies. It can only be found out in this specific context if
one enquires into the way in which fox-hunting, boxing, cricket, football and
other sports in fact 'developed'. I have used, provisionally and in quotes, the
expression 'mature' or 'ultimate' form of the game. It was one of the discoveries made in the course of enquiries of this kind that a game may reach in
the course of its development a peculiar equilibrium stage. And when this
stage has been reached, the whole structure of its further development
changes. For to have reached its 'mature' form, or however one cares to call

it, does not mean that all development stops: it merely means that it enters upon a new stage. However, neither the existence of this stage, nor its characteristics, nor, for that matter, its significance for the whole concept of social development, can be determined in any other way except through the empirical study of the evidence itself. On the other hand, the preliminary knowledge that what one is looking for if one studies the history of a sport is not merely the isolated activities of individuals or groups, and not only a number of unpatterned changes, but a patterned sequence of changes in the organization, the rules and the actual figuration of the game itself, leading over a certain period towards a specific stage of tension-equilibrium which has been provisionally called here the 'mature stage' and whose nature has yet to be determined. This knowledge itself, used flexibly and with the possibility of its inadequacy always in one's mind, can guide one's eye in the selection of data and help in perceiving connections.

17

GROUP CHARISMA AND GROUP DISGRACE

In October 1959 Elias went back to Germany for the first time after the war to give a lecture. In that lecture, about public opinion in England, he apologized for no longer being able to speak his mother tongue quite idiomatically: 'please don't hesitate to laugh if it sounds a bit quaint' (1960:7).

Five years later, 1964, was the first centenary of the birth of Max Weber. To commemorate that event, the German Sociological Association held its annual congress in his honour, in Heidelberg. Elias also attended – his first appearance since 1933 in the world of German sociology. He contributed a paper on 'Group Charisma and Group Disgrace'.

The paper was not included in the transactions, published as *Max Weber and Sociology Today* (Stammer 1971). This omission was no doubt a reflection on Elias's humble status in sociology; a quarter of a century after the publication of *The Civilizing Process*, few of his German colleagues were familiar with his work. Besides, the paper itself was not easy to accommodate in a volume of conference proceedings. Its format was rather long, and it contained some extremely lengthy quotations and footnotes. It broached several themes, without tying them up at the end in a neat summary or conclusion.

In the first part of the paper, Elias argued that the concept of 'clan charisma' as introduced by Weber could be extended into the more general concept of 'group charisma'. To substantiate this idea, he referred to the then forthcoming book by himself and John Scotson, *The Established and the Outsiders*, which showed that group charisma and its counterpart, group disgrace, far from being something exotic, could be observed even where one might least expect to find it – in the relationship between two working-class neighbourhoods in an English town. The second part, reprinted below, was a rather rare example in Elias's writings of a long textual critique and interpretation of another sociologist. It connected the discussion of group charisma to the problems of involvement and detachment (see above, pp. 84–91). In the third part he then made an effort to sociologize further the concept of charisma and to purge it of essentialist and normative associations.

I

Max Weber in his sociological studies on the religion of India has put forward a specific thesis about the relationship between group charisma and personal charisma.[1] My paper is, in part, a critical examination of Max Weber's thesis. An examination of theoretical concepts, however, is apt to remain sterile unless it is undertaken in close contact with empirical studies. The other part of my paper, therefore, will be concerned with the presentation of empirical material relevant to the more theoretical examination of Max Weber's ideas about group charisma and its relationship to the personal charisma of individuals. Max Weber himself developed his thesis in connection with macrosociological observations. It came to him when he studied the Indian caste system and the character of the kinship relationships which went with it. His own word is *Gentilcharisma*, which has been translated as 'clan charisma' and sometimes 'sib charisma'. But he uses the term not only with reference to kinship groups, but also with reference to whole castes or to aristocracies, to groups of 'noble blood', in short to groups of people bound by other than family ties. What he has to say about *Gentilcharisma* is, in some respects, of such a general nature that one does not stretch his concept unduly if one speaks of 'group charisma'; and as I wish to stress the general nature of the phenomenon, that is the term I propose to use here.

The empirical observations which led me to a re-examination of Max Weber's concept were made during a fairly intensive inquiry of modest dimensions, which I undertook together with Mr J. Scotson, and which forms the subject of a separate book, *The Established and the Outsiders*.[2] One would probably call it a microsociological study. It is concerned with the relationship between two neighbourhoods in an English community. One of these neighbourhoods, although hardly different from the other in its social composition and its occupational structure, treated the other as outsiders, and its members often spoke of them almost as if they all were moral reprobates and outcasts. What Max Weber observed when he studied the Indian caste system with its firmly established charismatic groups, especially the priestly castes, on the one hand, and its various outsider groups, with the pariahs at the bottom, on the other hand, appeared in the light of this small-scale enquiry as an extreme form of a type of relationship which – with varying degrees of complexity and exlusivity – can be found in many societies besides old India. The fact that one came across a variant of it even in a small European community made it seem worthwhile to re-examine Max Weber's concept of group charisma in the light of the additional evidence. If one draws alone on Indian sources, and particularly on materials from the relationship between Brahmins, lower castes and Pariahs, as evidence for group charisma and group disgrace, these phenomena may appear as unfamiliar and unusual. In fact, they are all around us. To study them on a small scale in familiar surroundings offered some advantages. The conditions under which the charismatic claims of the higher Indian castes developed, are less accessible, though by no means wholly inaccessible, to investigations. They lend themselves more easily to speculative interpretations. In the community of which I spoke, in Winston Parva, one could find reliable and fairly extensive first-hand evidence for the conditions under which the claim to a group charisma and the complementary ascription of a stigma, of a kind of communal disgrace to another group developed and maintained themselves. There is no need here to go into the details of this study which can be found elsewhere, but it will be useful to mention some of its aspects as an illustration in the discussion of the concepts of group charisma, and its counterpart, group disgrace.

Today, these phenomena tend to be discussed under a variety of different headings whose connections with each other usually remain unexplored. Max Weber himself conceptualized a variant of group charisma without conceptualizing to the same extent the reverse side of group charismatic claims such as group contempt, group ostracism, group disgrace and group abuse, which to this day command relatively little attention as sociologically significant phenomena. As a rule they are studied under a number of different headings, and as it were, in separate compartments. They may be classified as 'group prejudice' and in that case, they on their part are usually explored without reference to the charismatic claims of the 'prejudiced' groups. They may be studied under such names as 'racialism' or 'nationalism'. The group charisma to which Max Weber referred may be conceived elsewhere as 'class consciousness' or 'patriotism'. There are many different words for variants of the twin phenomena of group charisma and group disgrace, and for the various manifestations of an established–outsider relationship. One could probably discover a whole scale of differences in the degree to which groups can successfully claim, as an eternal gift, superior grace and superior virtues by comparison with others, and effectively condemn others for the inferior qualities ascribed to them collectively as eternal attributes. One might explore the varying conditions in which the belief in the charisma of one's own group and in the inferiority and disgrace of others moves from a relatively moderate and controlled to a more virulent and militant form and vice versa, or those others in which a group charismatic belief of established groups and its imposition on outsider groups gradually loses its power and conviction and finally disappears. Without some sense for the unity of the structure in the variety of relationships such as those, and of the corresponding attitudes and beliefs – which, at present, are usually classified under a multitude of separate headings often as if they had nothing to do with each other – the study of each of them must suffer. Sooner or later, one will have to develop a unified theoretical framework – a unified model or, to use Max Weber's own term, an 'ideal type' – of 'established–outsider relationships' with their concomitants, group charisma and group disgrace – probably in the form of a continuum extended between two poles. The discovery of one of its variants where one might least expect to find it – in the relationship between two working class neighbourhoods – and the opportunity to study it there *in vivo* was regarded by us as a step in that direction.

We have paid particular attention to one of the main weapons with which the superior group defends its charismatic claims and keeps outsiders or outcasts in their place. In the relationship between two neighbourhoods of a small community one usually refers to this weapon as 'gossip'. One can distinguish, we found, between 'praise gossip' – news items of communal interest which support a stereotyped belief in the special goodness of one's own group, and 'blame gossip' – news items which confirm the unfavourable standard beliefs about outsiders or deviants, and can be used as a device for controlling and checking them. But phenomena similar in structure and function to these types of 'gossip' can be found on other social levels apart from those of neighbourhoods and communities, for instance as stereotypes of collective self-praise and collective abuse of castes or classes on a national, or of nations on an international level. If one comes cross the standard forms of self-praise and of outsider contempt of the heroic invaders in the old Indian sagas, the ancestral forms of those used later by the higher Indian castes, one may not immediately recognize their affinity to forms of gossip in a small community. But the difference is more one of degree than one of kind.

The term 'gossip' has still largely the character of a pre-scientific term used, one may think, with reference to trivialities of everyday life, but of little interest to serious students of society. And specialized terms for related phenomena above the community level are almost lacking even in everyday language. To bring them into focus, one will have to standardize special terms such as 'group defamation', 'group disgrace' and, as one of their standing manifestations, the 'vocabulary of group abuse'. Seen in connection with specific relationships between groups, they all present sociological problems of considerable interest. It was striking to find that the techniques used by a superior group in a small community in order to preserve its own power, virtue and identity and to keep outsiders and deviants in their place, were not very different from those used on many higher levels of society. 'Gossip' was one of these techniques, and by no means the least effective. In Winston Parva, one could examine such phenomena at close quarters. One could see how closely the collective denigration and humiliation of outsiders in the form of blame gossip was connected with the collective belief of a group that their members, as members of this specific group, possessed superior virtues inaccessible to the outsider group. There, in a small community one could probe into the conditions of such charismatic claims made decidedly not with reference to an individual, but to the whole group, and could test, among others, one crucial aspect of Max Weber's concept of group charisma, which is significant for his general sociological approach – his ideas about the relationship between group charisma and personal charisma.

II

But it is time to consider Max Weber's thesis itself. He wrote that:

The Hindu social order, to a much larger extent than any other in the world, is organized in terms of the principle of *Gentilcharisma*. This means in this context that a personal qualification – a 'charisma' – which originally was thought to be purely magical and was generally regarded as extraordinary, or at least not universally accessible to man – was attributed to members of a clan as such and not only, as it initially always was, to a particular person. We have remnants of the sociologically very important conception above all in the hereditary rights of our dynasties to rule by 'the grace of God'. To a lesser extent every legendary tale about the special quality of the 'blood' of all kinds of aristocracies which regard themselves as pure whatever their origin, belongs to the same type. This conception is one of the ways in which the initially purely actual and personal charisma becomes routinized. The warrior king and his followers were heroes who distinguished themselves from other men by purely personal magical qualifications which had been demonstrated by their success; the authority of the warleader itself, just as that of the sorcerer, was initially based on a strictly personal charisma alone. The successor, too, claimed authority initially on the strength of a purely personal charisma. The need for order and regularity of succession which could not be denied opened up several possibilities . . . [One of them was] the victory of the obvious belief that the charisma was the property of a kinship group as such, that the qualified person or persons had to be found within this group. This formed the transition to the hereditary character of the *Gentilcharisma* with which it originally had nothing to do . . . In that way it became possible to evaluate as rooted in a magical group charisma not only heroic and priestly-ritual qualifications . . . but positions of authority of many kinds. . . . This development reached in India a point far beyond that which it reached anywhere else. It did not become dominant all at once . . . ; it struggled with the old charismatism which treated as valid only the supremely personal gift of a single individual . . . The 'sib charismatism' captured particularly the representatives of the hierocratic (priestly) power . . . In the case of the Aryans, the ancient priests, the performers of sacrifices, had become a high ranking nobility already at the time of the old Vedic hymns. As a result of the great prestige of the magic group-charisma which they claimed for themselves, they and their heirs, the Brahmins, became the most important agents for the diffusion of this principle [of group charisma] through Hindu society. . . . All groups within that society who claimed for themselves an elevated rank (by comparison with others) were induced to model themselves on the highest groups . . . and the principle of the heredity of social position, ritual duties, way of life and occupation gave to the group charismatic principle as an attribute of every position of authority its final and decisive sanction.[3]

Max Weber's reflections about individual and collective charisma have a number of implications which have not been fully explored. They are potentially useful as a point of departure for further discussions and further research. But the fuller use of these potentialities is greatly hampered because in Max Weber's usage the concept has acquired some highly personal implications connected with his own transient partisan ideas in the struggles of his own time. One cannot proceed with the use and development of the concept charisma as a general sociological concept without glancing at some of the older magical associations which Max Weber himself was not able to cast aside.

The explanation of what he meant by 'charisma' which Max Weber gave in the passages that have been quoted appears to be one of the earliest of several he has left. It shows clearly the initial ambiguity of Weber's concept; is charisma, in point of fact, an extraordinary, unexplainable and somewhat mysterious gift of certain individuals which Max Weber himself accepted as such and which we are meant to accept in the same way? Or does the concept refer to the fact that in certain situations the followers or individuals who play, or aspire to, a leading role in their group – and perhaps these individuals themselves – *believe* that they have been graced with a special gift which cannot be explained in the way in which one explains the faculties of ordinary men? In other words: does the concept 'charisma' refer to a specific – not, however, explainable – quality of people, or to certain social configurations within which people who are able to possess these qualities assume or perform the role of leader and exercise authority?

The definition which has been quoted does not provide a clear answer to these questions. Another which Max Weber presented in the Introduction to 'The Economic Ethics of the World Religions', shows traces of the same ambiguity. He wrote:

In the studies that follow, charisma shall mean an extraordinary quality of a person regardless of whether it is real or supposed or imagined.[4]

But in what was probably the last, and certainly the most concise and elaborate presentation of the theory of charismatic rule the question of the magical or psychological reality of the charisma disappeared from view. There Weber referred only to its sociological reality. He carefully defined charisma as a quality.

> ... *evaluated*[5] as something out of the ordinary on account of which a person is *assessed* as having super-natural or super-human, or at any rate extraordinary powers or properties not accessible to any other person and for that reason as 'leader'.[6]

He added

> How this kind of quality might have to be evaluated correctly from an ethical, aesthetic, or any other kind of view has, of course, conceptually no bearing on this whatsoever; the only relevant point is how the quality, in point of fact, *is* evaluated by the ruled – the 'followers'.[7]

Thus some of the ambiguities concerning the concept of charisma were gradually eliminated.[8] Up to a point it became an example of what Max Weber meant by 'value neutrality':

> It is understood that the expression 'charisma' is used here in a completely value-free sense. From a sociologist's point of view the attack of manic rage of a Nordic 'berserker', the miracles and revelations of a sham prophet, the demagogic gifts of a Cleon are as significant instances of 'charisma' as the qualities of Napoleon, Jesus or Pericles. Decisive for us is whether people recognized and evaluated them as 'charisma' and acted accordingly.

But Max Weber did not attain the relatively high degree of emotional detachment manifest in such utterances without a struggle. One cannot doubt that for him personally, as for many other people brought up in the German tradition during the last 160 years or so, the figure of the strong, the extraordinary, the 'charismatic' leader had a very great fascination (not unconnected with the peculiar historical fate which drove Germany for centuries from crisis to crisis and, with short interruptions, from defeat to defeat, so that permanent residues of insecurity and fear could often only be stilled magically and, alas, deceptively, by the rule and protection of a 'strong man' who seemed greater than life).

Max Weber in his attachment to the ideal of a great leader was thus an individual representative of a specific social and national tradition. The attachment had strong emotional roots; it was closely associated with his patriotism, with his overriding concern for Germany's fate, particularly in the years just before and after the end of the 1914–18 war.[9]

This specific emotional involvement undoubtedly provided the driving force for Weber's interest in the problems of great leader figures. That he could gradually detach himself from the emotional core of his experience – that he was able in his reflections to tone down the warmth of his partisanship and to develop the concept of charismatic leadership into a tool of sociological research which could be used by people belonging to different social and national traditions who might have different ideas – points to the specific propensities of Max Weber as a social scientist.

It also points to the solution of one of the great unsolved problems of the contemporary sociology of knowledge. The concept of charisma as presented by Max Weber was bound to be ambiguous, since it combined pre-scientific and almost mystical features stemming from Weber's involvements, with more impressive scientific views resulting from his strenuous efforts at greater detachment. This shows how illusory are the traditional static and absolute polarities with which one usually operates today in this context – polarities such as 'ideology' and 'truth', 'subjectivity' and 'objectivity', 'value judgement' and 'value-free judgement'. On the basis of such absolute priorities one is compelled to ask: if Weber's concept of charisma was 'socially conditioned', if it was the elaboration of a social ideal and part of a political ideology, how can it be 'true' or objective? How can it have any scientific function and relevance? The answer is simple; it would be obvious enough if our habits of thinking did not enjoin us to expect an answer in terms of exclusive and static alternatives, and did not block as almost irrelevant the perception of what occurs in actual fact – of what could be observed and demonstrated if our traditions of thinking allowed it – of the fact that, under certain conditions, men can improve the appropriateness of their thinking and the correspondence of their concepts to observable data. Weber's introduction of the term 'charismatic' as a sociological term for a specific type of leadership was such a step. He developed a magic-theological into a scientific concept. But as he remained to some extent a captive of one of the social religions of his time his concept in turn remained a hybrid – it remained magic-scientific in character. One has to go beyond him; one can improve the concept still further.

The relationship between ideological and scientific, fantasy-centred and reality-centred, involved and detached ways of thinking is not an 'either–or' relationship; it has not the form of a static polarity between two opposites of which one can apply in any particular case only to the complete exclusion of the other, but that of a process of changes in a specific direction – of a development with many transitional stages. At present one can diagnose such stages only as blends or alloys of polar conceptual structures from which a concept moves away or towards which it moves at a given stage of its development and which blend or amalgamate at different stages in different forms and degrees. The question whether or not such processes are finite – the quest for an 'absolute truth' – which as one of the residues of theological forms of thinking still exercise people's minds, has in its application to the advance of sciences at the most a marginal significance. The answer cannot be given in the form of the expected static polarity between absolutes which, in this case too, seems to preclude any other solution in the form of a 'yes' or 'no'. In the sciences congruence between thinking and the objects of thinking can become less great or greater. Whether it can become absolute depends among other things on whether the world is finite. What one can actually observe if one takes sciences, or scientific concepts such as 'charisma', as one's object of studies is a development, an advance from lesser to greater congruence between modes or models of thinking and observable data over a steadily growing area. But concise empirical studies of such developments over long, and even over short periods are still lacking and their specific techniques such as the developmental analysis of concepts and modes of thinking are still in their infancy.

One of its procedures is the diagnostic separation of different connotations with the hallmark of different stages in the development of thinking which often amalgamate in the use of one and the same concept at a given period of time. Max Weber's concept charisma is an example. In its use, as has already been mentioned, the connotations flow into each other. One of them, born from Weber's efforts at greater detachment, gradually prevailed. But even in his most mature version of the theory of charismatic leadership the other, born from his personal involvements, often came to the surface and dictated the course of his arguments.

The interference of transient personal feelings and values in his manner of reasoning made itself most strongly felt in his presentation of what he called *Gentilcharisma* or 'hereditary charisma' – the belief in a special 'charisma' not of an individual leader but of a whole group. He probably first became aware of such phenomena when he studied Indian and Chinese religions, and the passages which have been quoted before from his work on Hindu religion[10] give an idea of his approach. He extended its use in *Economy and Society*. Today one can see that the concept of a special grace, a 'charisma' claimed by whole groups with all that it involves has even wider applications than he saw. But one cannot prepare the concept 'group charisma' and its counterpart 'group disgrace' for the wider use for which they are needed without removing from the term 'charisma' the magical and pre-scientific connotations left in Weber's use of the term in connection with his own involvement.

18

THE BREAKDOWN OF CIVILIZATION

The trial of Adolf Eichmann, in 1960–61, made Elias reflect once again on the social political trauma of National Socialism which had so deeply affected his own life. He noted the tendency to regard the atrocities committed under National Socialism as an anomaly, unique and not in any way related to the normal structure of modern industrial societies. This view, he feared, might well be an illusion. Rather than embracing such an illusion we should be prepared to admit the possibility 'that National Socialism revealed, perhaps in an especially blatant form, what are normal conditions of contemporary societies, tendencies of acting and thinking which can also be found elsewhere' (1996:303).

Elias committed a long series of comments to paper, in English, under the title 'The Breakdown of Civilization'. He never finished that essay to his own satisfaction, however. The text remained unpublished until the late 1980s when he decided to compile a book of essays on the Germans, one chapter of which would be devoted to 'The Breakdown of Civilization'. Together with his assistant and editor, Michael Schröter, he prepared a German translation, making numerous revisions and additions as he went along. The following excerpt is from the beginning of the essay. It corresponds to the original English text written in the early 1960s.

I

The attempt to wipe out the entire population of Jews in the lands under German rule remained half completed only because of Germany's defeat. It was not by any means the only regression to barbarism in the civilized societies of the twentieth century. Others could easily be pointed out. But of all these regressions, it was perhaps the deepest. Hardly any other example shows the vulnerability of civilization so clearly or reminds us so strongly of the dangers of contemporary growth processes and the fact not only that processes of growth and decay can go hand in hand but that the latter can also predominate relative to the former.

One of the reasons for the slowness with which people are beginning to recognize the treatment of the Jews by the National Socialists as a symptom of one of the severest breakdowns of civilization in recent European history, is a concept of civilization that is flawed. Many Europeans seem to be of the opinion that it is part of their nature to behave in a civilized manner – more or less in the manner in which aristocrats used implicitly to consider their specific manners and ways of behaving as inborn. Sometimes they even characterize themselves in their speaking and thinking as members of 'civilized races' in contrast to 'uncivilized races', as if civilized behaviour were a genetically inherited attribute of specific human groups and not of others. It was partly due to this idea of civilization as a natural inheritance of the European nations that many people reacted to events such as the open relapse of the National Socialists into barbarism at first with incredulity – 'that cannot happen in Europe' – and then with stunned surprise and dejection – 'how was it possible in a civilized country?' The experience seemed to justify the many voices which had been murmuring about the inevitable decay of Western civilization and threatened to drown out completely the fading belief in its eternal progress and superiority. And in fact, people who as children had been brought up in the idea that their own, higher civilization was a part of their 'nature' or their 'race', might very well have fallen into despair and been driven to the opposite extreme when, as adults, they noticed that this flattering belief was contradicted by events. Every war was clearly a regression to barbarism.

Up till then, however, European wars had always been relatively limited regressions. Certain minimum rules of civilized conduct were generally still observed even in the treatment of prisoners of war. With a few exceptions, a kernel of self-esteem which prevents the senseless torturing of enemies and allows identification with one's enemy in the last instance as another human being together with compassion for his suffering, did not entirely lapse.

In the attitude of the National Socialists towards the Jews none of this survived. At least on a conscious level, the torment, suffering and death of Jews did not appear to mean more to them than that of flies. Along with the whole way of living which the SS allowed themselves in the concentration camps and that which was forced on the prisoners there, the mass murder of Jewish people, as has been said, was probably the deepest regression into barbarism in twentieth-century Europe.

One might think that the Nazis decided on these measures because of the war. However, although it took place during the war and was partially facilitated by it, the extermination of the Jews had little to do with the conduct of the war. It was not an act of war. Eichmann and others have compared it with the killing of Japanese civilians through the first American atomic bombs. But the Japanese had attacked the United States; Pearl Harbour came before Hiroshima. The attack by the National Socialists on the Jews was almost entirely lacking in the reciprocity which, according to present conceptions, lends an element of realism to enmity and group killings during a war. Their hatred towards the Jews was, at that stage, an unrequited hatred. For the majority of Jews, it would have been difficult to say why the Germans treated them as their worst enemies. The only sense which they could give to these experiences came from their own tradition. They had been persecuted since time immemorial. Hitler was a new Haman, one of a long line, perhaps a little more menacing than his predecessors. The military usefulness of the pogroms and gas chambers was absolutely nil. All population groups in the conquered territories of Europe constituted a certain danger for their German masters and exploiters, that of the dispersed Jewish groups hardly more than others. Their death did not free land for German settlers. It did not in the slightest increase the political power of the Nazis inside Germany or that of Hitler's Germany among the states of the world. Nor did it any longer have the social function in the tensions and conflicts between various sections of the German people which attacks on the Jews had undoubtedly had for the Nazis in their struggles before they seized power. Its propaganda value was in this phase trivial or negative. In no way was the considerable outlay of labour power and resources which the transport and killing of millions of Jews involved rewarding – at the height of the war when both were growing more expensive.

Indeed, the more one learns about the facts, the clearer it becomes that our standard explanations have failed.

II

The question why the Nazi leadership decided at the beginning of the war to exterminate all the Jews under their dominion has an answer which is simple and ready to hand. However, it almost seems as if, in the eyes of many people, this answer does not make any sense. Apart from some incidental reasons – such as, for example, the reinforcement which it gave to Himmler, the

Reichsführer SS, and his faction in the continuing manoeuvring for position which took place at the top levels of the party and the state – the decision to implement the 'Final Solution of the Jewish problem' had no basis of the kind which we are accustomed to describing as 'rational' or 'realistic'. It was simply a question of the fulfilment of a deeply-rooted belief that had been central for the National Socialist movement from the beginning. According to this belief, the present and future greatness of Germany and the whole 'Aryan race', of which the German people were the highest embodiment, required 'race-purity'; and this biologically conceived 'purity' required the removal and, if necessary, the destruction of all 'inferior' and hostile human groups who could contaminate 'the race', above all people of Jewish stock.

Hitler and his followers had never concealed the fact that they regarded the Jews as their own and Germany's worst enemies. For this, they required no specific proof. It was simply their belief that this had been decreed by nature, by the world order and its creator. They believed that the Jews, on account of their inborn racial characteristics, were bound to hate the superior, Aryan–Germanic people, and, if they were allowed to, to destroy them. Whoever wanted to save the crown of humanity, the Aryan race, from destruction by the Jews and other inferior 'races', had therefore to see it as his noblest task and mission to destroy the Jews themselves. The speeches of Hitler and many other Nazi leaders, together with the whole National Socialist literature, testify to the strength and consistency of this doctrine. One could read there how all the misfortunes experienced by Germany, including the defeat of 1918 and the iniquitous impositions of the Treaty of Versailles, could in the last instance be traced to the machinations of the Jews.[1] One could read how a Jewish conspiracy prevented the renewed rise of Germany after the defeat; how, after the First World War, Jewish warmongers had repeatedly tried to sow the seeds of increasing discord between Germany and other countries; how their plans were foiled in 1938 when Chamberlain came to Munich; how world Jewry reacted to this failure with an outcry of fury, redoubled their efforts and in 1939 finally succeeded in unifying a number of neighbouring nations to attack Germany in the interests of the Jews. All of this had been said with different words again and again. To end the conspiracy of the Jewish race was the often declared goal of Hitler and the National Socialist movement. Since the early days of the movement it had found popular expression in slogans such as 'Croak, Judah' or in the lines which anticipated the great *volte face*, 'when Jew-blood spurts from the knife'.

Uninhibited threats and the systematic use of physical violence – in a society in which many people were still contemptuous of non-violent forms of politics – were among the most important factors to which Hitler owed his eventual success. Although the 'racial purity' of Germany and the elimination of 'inferior' groups, above all of people of Jewish stock, were central to the political programme of the National Socialists, they had refrained from a fully logical pursuit of their aims so long as they regarded it as necessary to take account of the potential effects of their actions on public opinion in other countries. The war removed these constraints. Inside Germany, the National Socialist rulers were now firmly in the saddle: they were the undisputed leaders of a nation at war. Under these favourable circumstances, Hitler and his closest collaborators decided to put into practice what they believed in and had long since preached. They decided to destroy all people of Jewish stock, regardless of their religion, once and for all. After the war there was to be in Germany – and in the 'great German empire' (*grossdeutsches Reich*) they were striving for – no Jewish conspiracy and no more pollution of German blood by Jewish blood.

The question why, in 1939 the path was taken toward the murdering of all Jews is thus not difficult to answer. The decision itself and its implementation followed directly from a central doctrine of the Nazi belief system. Hitler and his followers had never made a secret of their total and irrevocable enmity towards the Jews or of their wish to destroy them. It is not surprising that, when the risk no longer seemed too great, they finally began to translate this destruction-wish into fact.

What is more surprising is the fact that for a long time only a few people, and above all only a few statesmen from leading countries, were able to imagine that the National Socialists might one day put into effect what they had announced. There was then, and there still is today, a widespread tendency to underrate political and social beliefs, to see them as mere froth – as 'ideologies' which have as the only real substance at their basis the interests of the carrier groups as these are defined in their own understanding. According to this assumption, the actions and aims of social units must be explained in the first instance by reference to current 'group interests', while expressed goals and doctrines only have a secondary explanatory value in so far as they serve these interests which they often conceal.

Numerous attempts to explain the murder of millions of Jews correspondingly proceed from the expectation that it is possible to discover a kind of realistic 'interest' which this policy served. The search is for grounds that can be regarded as more or less 'rational', as derivable from a 'realistic' goal other than the fulfilment of the belief itself, and which point in this sense, for example, to the elimination of potential economic competitors and the opening of new income-chances for party members, the cementing of the unity of one's own followers through the channelling of all dissatisfactions on to an external scapegoat, or, purely and simply, to the improvement of one's chances of victory in the war by the killing of as many enemies as possible.

It is certainly not unjustified to suppose that some of these or other, similarly 'realistic' interests played a part as driving forces of the anti-Semitic propaganda of the Nazis and as reasons for their adoption of anti-Jewish measures in the phase of their ascent to power or later when Hitler ruled

Germany but his power was not yet secure. However, there is little evidence that the decision to kill all the Jews and to undertake the sustained and costly effort necessary to achieve this goal, which was taken during the war, that is when Nazi rule had been secured, was based decisively on 'realistic interests' of this kind and for which the anti-Semitic beliefs served merely as an ideological smokescreen. In the final analysis, it will be found that the mass murder of Jews did not serve any purpose which one might call 'rational', and that the National Socialists were driven to it above all by the strength and unshakeable character of their belief itself. It is here that the lesson to be drawn from this experience lies.

This is not by any means to imply that professed irrational beliefs are *always* to be taken at face value as the primary factors in group actions but only that there are *also* figurations where they do work as primary determinants.[2] Professed aims and beliefs are quite often at most secondary impulses to action and perhaps merely an ideological weapon or an ideological screen which hides other, more narrowly sectional interests which today, lacking more adequate concepts, we describe as 'realistic' or 'rational'. In these cases, the explanation of group actions in terms of such aims and doctrines is deceptive, illusory or at least highly incomplete. Sometimes, however, a course of action is determined by nothing stronger than a goal derived from a set of professed beliefs. The beliefs in question may, as we say, be extremely 'unrealistic' and 'irrational'. They may, in other words, have a high fantasy content so that the fulfilment of aims demanded by them promises the acting group a high degree of immediate emotional satisfaction. As a result – at the level of social reality and in the longer term – such a fulfilment brings the carrier group no advantages other that the realization of their belief. It may even harm them. The attempt of the National Socialists to destroy the Jews belongs to this category. It was one of the most striking examples of the power which a belief – in this case, a social or, more properly, a national belief – can gain over people.

It was this possibility for which in the 1920s and 1930s many people inside and outside Germany were hardly prepared. Their conceptual equipment led them to the idea that human groups – especially groups of people in power, including the rulers and statesmen of the world – however fantastic their professed beliefs were, would in the long term always orientate themselves towards hard 'reality', towards their so-called 'real interests'. No matter how savage their creed, no matter how absolute the enmity they preached, in the end they would recognize the merits of moderation and come to conduct their affairs in a more or less 'rational' and 'civilized' way. Evidently something was very wrong with a way of thinking which blocked the insight that a nationalistic movement in whose programme the use of violence and the total destruction of enemies loomed large, whose members ceaselessly emphasized the value of cruelty and killing, might in fact commit savage acts and kill.

It is not usual to hold an inquest in order to test in the light of the factual course of events what was wrong with one's own earlier ways of thinking and acting. If one were in this sense to investigate the systems of ideas, dispositions and beliefs which led so many people to be so ill-prepared for events such as the Nazi concentration camps and the mass murder of the Jews, then one would have to place at the centre the basic flaw in the dominant conception of contemporary civilization that has already been mentioned. Contemporaries did not then conceive of civilization as a condition which, if it is to be maintained or improved, requires a constant effort based on a degree of understanding of how it works. Instead, like their 'rationality', they took it for granted as one of their own permanent attributes, an aspect of their inborn superiority: once civilized, always civilized. So, in Germany and elsewhere and at first with a shrug of the shoulders, they swept the barbaric doctrines and deeds of the Nazis under the carpet because it seemed to them unimaginable that people in a civilized country could behave in such a cruel and inhuman way as the adherents to National Socialist beliefs had announced they were going to act, proclaiming it to be necessary and desirable in the name of their country. When members of tribal groups such as the Mau Mau in Kenya unite in a belief which demands the killing of others, people are fully prepared by the beliefs they hold about them for the possibility that they will do what they say and hence take the appropriate defensive measures. When the members of more advanced industrial societies, such as the National Socialists, unite in a no less barbaric belief, people are led by their conceptual inheritance to the judgement that they have an 'ideology', that they will not act as brutally as they talk.

That was the position. Because of their conceptual equipment, observers of the German scene before but also after 1933 did not reckon with the possibility of a genuine recrudescence of barbarism in their own midst. They had at their disposal specific techniques for dealing intellectually with the wilder and more strongly emotionally laden beliefs which they encountered in some political movements. Hitler and this people were classified as 'agitators' who used the Jews in their propaganda as 'scapegoats' without, however, themselves necessarily believing everything that they said about them. 'Underneath it all', such commentators seemed to imply, 'these Nazi leaders know as well as we do that much of what they say is rubbish. When it gets serious', that was the implicit assumption, 'these people think and behave just like us. They simply need all this propaganda talk in order to gain power. That is why they do it'. The belief was seen as the means to a rational end. It was conceived simply as an instrument which the Nazi leadership had developed in order to gain power. And the goal of gaining power appears to people all over the world who have power as eminently 'rational'.

Then, as now, numerous people, among them certainly many statesmen, had no understanding of a mentality that was different from their own. They could not picture to themselves that, in civilized countries, anything other than an at least moderately civilized belief system could be seriously advocated by its adherents. If a social creed was inhuman, immoral, revolting and demonstrably false, they thought it could not be genuine: it was a made-up goal of ambitious leaders who wanted to gain a mass following for their own ulterior ends. Perhaps they were vaguely aware that the National Socialist movement was mainly led by half-educated men. But they did not, so it seems, wake up fully to the fact that Hitler and his closest collaborators believed deeply in the majority of what they said.

Even in the most advanced industrial societies of our age, the gap between the highest and the lowest educational levels is extraordinarily wide. The number of illiterates has declined, that of 'half-educated' people has increased. A great deal of what is regarded as characteristic of twentieth-century civilization carries their stamp – as a consequence of the deficiencies of contemporary educational systems with all the frustrations and wastage of abilities they entail.

Among the more or less surface factors in the rise of the National Socialist movement were the peculiar social characteristics of its elite. The majority of party leaders were, in fact, 'half-educated'. They were – and this is in no way unusual for a movement of this type – outsiders or failures in the older order, often filled with a burning ambition which made it impossible for them to bear their inadequacies and admit them to themselves. The Nazi belief system with its pseudo-scientific varnish spread thinly over a primitive, barbaric national mythology was one of the more extreme symptoms of the moral and intellectual twilight in which they lived. That it could not withstand the judgement of more educated people, and with few exceptions had no appeal for them, was probably one of the reasons why such people often underestimated the seriousness of the belief itself and the genuineness of the feelings vested in it. Few of the social and, especially, the national myths of our age are free of similar falsehoods and barbarisms. The National Socialist doctrine shows, as if in a distorting mirror, some of their common features in a glaring form.

That Hitler and his helpers were masters of dissimulation and the spreading of deliberate lies, that their preachings contained a strong dose of hatred, humbug and hypocrisy, was in no way imcompatible with their fervent belief in the ultimate truth of their creed. In fact, National Socialism combined many of the traits of a religious movement with those of a political party. To see it as such, as a movement resting on a very sincerely held belief, is one of the first preconditions for understanding what happened. The movement began as a sect. Its leader believed from early on in his messianic mission, his mission for Germany. So did many of its members. And, carried miraculously to the top on the crest of a prolonged crisis, their certainty that their beliefs were true, their methods justified and the success of their mission preordained became absolute and unshakeable.

It is understandable that many representatives of the older educated elite experienced the extent of the regression under the Nazis as a shock out of the blue, because they could not discern beneath the lies, the propaganda tricks and the deliberate use of falsehoods as a weapon against enemies, the sincerity with which the standard bearers of the movement believed in ideas which appeared to them themselves as doubtful or patently absurd. They were also inclined to understand the kernel of the Nazi belief system, especially its wild and extreme anti-Semitism, as propaganda or as a well-planned means for unifying the German people, but not as a deep conviction of religious strength.

Even today the gulf separating the 'educated' higher strata, whose ways of thinking steer their interpretation of social events, and the great mass of 'less-educated' people whose interpretation of such events is often quite different, leads recurrently to the former perceiving the latter in a distorted form. One can understand better why so many 'educated' people, brought up on the tacit assumption that civilized behaviour would continue in European societies without any effort on their part, were so ill-prepared for the forthcoming breakdown of this civilization, if one looks into some of the conditions in Germany which gave the National Socialists their chance.

PART IV

A EUROPEAN
SOCIOLOGIST,
1966–1990

19

THE CIVILIZING PROCESS REVISITED

When, in 1962, Elias reached retirement age, he did not retire from sociology. On the contrary. He began by accepting a two-year appointment as Professor of Sociology at the University of Ghana in Lagos. After his return to England in the summer of 1964, he settled again in Leicester, where he was now able to buy a house, while keeping an office at the university. He continued to take an active part in the activities of the Department of Sociology, attending staff seminars, conducting a postgraduate seminar, and, above all, engaging his colleagues and students in never-ending discussions.

Still, his position had become different from what it had been before his stay in Ghana. He was now released from regular teaching duties; he had at last attained the official title of Professor; and, aided by financial compensation from Germany, he could afford a level of material comfort that had been beyond his means for most of his life. These various circumstances enabled him to enter into a stage of prolonged productivity which lasted virtually till the day of his death in 1990.

The new stage was heralded, in 1969, by the appearance of the second German edition of *The Civilizing Process*. It was a facsimile reprint, in which not a word was changed. Elias had added a long introduction, however, explaining both what he himself held to be the importance of the book, and what were the reasons for its lack of resonance among sociologists.

In the section that follows, Elias ascribes the lack of response mainly to the tendency prevailing in the sociology of the 1950s and 1960s to conceive of human societies as structures or systems tending to a state of equilibrium. He singles out Talcott Parsons as the major representative of this essentially static approach. While his argument is in many respects well taken, it may be noted that he failed to take into account the simple fact that his own book on the civilizing process was available only in German, in an edition which had received very little publicity. It was only after 1969 that Elias himself, and a few others, began to make serious attempts to make his work more widely known in the English-speaking world.

I

When I was working on *The Civilizing Process* it seemed quite clear to me that I was laying the foundation of an undogmatic, empirically based sociological theory of social processes in general and of social development in particular. I believed it quite obvious that the investigation, and the concluding model of the long-term process of state formation to be found in the second volume, could serve equally as a model of the long-term dynamic of societies in a particular direction, to which the concept of social development refers. I did not believe at that time that it was necessary to point out explicitly that this study was neither of an 'evolution' in the nineteenth-century sense of an automatic progress, nor of an unspecific 'social change' in the twentieth-century sense. At that time this seemed so obvious that I omitted to mention these theoretical implications explicitly. The introduction to the second edition gives me the opportunity to make good this omission.

II

The comprehensive social development studied and presented here through one of its central manifestations – a wave of advancing integration over several centuries, a process of state formation with the complementary process of advancing differentiation – is a figurational change which, in the to-and-fro of contrary movements, maintains, when surveyed over an extended time span, a constant direction through many generations. This structural change in a specific direction can be demonstrated as a fact, regardless of how it is evaluated. The factual proof is what matters here. The concept of social change by itself does not suffice, as an instrument of research, to take account of such facts. A mere change can be of the kind observable in clouds or smoke rings: now they look like this, now like that. A concept of social change that does not distinguish clearly between changes that relate to the structure of a society and those that do not – and, further, between structural changes without a specific direction and those which follow a particular direction over many generations, e.g., towards greater or lesser complexity – is a very inadequate tool of sociological inquiry.

The situation is similar with a number of other problems dealt with here. When, after several preparatory studies which enabled me both to investigate documentary evidence and to explore the gradually unfolding theoretical problems, the way to a possible solution became clearer, I was made aware that this study brings somewhat nearer to resolution the intractable problem of the connection between individual psychological structures (so-called personality structures) and figurations formed by large numbers of interdependent individuals (social structures). It does so because it approaches both types of structure not as fixed, as usually happens, but as changing, and as interdependent aspects of the same long-term development.

III

If the various academic disciplines whose subject matter is touched on by this study – including, above all, the discipline of sociology – had already reached the stage of scientific maturity at present enjoyed by many of the natural sciences, it might have been expected that a carefully documented study of long-term processes, such as those of civilization or state formation, with the theoretical proposals developed from it, would be assimilated, either in its entirety or in some of its aspects, after thorough testing and discussion, after critical sifting of all unsuitable or disproved content, to that discipline's stock of empirical and theoretical knowledge. Since the advance of scholarship depends in large measure on interchange and cross-fertilization between numerous colleagues and on the continuous development of the common stock of knowledge, it might have been expected that thirty years later this study would either have become a part of the standard knowledge of the discipline or have been more or less superseded by the work of others and laid to rest.

Instead, I find that a generation later this book still has the character of a pioneering work in a problematic field which today is hardly less in need than it was thirty years ago, of the simultaneous investigation on the empirical and theoretical plane that is to be found here. Understanding of the urgency of the problems discussed here has grown. Everywhere gropings in the direction of these problems are observable. There is no lack of later attempts to solve problems to whose solution the empirical documentation in the two volumes endeavours to contribute. I do not believe these later attempts to have been successful.

To exemplify this, it must suffice to discuss the way in which the man who at present is widely regarded as the leading theoretician of sociology, Talcott Parsons, attempts to pose and solve some of the problems dealt with here. It is characteristic of Parsons's theoretical approach to attempt to dissect analytically into their elementary components, as he once expressed it,[1] the different types of society in his field of observation. He called one particular type of elementary component 'pattern variables'. These pattern variables include the dichotomy of 'affectivity' and 'affective neutrality'. His conception can best be understood by comparing society to a game of cards: every type of society, in Parsons's view, represents a different 'hand'. But the cards themselves are always the same; and their number is small, however diverse their faces may be. One of the cards with which the game is played is the polarity between affectivity and affective neutrality. Parsons originally conceived this idea, he tells us, in analysing Tönnies's society types *Gemeinschaft* (community) and *Gesellschaft* (society). 'Community', Parsons appears to believe, is characterized by affectivity and 'society' by affective neutrality. But in determining the differences between different types of society, and between different types of relationship within one and the same society, he attributes to this 'pattern variable' in the card game, as to the others, a wholly general meaning. In the same context, Parsons addresses himself to the problem of the relation of social structure to personality.[2] He indicates that while he had previously seen them merely as closely connected and interacting 'human action systems', he can now state with certainty that in a theoretical sense they are different phases or aspects of one and the same fundamental action system. He illustrates this by an example, explaining that what may be considered on the sociological plane as an institutionalization of affective neutrality is essentially the same as what may be regarded on the level of personality as 'the imposition of renunciation of immediate gratification in the interests of disciplined organization and the longer-run goals of the personality'.

It is perhaps useful for an understanding of this study to compare this later attempt to solve such problems with the earlier one reprinted in unchanged form here. The decisive difference in scientific approach, and in the conception of the objectives of sociological theory, is evident from even this short example of Parsons's treatment of similar problems. What in this book is shown with the aid of extensive empirical documentation to be a process, Parsons, by the static nature of his concepts, reduces retrospectively, and it seems to me quite unnecessarily, to states. Instead of a relatively complex process whereby the affective life of people is gradually moved toward an increased and more even control of affects – but certainly not toward a state of total affective neutrality – Parsons presents a simple opposition between two states, affectivity and affective neutrality, which are supposed to be present to different degrees in different types of society, like different quantities of chemical substances. By reducing to two different states what was shown empirically in *The Civilizing Process* to be a process and interpreted theoretically as such, Parsons deprives himself of the possibility of discovering how the distinguishing peculiarities of different societies to which he refers are actually to be explained. So far as is apparent, he does not even raise the question of explanation. The different states denoted by the antitheses of the 'pattern variables' are, it seems, simply given. The subtly articulated structural change toward increased and more even affect control that may be observed in reality disappears in this kind of theorizing. Social phenomena in reality can only be observed as evolving and having evolved; their dissection by means of pairs of concepts which restrict the analysis to two antithetical states represents an unnecessary impoverishment of sociological perception on both empirical and theoretical levels.

Certainly, it is the task of every sociological theory to clarify the characteristics that all possible human societies have in common. The concept of the social process, like many others used in this study, has precisely this function. But the basic categories selected by Parsons seem to me arbitrary to a high degree. Underlying them is the tacit, untested, and seemingly self-evident notion that the objective of every scientific theory is to reduce everything variable to something invariable, and to simplify all complex phenomena by dissecting them into their individual components.

The example of Parsons's theory suggests, however, that theorizing in the field of sociology is complicated rather than simplified by a systematic reduction of social processes to social states, and of complex, heterogeneous phenomena to simpler, seemingly homogeneous components. This kind of reduction and abstraction could be justified as a method of theorizing only if it led unambiguously to a clearer and deeper understanding by men of themselves as societies and as individuals. Instead of this we find that the theories formed by such methods, like the epicycle theory of Ptolemy, require needlessly complicated auxiliary constructions to make them agree with the observable facts. They often appear like dark clouds from which here and there a few rays of light touch the earth.

20

THE CONCEPT OF FIGURATIONS

Elias was always very sensitive to the subtle implications of terms and concepts. In the original foreword to *The Civilizing Process* (see above, pp. 39–45) he apologized for the fact that he had to use a series of unfamiliar expressions such as sociogenesis, threshold of embarrassment, and monopoly mechanism. What he did not mention was the equally significant fact that there were at least as many terms which are generally accepted in philosophical and sociological jargon which he deliberately avoided. Thus, apart from an occasional critical comment, such terms as transcendental, or system, or actor (in the technical sociological sense), are conspicuously absent from Elias's writings. Throughout his work, he tried to restrict himself to concepts which would not entangle him in one of the many 'frozen dichotomies' of academic discourse.

At the same time, he continued coining new concepts. In the highly polemical introduction to the second edition of *The Civilizing Process* he introduced the notion of *homo clausus*, 'the closed person', to characterize the current image of the individual as a self-contained being, isolated from the outside world, including all other people. He found the idea of *homo clausus* in a particularly pronounced form in philosophy where, in Elias's words, it took the form of *homo philosophicus* – a phantom apparently thrown into the world as an adult and naturally endowed all by himself with powers of perception, reason and conscience.

In order to do away with the individualistic and static connotations of *homo clausus*, Elias proposed as a central notion the concept of figurations. Derived from 'configuration', a central concept in *Gestalt* psychology and used more than once in the original text of *The Civilizing Process*, the term figuration is intended to convey a cluster of important insights. First, that human beings are interdependent, and can only be understood as such: their lives develop in, and are significantly shaped by, the social figurations they form with each other. Second, that these figurations are continually in flux, undergoing changes of different orders – some quick and ephemeral, others slower but more profound. Third, that the processes occurring in such figurations have dynamics of their own – dynamics in which individual motives and intentions play a part but which cannot possibly be reduced to those motives and intentions alone. The following small excerpt gives in one single paragraph a lively picture of what Elias meant by 'figurations'.

What is meant by the concept of the figuration can be conveniently explained by reference to social dances. They are, in fact, the simplest example that could be chosen. One should think of a mazurka, a minuet, a polonaise, a tango, or rock 'n' roll. The image of the mobile figurations of interdependent people on a dance floor perhaps makes it easier to imagine states, cities, families, and also capitalist, communist, and feudal systems as figurations. By using this concept we can eliminate the antithesis, resting finally on different values and ideals, immanent today in the use of the words 'individual' and 'society'. One can certainly speak of a dance in general, but no one will imagine a dance as a structure outside the individual or as a mere abstraction. The same dance figurations can certainly be danced by different people; but without a plurality of reciprocally oriented and dependent individuals, there is no dance. Like every other social figuration, a dance figuration is relatively independent of the specific individuals forming it here and now, but not of individuals as such. It would be absurd to say that dances are mental constructions abstracted from observations of individuals considered separately. The same applies to all other figurations. Just as the small dance figurations change – becoming now slower, now quicker – so too, gradually or more suddenly, do the large figurations which we call societies. *The Civilizing Process* is concerned with such changes. Thus, the starting point of the study of the process of state formation is a figuration made up of numerous relatively small social units existing in free competition with one another. The investigation shows how and why this figuration changes. It demonstrates at the same time that there are explanations which do not have the character of causal explanations. For a change in a figuration is explained partly by the endogenous dynamics of the figuration itself, the immanent tendency of a figuration of freely competing units to form monopolies. The investigation therefore shows how in the course of centuries the original figuration changes into another, in which such great opportunities of monopoly power are linked with a single social position – kingship – that no occupant of any other social position within the network of interdependencies can compete with the monarch. At the same time, it indicates how the personality structures of human beings also change in conjunction with such figurational changes.

21

African Art

During his stay in Ghana from 1962 to 1964, Elias developed a lively interest in African art. On his return to England he brought with him a large collection of pieces from various regions of West Africa. From now on, wherever he lived he would be surrounded by figures and masks reminding him and his visitors of a world very different from modern Europe.

In the spring of 1970, the Leicester Museum and Art Gallery organized an exhibition from Elias's collection. Elias himself wrote the text for the catalogue: brief comments about the 250 pieces on display, and a general introduction. The introduction clearly reveals how intrigued Elias was by so-called primitive art – a long-standing fascination which was already evident in his expositions on Thurnwald and on kitsch (see above, pp. 8–11 and 26–35). The text is also interesting because it conveys something of the didactic stance Elias used to take in his oral presentations to students and laymen: a deliberate effort to state the problems at hand as explicitly as possible and to connect them with first-hand experience on the part of the audience. He accepted the risk that this stance could be interpreted as bordering on pedantry and condescension.

I began to collect the pieces which you see here while I lived in Africa teaching sociology at a University. I collected them in an haphazard manner and, at first, without much knowledge. Traders brought samples to my door. Occasionally I bought one or two partly out of curiosity, partly because I liked them. I did not know and I was not particularly interested to know whether any of these pieces had a commercial value on the international art market. I was fairly familiar with the work of the great masters of contemporary European art and was struck by the strange kinship which some of the African pieces bore to these trends in non-African painting and sculpture. My own taste lies very much in that direction and I was delighted to be able to acquire in Africa sculptures, many of which I found artistically satisfying, and for me often novel in conception – as one says – at prices which I could afford. Most of the contemporary European art which I liked was decidedly beyond my reach.

I could rely entirely on my own taste, but my taste so far as African figures were concerned was at first untrained; I made mistakes, that is to say I was misled by the novelty of the artistic experience with regard to its intrinsic quality. To assess this quality needs time. Some visitors to this exhibition may find that too. It requires a certain training of one's perception. At first I bought only every now and then a few figures; I had no intention of starting a collection. After I had some figures in my house for a month or two I began to be able to distinguish differences in their artistic quality. I learned while I went along.

As I became more discriminating in my judgement I gradually discovered that one can distinguish, broadly speaking, four types of traditional African sculptures. The distinction can serve as a rough guide to one's assessment though, of course, the types shade into each other, there are no sharp dividing lines. Roughly speaking, these four types may be described as follows:

1   Relatively old ritual objects
2   Relatively new ritual objects.
3   Objects derived from the former categories, and still made by traditional craftsmen with a relatively high standard of craftsmanship, though not for any known purpose or person in their own village circle, but for unknown, largely European buyers.
4   The same as 3, but produced more quickly with a declining standard of craftsmanship and artistic quality.

It took me some time before I was able to assess with a reasonable degree of certainty to which of these four categories a particular piece belonged. As I said before, I made mistakes, that is to say, I acquired pieces which I would now allot to Class 4. In this exhibition I have not concealed from you all my mistakes. I thought it might be instructive as well as amusing for you to see whether you can spot them. In fact looking back, I am glad I acquired these pieces too.

Among the most instructive problems of art is the change in the shape of figures which the traditional craftsmen's art undergoes in connection with a modernization process. My way of collecting enables me to show side by side older and newer pieces of the same type so that everyone is able to assess for himself the changes in the form of a traditional work of art that go hand in hand with a change in their society in this direction.

Art everywhere is dependent on special social conditions which make its continued production possible. The traditional craftsman's art in Europe declined – in spite of the efforts of men like William Morris – and finally disappeared with the advance of urbanization, of long distance commerce and industry and the corresponding changes in the conditions of living. African countries are bound to be increasingly drawn into the whirlpool of modernization. Nothing could be more fallacious and more irritating to the peoples of Africa themselves than the regret some Europeans seem to feel about the passing of the old order in Africa. Anything that can be done to speed up this process and to help in lowering the temperature of the tensions and conflicts inherent in its structure should be done. But that does not absolve Europeans as well as our African friends themselves from the task of gaining as much understanding of the old order, and preserving as much of the immensely rich artistic heritage left to us, before it is too late.

In Africa, and in a number of other places, we are still able to see with our own eyes types of art and types of art production which have disappeared in the more developed sections of mankind. Most of these works are made of wood and of other perishable materials. The majority of them are made for use in the rituals and ceremonies of relatively small and largely self-supporting peasant, hunting or fishing communities with – at the most – a sprinkling of trade and market connections over longer distances. In this social setting the people of the traditional art producing areas of Africa, which are almost exclusively to be found in black Africa, not for instance in the Muslim areas, have evolved thousands of sculptures and other pieces of art whose ritual and ceremonial significance is confined to one or the other small scale community. But their artistic significance goes far beyond these enclosed communities (though their members can hardly be aware of it). Seen as a whole it must be regarded as one of the great phases in the development of man's artistic production and its products as a significant part of the artistic heritage of mankind. Yet only a very small percentage of all these works which have been, and which to a diminishing extent are still produced in Africa, have a chance of being preserved.

Metal and terra-cotta pieces may still be found in considerable numbers when a systematic search is made for them; they lie buried in the houses of chiefs and, no doubt in graves. But of pieces made of wood and other similar material only those will remain which have already been collected and been brought to safe places where they can be preserved. For the rest their production is likely to come to an end in the course of the next two or three generations. One can often read fairly romantic accounts of the reason why traditional art in Africa is declining. But in fact the reason is obvious. When the social order changes and disappears in which traditional art and traditional craftsmen have their function and their place, this type of art and of occupational skill is bound to change and to disappear too. Being a sociologist by profession as well as predilection, perhaps I was more acutely aware than one usually is of this connection between function and form. If it was in the first place simply my enjoyment and appreciation of individual pieces of African art which induced me to acquire some of them, they were soon reinforced by the realization that the social setting within which the traditional religious African art has its place and its function would gradually disappear as modernization of African societies progressed, and with it would disappear this art-form itself. One could foresee that it would give way to more individualized, more secular types of sculptural art with the same functions and general characteristics as art in other industrial nation states of this world though, like that of these other societies, with its own national and perhaps continental distinctiveness. And the realization that traditional African art, like the traditional craftsman's métier, was doomed, made me acquire more figures and masks than I had ever intended to acquire. It added to my personal liking a great sense of urgency. It accounts for the fact that I did not acquire any works of the growing number of African artists although I could appreciate the work of some of them too. Their art, I felt, though still in its infancy was more likely to be preserved. But according to my estimate by far the greater part of traditional African art has never been preserved in the past and is not likely to be preserved in the future. Its wealth and variety is immense. A good number of art producing groups have hardly been explored. Their figures, their masks, their dancing staffs and the other works of their craftsmen are used in the annual round of their rites, their ceremonies and festivals. Perhaps they are kept for a while in a store-room. But if they break or decay their owners are likely to throw them away or to bury them; they have often no incentive and no means to repair them and to preserve them. In that situation single individuals cannot do much. Nor does it seem likely that without aid each of the art-producing African countries alone can provide the incentives, the stimulus and the resources for the restoration and preservation of its wealth of traditional art, the greater part of which is stored ineffectually or thrown away.

One of the most beautiful and most efficient African Museums, that of Lagos, Nigeria, already houses and preserves in its stores so many pieces that it may find it difficult to receive others, which today simply seem repetitive. This is a pity because they are bound to get scarcer and craftsmanship is bound to decline. The eventual decline and disappearance of traditional religious art is simply a price that has to be paid for the increasing modernization of African societies, and it is in no way too high a price. But one cannot see the problem that arises here simply in national terms. Ours may well be the last period in the development of mankind in which this type of art, the craftsman's traditional art, is produced anywhere on earth. As long as it is still alive, much could be learned about it that is unknown or ill understood. The comparative period of European art has left some of its silent masterpieces behind, but the greater part of the work has disappeared. The men who made it, the people for whom it was made, can no longer talk to us. One is rightly concerned about the possible disappearance of animal species in Africa as elsewhere. The problems of a dying form of art are different. One cannot ensure its survival if the societies where it flourishes transform themselves. But one can try to preserve as much of it as is possible and to understand much more fully the people by whom and for whom they were made. Without understanding them and their art we can hardly hope to understand ourselves and our art.

I have often asked myself what distinguishes the traditional African craftsman's art from the artist's art which in Europe began to emerge from that of European craftsmen, broadly speaking, in the fifteenth and sixteenth centuries. What are the differences between these two types of art? What accounts for the similarities which make us experience both as forms of art – for the fact that these figures and masks produced by mostly anonymous craftsmen, whose experiences and manner of life are in many respects very different from our own, can nevertheless in their own way speak to us as strongly as works of art produced in a social setting more nearly akin to ours?

The problem that one encounters here, as one can see, concerns the perception of art in general. It may be of help if I mention it, though I do not pretend to be able to answer it adequately. Many visitors to this exhibition may at first only see and feel the strangeness of the figures and masks they see here. At that stage one may try to build a bridge for one's understanding by seeking an explanation of the strange object in terms of the use people made of it. One may ask: what is the purpose of this shape or this pattern? But as most of these figures and masks are used in the context of beliefs with which we are not familiar, this explanation may often be as strange as the shape and pattern itself. One may have to say, this is a figure used for driving out witches or perhaps as part of an initiation ceremony – and an answer of this type still leaves you in a void.

But it is also possible to look at these shapes and patterns for a while without asking what their purpose is and allow them to speak directly to one's own imagination. Then one may become aware that they communicate something to those who look at them, that they convey some unspoken message even though it is perhaps difficult to put it into words. On that level, thus, the figures and masks you see here are not very different from any contemporary works of art. In their case too, shape and pattern alone can speak to those who look at them even though the artist gives no clue to their meaning for himself and simply calls his work 'Composition 3' or 'Seated King and Queen'.

If one is able to establish rapport not with all, but with some of the figures and masks in this exhibition, one comes face to face with one of the basic problems of the visual arts. It concerns the nature of the rapport which a sculptor or a painter can establish with other human beings through the shapes and patterns he conjures up before them. They may not know the associations which guided his eyes and his hands. To some extent their associations may be different from his. Yet the work he has created has a life and speaks a language of its own. It communicates a message from the maker to the viewer which is not entirely subject to the latter's arbitrary interpretation.

It is the test of the quality of a work of art that its maker, by means of the patterns of shapes and colours he invents, can appeal to those who see his work and can establish rapport with them. Perhaps it may not seem particularly surprising if contemporary English artists, like Henry Moore, are able to do that (although in their case too this rapport raises considerable problems). But that African craftsmen living in relatively simple and undifferentiated societies can communicate and establish rapport through their work with people living in very different circumstances who may not have the slightest ideas of the original associations surrounding these works or of the purpose for which it was made, is a little more surprising. It raises the problem whether visual patterns and shapes can appeal to a level of human understanding, to sources of human feeling which transcend the frontiers of ethnic and national differences and are common to all men. Not only the collections of African art in Europe and America, but even more the increasing popularity of books reproducing photographs of pieces such as those you see here, underline this problem.

It is complicated by the fact that figures and masks of the type you see here, as far as we know, evoked no aesthetic resonance whatsoever in members of the more developed societies of America and Europe until recent times. I cannot remember reading of any figure like these here adorning a Victorian drawing room. A considerable number were collected for museums during the nineteenth and twentieth centuries, but with few exceptions they were regarded simply as ethnological curiosities. Just as 'gothic' as a term for the craftsmen's art of the European Middle Ages was initially a term with strong negative value implications, so was the aesthetic reaction of our forebears to the art of African craftsmen mainly negative. It was the far-reaching transformation of taste starting in Europe at the turn of the twentieth century which led in the course of sixty or seventy years to an increasing appreciation of traditional African sculpture as a type of art in its own right. People buy pieces such as these you see here because they like having them in their homes, and books with pictures of African masks and figures are bought in increasing numbers evidently because people like to see them and are, as I said, in emotional rapport with them. So were some of the leaders of the modern art movement. This kind of evidence makes the problem I have raised before all the more intriguing. How is it possible that works produced in simpler societies can influence and can find a strong resonance in highly differentiated societies? What is the common ground?

I have permitted myself to mention this problem here because it has occupied my mind a good deal. The answer is elusive. But two or three points are worth mentioning. They may be of help.

The first concerns the problem of time. Many of the pieces here have been made by and for people with a sense of time which is rather different from ours. Many, though by no means all of them, are made from the very hard and heavy wood abundantly growing in African forests, one or two even from the so-called 'lignum vitae' said to sink in water. One of the first changes which occur when less differentiated peasant and hunting communities are drawn into the whirlwind movement of industrialization and nation-building processes is the much more acute awareness of the economic, the monetary value of their time.

I first became aware of this factor in this context when I paid a visit to the shop of a former Nigerian ivory carver whom I knew. He sold mostly rather indifferently made curios but occasionally he had a well made piece which I liked. Pointing to one of those one day I asked him why he had not more of this type. I remember him shaking his head: 'such pieces', he said 'are made by old men. Now we no longer have the time'.

I understood this remark and followed it up. When a trader asks a wood-carver in a bush village to make him in a fortnight twenty masks of a type of which he made before perhaps two or three every year for personal acquaintances in his village, the carver can of course earn what is for him a small fortune. For a time he may try to work a little quicker without abandoning his traditional standard of skill of which he is proud. But when the merchant badgers him sufficiently he may allow his work to deteriorate after a while. That is how it starts. The best work you see here is made without haste. The traditional wood carver does not see the wood as a dead piece of material. A good deal of affection goes out from the carver to his material. The shape is already there. He brings it out in a kind of emotional dialogue. The spirit of the wood must help. Or else it can resist and the work has to be interrupted. All that takes time. Although I cannot put my finger on the details I am sure that this way of making a mask or an ancestor figure, the peculiar intimacy between the maker and his material, the gradual working out of a personal relationship between the two shows itself in the shape of the product. Then there is the problem of self-consciousness. Artists in the more developed societies try very consciously to produce a work of art, i.e. shapes and patterns of their own invention which, as far as possible, are unique and unlike any others that have been made before. Their sculptures and paintings are valued particularly highly if they are without precedent and bear the imprint of an individual personality whose distinct personal style is easily recognizable. Although we may not be aware of it, this type of art shows quite unmistakably the high degree of self-consciousness with which it is produced. On occasions, some of its representatives, particularly Picasso indicate in their work quite directly their own awareness of the artist's struggle between his self-consciousness and his spontaneity.

African crafstmen have no such problems. Their hand is guided and held by their tradition. Their ambition is not to create a shape and a pattern which is different from those anybody has created before, but rather to create the same or almost the same shape and pattern as their ancestors and masters with particular skill and perfection. That does not mean that there is no scope at all for individual variations and certainly not that there is no sense of individual achievement. But the achievement does not consist in the assertion and representation of one's unique personality through one's work; it consists instead in the perfection of the traditional paradigmatic shape which normally has firm emotional roots in the ritual associations and requirements of the community. The perfection of a shape such as that of the Bambara antelope masks can only be understood as the product of generations of craftsmen experimenting, often unintentionally, with small variations of a traditional form, thus evolving in small steps a shape which by communal consent agreed best with their emotional needs and their imagination.

Thus the African craftsman's art is produced far less self-consciously, and the innocence, the unselfconsciousness with which it is made shows itself in its form. If one is sufficiently in rapport with it, one can feel the directness with which its shape and its pattern speaks to us; one can feel the emotional spontaneity of its appeal.

All this together, I believe – the relative simplicity, the lack of affectation, the unselfconscious and direct emotionality – accounts, to some extent, for the growing attraction of these figures and masks in a society which lacks most of these attributes. One can like them without nostalgia, without implying that one wishes to restore these qualities either in one's society or in oneself. The response to their appeal entails a widening of one's emotional horizon, an enrichment of one's imagination beyond the limits of our self-conscious art.

Perhaps the most immediately obvious expression of this relative unselfconsciousness of traditional African art is the way in which the naked human body is shown here. In European art, you find again and again that the human body, particularly the female body, was made visible in art under some literary disguises. One had to allude to the Bible or perhaps to classical antiquity if one wished to show it in the form of a sculpture, in order to protect oneself and one's public against the embarrassment of showing or seeing in public what was otherwise largely debarred from public view and relegated to people's private lives. Even today when the severity of the taboo against showing or seeing the naked body in public has somewhat diminished, the loosening of the old taboo is done most self-consciously. One can always feel the effort that has to be made by people if they are exposed to seeing what is normally prohibited in public.

In traditional African sculpture the naked body is shown very simply and in all innocence, as it might have been shown 'before the fall'. It does not entail an effort. But in this respect too the development of African societies is producing a change.

Closely connected with this aspect is another difference between traditional African and contemporary European art. As you can see here, the barrier separating dream and reality is less hard and fast. In the everyday life of more differentiated societies this barrier is normally very stable and strong. Children are trained early to distinguish between fantasies and facts. Even many artists have to make a conscious effort in order to open the gates to their imagination and let it flow spontaneously into their work. Traditional African art reflects the fact that in its society dream and reality flow more easily into each other. The spirits are alive, they may take possession of one of the masks you see here and cure or threaten, punish or reward. And their faces show it. They show the intensity and spontaneity of the feeling which surrounds them and which they evoke. This, the more effortless, more spontaneous mingling of dream and reality too I think can contribute to the appeal of this type of art.

22

An Interview in Amsterdam

Elias had a long-standing connection with the Netherlands. One of his first publications, the essay on kitsch, appeared in an émigré journal published in Amsterdam; it caught the attention of a leading Dutch literary critic, Menno ter Braak, who also wrote a very favourable review of the first volume of *The Civilizing Process*. That book also received high praise from the sociologist and criminologist W. A. Bonger.

When, in May 1940, the German army overran the Netherlands, both Ter Braak and Bonger committed suicide. Their recommendations of *The Civilizing Process* had not been in vain, however. Whereas the German, English, and French reviews by such men as Foulkes, Borkenau, and Aron left few traces, in the Netherlands *The Civilizing Process* continued to be read and discussed by small circles of literary people, psychoanalysts, and sociologists.

Although the interest in Elias's work in the 1940s, 1950s and 1960s may be described as dispersed and eclectic (Goudsblom 1977a: 63), it provided the background for a strong upsurge around 1970. At that time, three books by Elias were published in Germany in the span of one year: the second edition of *The Civilizing Process*, the revised version of his unpublished *Habilitationsschrift* on *The Court Society*, and *What is Sociology?* – an entirely new text, based upon manuscripts originally written in English, which were translated into German by Elias himself and edited to form a general introduction to sociology. Together those three books offered a broad spectrum of ideas which some members of a younger generation of Dutch sociologists hailed as 'paradigm regained' (Goudsblom 1990: 15).

The impact of Elias's books was greatly enhanced by his personal presence. Between

1969 and 1971 he spent three autumn terms in succession as a visiting professor in the Netherlands. In retrospect those visits appear to have been particularly well timed. It was the beginning of a period when intense debates were going on in the social sciences, especially in sociology. On the one hand, there were the proponents of such established theories and practices as structural functionalism and survey research; on the other hand, there were radical critics of various persuasions who, mostly in the name of Marxism, decried all prevailing social science as positivistic. Amidst those discussions, Elias's work promised to offer, to a minority of Dutch sociologists, a viable alternative.

At the end of Elias's first stint as a visiting professor, on 23 December 1969, one of the present authors interviewed him for a Dutch sociological journal. Confronted with statements by some then prominent figures, such as Amitai Etzioni and Herbert Marcuse, Elias responded, typically, with reservations about the way the questions were phrased, but also with some unambiguous comments on the current state and challenge of sociology.

> *Goudsblom:* To begin this interview I should like to read you a quotation from Amitai Etzioni's recent book, *The Active Society:* 'the institutionalized control of the means of violence is largely a macro-variable; it has only minimal application in micro-theory and next to none in intra-role and intra-personality analysis.'[1] I would think that you will have something to comment on this.
>
> *Elias:* Yes, I am quite surprised that so intelligent a sociologist uses the categories micro and macro sociology without asking himself how these two types of sociology are connected, because the facts, the data with which they are concerned obviously do not stand unconnectedly side by side in reality. Therefore their problems and findings too must be somehow connected.
>
> *G:* And then, the example he gives seems to be particularly ill-chosen.
>
> *E:* That is perfectly true, but it is his evident inability to see how the structure of violence control in the individual and the structure of violence control in the state can be linked to each other. I do not know why so many sociologists overlook so simple a thing, but I think I have succeeded in embodying it in my own theory.
>
> *G:* Yes. I suppose that Etzioni and most other sociologists would agree that, at closer inspection, these things do belong together, but they say they can treat them separately for the purpose of analysis. One of the formulae they often use is the formula 'other things being equal,' as if by invoking this formula they can simply concentrate on either a macro or a micro level.
>
> *E:* Yes. I think the decisive point in all this is that, as long as you consider what one calls 'for the purpose of analysis' both levels statically, you can analyse them in separation and you will not find the links. But as soon as you use a developmental model, that is to say, see both levels as being in a state of structured flux, not only a historical flux, the separation becomes impossible and you see the unity between them. If you use a dynamic model, it becomes

very simple. You can of course ask: 'Why do not people have developmental or dynamic models?'

G: Well, you raise the question yourself!

E: My inclination would be to say that there are two main reasons. The first is that the whole trend of our reflection, the whole tradition of our conceptualisation, is so much attuned to what I call in German *Zustandsreduktion*. There is no corresponding word which I can at the moment find in English. It means the reduction in thought of all things that you observe as being dynamic to something static. Our whole conceptual tradition, particularly our philosophical tradition, pushes our thinking in that direction and makes us feel that one cannot come to grips with observed happenings as flowing events in speaking and thinking. The second reason is an ideological one, that is to say, a great deal of our thinking has strictly conservative ideological undertones and, if that is so, one inevitably tends to think of society as it *is*, rather than of society as it *becomes* – *has become* in the past, *is becoming* in the present, and *may become* in the future.

G: When I hear you mention these two reasons, it seems to me that they are actually linked to each other. I mean that the tendency towards *Zustandreduktion* in social science is very much connected with the ideological tendency.

E: Not wholly. I can give you a very short example. Physicists still have not got over their surprise that they cannot operate with the concept of cause and effect on the subatomic level. They do not see the concept of blind mechanical causality as a specific type of perceiving connnections which has developed at a certain time in a specific phase in the development of our knowledge. As long as they consider the concept of cause and effect as an eternal category, they cannot get over their surprise that this category does not apply when we gain further knowledge and especially when we open up new levels of our universe. They then make hundreds of guesses as to how this is possible, while in fact the opening up of new levels of the universe requires a new effort to study the different types of connections we encounter there and to develop not only new mathematical but also new non-mathematical forms of thinking to fit them.

G: The words cause and effect come to us very easily and it is very difficult to conceptualise an alternative to cause and effect.

E: But only because the idea that our forms of thinking are unchanging and eternal has taken such a hold over us that, if I say we cannot always use the term cause and effect in sociology, or we cannot identify explanation with cause-and-effect explanation, everybody says 'this is impossible.' While in fact we must constantly reflect not only on the observations we make on the empirical level, but also on the forms of thinking we use to cope with what we observe. And if we find that our present forms of thinking do not fit what we observe, we have to develop new instruments of thinking.

G: And do these have to be entirely new? I am thinking of Max Weber's definition of what sociology should be. He said that sociologists have a double task, consisting of *deutend verstehen* (or interpretative understanding) and *kausal erklären* (or causal explanation). And *deutend verstehen* was apparently something he considered necessary, because *kausal erklären* is not enough in sociology.

E: I will, if you want me to, come back to this *deutend verstehen*, but I want to say something else first. I think that all those definitions are too learned and too abstract. For me, sociology is an undertaking in which the primary task is to help us to orientate ourselves in this social universe of ours – to orientate ourselves better than we are able to do now, and accordingly also to act less blindly. That goes for both empirical and theoretical levels. Both are necessary in order to orientate ourselves, and the first step in that direction is the step which makes us aware that we are dis-oriented, that we do not really understand the universe which we form with each other. So I am not satisfied with this rather academic way of regarding sociology. I think we must be strictly scholarly, of course, but always with the knowledge that a sociologist has the hard task of helping to orientate ourselves in the unknown social universe which we form with each other.

G: Homans has called this 'the familiar chaos of daily life'.

E: Yes, daily and not daily.

G: Don't you like the words 'familiar chaos'?

E: No, he means something quite different. One must clearly say that what seems most familiar to us covers our ignorance, so the question is not whether this is a chaos, but whether or not we are aware of our own not-knowing.

G: So actually, it is not a chaos, but an unfamiliar order.

E: It is unfamiliar and it is not a chaos. Quite. But in any case, unless we are able to make that which seems most familiar to us completely unfamiliar, we shall never be able to find our way in it.

G: Is that not what you mean by 'detachment'?[2]

E: By 'distantiation': to step away from it, to look at it again, to get away from the idea that we know all about it – then perhaps we can get to know it anew.

G: Is this in any way parallel to the alienation effect that has been used in the theatre by Berthold Brecht?

E: Yes, but the term 'alienation' as it is used today has very strong romantic undertones, as it had when the young Marx brought it into favour. The young Marx *had* strongly romantic leanings, that is to say, a longing for a utopian paradise in which no alienation would ever exist. Speaking only of the more psychological aspects of the concept 'alienation', one has to say that *every* form of reflection requires a 'standing back' at a distance from the reflected object. If people feel so inhibited by this reflection that they suffer from it, then the self-control needed for distancing and reflecting is built in wrongly. There is no reason why one should not be able to stand back, to reflect, to 'alienate oneself', as it is called, and then go into action with the full impetus of one's spontaneity. That is why I don't like to use the term 'alienation', because it is always used with the undertone of 'something from which we suffer'.

G: Well, not always. That is why I mentioned Brecht.

E: Yes, you are right there, but it seems to me that this aspect of Brecht is getting lost. If one speaks of alienation today, one no longer realizes that he gave it a relatively positive meaning in the theatre. But today 'alienation' is only used in a negative sense.

G: I am reminded now of a remark by the American sociologist Maurice Stein in his book, *The Eclipse of Community*. There is one sentence which goes something like this: 'the feeling of being alienated may be our last shared experience.'[3] This sums up very concisely an image of people being entirely cut off from each other; the only thing that still connects them is their common experience of being alienated.

E: A terrible picture, a completely unrealistic picture. It sounds as if affectionate love had completely disappeared from our world. Which is obviously wrong!

G: Not only love, but also hatred.

E: Certainly, but let us say affectionate love had disappeared. In fact, our world has become even richer in this spontaneity of affection than it was earlier, but it was never lost. When I think of my parents' or grandparents' marriages, both were full of warmth and affection. So, what the heck?

G: And do you think there has been a turning-point recently, that the idea that everyone is so very much on his own, a sort of small closed human universe, is beginning to loosen its hold over the younger generation?

E: The *feeling*.

G: All right.

E: It may very well be so, but let me say something about the theory of the civilizing processes in this connection. So far, the civilizing of human beings and the standards of civilization have developed completely unplanned and in a haphazard manner. It is necessary to form a theory so that, in the future, we may be able to judge more closely what kind of restraints are required for complicated societies to function and what type of restraints have been merely built into us to bolster up the authority of certain ruling groups. What I have done is not enough, it is only one step. We must find out more about it. We do now know. I do not believe that we can live entirely without restraints, as some communes today try to do. But I firmly believe that the ways in which restraints are built in today are wasteful and uneconomical.

G: This has a certain similarity with what Herbert Marcuse calls repression and surplus repression.

E: I must decline any relationship. That is all philosophy, and we must investigate these problems empirically as well as theoretically. We cannot do it with philosophies; we need both more experiments and more theoretical *understanding*.

G: I agree, Marcuse seems to believe that he has already solved the problem. He seems to know where the boundary between necessary and surplus repression lies . . . I have here a quotation from a book by R. D. Laing, *The Politics of Experience*, that I meant to show you. He says: 'From the moment of birth, when the Stone Age baby confronts the twentieth-century mother, the baby is subjected to the forces of violence called love, as its mother and father have been and their parents and their parents before them. These forces are mainly concerned with destroying most of its potentialities. This enterprise is, on the whole, successful. By the time the new human being is fifteen or so, we are left with a being like ourselves, a half-crazed creature, more or less adjusted to a mad world. This is normality in our present day!'[4]

E: Yes, but I dislike the description. The sort of general description of our society with complete hostility is as harmful as the description which rests content with what *is*, and regards it as wonderful. We have to sit down and do some hard work and hard thinking in order to find out what is wrong. But if one just sits down and calls our world mad, this helps as little as when one says, 'How wonderful our world is'.

G: He is, of course, thinking of some very concrete reasons, like the Vietnam war, for calling this world mad.

E: But this means proceeding as if he knew why there are wars! As if, by simply crying 'There shouldn't be any wars', we shall stop wars! This is an illusion and a very dangerous one. Moreover, if you only accuse one side of being guilty of wars, you increase the chances, the danger of future war.

G: Now you say that we should investigate empirically and theoretically how much restraint will be necessary for people in order to live together in a complicated social world.

E: Not only how much. What *kind*. The whole pattern of conscience-formation, the whole pattern of taboos. Not only how much. I have no idea what built-in restraints with regard to sexuality are really economic or fruitful in terms of our living together. I simply do not know. I can only guess that what we have today is entirely wasteful.

G: But don't you think that at the moment the restraint on sexuality is becoming less of a problem than the restraint on violence?

E: All types of restraints require a far more thorough investigation, *not* in the form of present-day psychology, but in the form of a unified human science which embraces the social as well as the psychological aspects.

G: And should one consider the psychological aspects especially in psychoanalytical terms?

E: Yes. But psychoanalysis, while it was an enormous breakthrough, has a theoretical framework which is also an example of *Zustandsreduktion*. While it goes into individual dynamics and appears to be dynamic from the psychological point of view, it is *Zustandsreduktion* because a kind of super-ego formation and Oedipus situation which can be found in middle-class people of our society is theoretically presented as eternal, as a nature-given formation of man in general. In that sense it is static.

G: But still, as you have demonstrated yourself in your book on the civilizing process, you can use the basic theoretical ideas of psychoanalysis very well in a dynamic perspective. I mean, you can show the changing emotional economy and the changing relation between ego, super-ego and id without treating them as fixed entities.

E: Yes, but psychoanalysts often proceed as if, for example, super-ego structures were unchanging. Further developments of psychoanalytic theory will be necessary for the practical problems which I have raised. Again, I am not saying Freud is wrong, because he was an enormous breakthrough. But today, psychoanalysis is one of the few branches of knowledge acquisition which still follows the ancient pattern in which the practitioner and the person doing research are not differentiated. And while I think research in all fields should be done in close relation with experimentation and practice, I also think it requires a degree of specialisation. If research is entirely in the hands of those who are at the same time doctors, the future of this branch of science is severely handicapped. My own friends who are psychoanalysts realize that psychoanalysts will have to collaborate far more with sociologists in the future than is the case today. There is no fruitful way to further development of psychoanalytic theory except by interdisciplinary collaboration.

G: In your book on the civilizing process you also used two words that are not at all technical: shame and embarrassment, referring to thresholds of shamefeeling and of revulsion. Although they sound very innocuous and easy, these words seem to lie at the crux of the whole problem of personality and social control. At first sight, one may be inclined to think that they refer to personal feelings but, on closer analysis, one is inclined to think that shame and revulsion are not personal feelings, but functions of social control.

E: They are both.

G: I was leading to that. Isn't it – and that is why I called it the crux of the matter – isn't it right to say that we should get away from the idea that we are faced with a dilemma? Shouldn't we reconceptualize the issue with the idea that, as you said, they are both?

E: Yes, I don't think for a moment that one could say that shame feelings and feelings of revulsion are *not* personal feelings. They are highly personal feelings. But they are at the same time built-in personal feelings, built-in in accordance with social controls. You cannot say they are *not* personal feelings. So there is no one or the other. Wasn't this your question?

G: No, my question was rather: shouldn't this awareness be the starting-point of a whole reconceptualization of a great many categories? For most of the categories that we are using in sociology and psychology today refer to *either* personal *or* social characteristics.

E: Well, I fully agree with that. We are bound by classifications which correspond to autonomous academic disciplines and we think that the corresponding factual data are as autonomous as the two occupational groups wish to be in relation to each other. Psychologists and sociologists wish to be academically autonomous, and our conceptualization of either 'social' or 'psychological' is really a reproduction of the professional ideology of two different academic groups.

G: Yes, but doesn't it go back even further? I mean, today it may be the ideology of two professional groups. But the whole way of thinking, of contrasting individual and society goes back much further.

E: Yes, you are absolutely right, it goes back much further and much deeper. Undoubtedly. But let us reformulate it and say a very old *Weltanschauung* division has become petrified and reinforced through its institutionalization into different disciplines.

G: The basic theme in all your work is the unity of all the apparently diverse phenomena that have been the subject-matter of history, sociology, psychology, psychoanalysis, economics, political science. The problem to many of your readers who may wish to continue with such studies is that when they see this unity, they may lose the firm grasp that a more narrow disciplinary approach might give them.

E: Well, if people have become socialized with a particular scheme of classification, they feel thrown into the sea of uncertainties if someone tells them that this scheme of classification does not correspond to the structure of what we are actually observing. Formerly people linked a particular plant, a particular type of direction of the sky, a particular type of illness, a particular type of animal with one tribe, and another animal, another direction of the sky and other aspects of the world with another tribe; people who used such a classificatory scheme were probably also very unwilling to abandon something that gave a really firm security in their whole thinking. So I can understand that people feel thrown into the sea of uncertainties if they are told that these types of divisions do not correspond to what we are observing, but are merely remnants of an old tradition of thinking. But my whole conviction is that our image of and orientation in our social world will become very much easier once we realize that human beings are not economic in one of their pockets, political in another and psychological in another, in other words that no *real* divisions correspond to the traditional divisions. I think that one can give a new, greater certainty if one abandons this classification.

G: Yes, but the reply to this would be that the method of science in general is analytic, that is, one does not face reality with all its possible aspects at once, but tries to isolate the aspects that seem to have regularities, hoping that this will enable one to predict – always with the condition 'other things being equal'. Now physical sciences have gone a long way along this analytic line, because there is a practical possibility to rule out disturbing conditions.

E: I think the term analytic method is a disguise for something quite fictitious. If analysis means cutting off one thing from another, it is obviously very important what scheme you use for dissecting. And my argument is that, if you dissect according to the traditional classificatory scheme, psychology here, economics there, politics there, God knows what there, then this type of dissection is obviously inadequate for what we actually observe; as we get along, it becomes more and more inadequate. Moreover, I do not agree with the theory of science that all science has to do is to analyse. True, analysis is one step, but synthesis is another. You cannot have an analytic method which does not have models for putting together again what you have dissected. Therefore, I think all the human sciences will in the end have to build an overall model of interdependent human beings, which can be improved and changed in accordance with the evidence – in any case a model which shows how the dissected parts belong together, or can be fitted together. But today, no one shows me how psychology, sociology, economics, politics are really connected with each other.

G: But they say that, by dissecting social reality in this manner, certain partial developments can be predicted. Especially economists and also demographers claim that they can make prognoses and predictions.

E: Yes, I think that in our present theory of sciences we do not distinguish clearly enough between the application of human sciences for purposes of short-term administrative planning, and scientific work without regard for its immediate application. Today many people take it for granted that the main task of science is to provide predictions for state or business planning. Let me give you an example. Econometrics is extremely useful in providing techniques for enabling administrators of the state and in business to make short-term forecasts and, thus, to plan for the near future. This is very useful and very necessary, but we must not confuse these techniques with prediction in the sense used by people like Popper, who seems to consider it the main criterion of anything that aspires to the status of a science.

G: But what other criteria could you mention?

E: The other criteria, vastly underplayed today are, for instance, the criteria of explaining, and in particular for explaining long-term processes. I know that every type of explaining is linked to the possibility of forecasting, but the present emphasis on forecasting alone creates an imbalance which in the human sciences is surely due to the immediate need to legitimize themselves through the short-term help which they give administrators in their practical tasks. So, my answer is that I would rectify this imbalance by saying that there are many different types of forecasting. At present the emphasis on short-term forecasting threatens to stifle basic or long-term research and theory building in sociology, without which a good deal of social action, as well as short-term sociological research, is inevitably misconceived and misdirected. We need more basic research into the largely unknown human universe, in order to find out *why* things have happened, and *why* they are happening today.

G: Could you go on a little more in this direction? There are so many ways of conceiving of the 'why.' Some people feel satisfied when they have had an historical report, others think that they understand when they have an explanation in terms of human motives, again others think they understand if they can give a functional analysis of the social system . . .

E: My own formulation would be that our primary task is to see that the human sciences provide us with a more adequate, better fitting faculty to diagnose the present events in the social universe. Once we have a more realistic diagnosis, we can really determine what we should do about things. One can only make a better fitting diagnosis if one has long-term processes in mind. They cannot be made, as is so often done today, simply by means of short-term, makeshift predictions. In the book on the civilizing and state formation processes I put forward for the first time a model for diagnosing the nexus of events in long-term processes, by showing how the development of standards and types of restraints are connected passively as well as actively with certain aspects of the state-formation process. This provided both an explanatory and a diagnostic model. One could continue it by, for instance, asking why the power of governments has increased in the last hundred years even in parliamentary democracies, as shown by the increase in personnel and in the functions of government. We must have a clear picture of why this is so. This is just one long-term problem among hundreds, which requires long-term developmental sociological research.

G: And would then the sociological solution to such problems lie in a diagnosis of the underlying interdependencies of the human beings who together form a specific social configuration, as in this instance a configuration of 'the rulers and the ruled'?

E: Yes: but this is in itself a pretty wide subject.

G: I know, but I am trying to fill in more fully what you mean by 'more adequate explanation . . .'.

E: . . . than those we have today.' Well, I mean that we can see the facts. We can demonstrate the fact that in 1850 what were regarded as functions of governments in industrial nation states were far more limited than those we have today. May I say that I think that you formulated your question a bit too abstractly? On a very empirical level it is quite possible to find relatively simple answers to the question: 'what is the explanation for the general extension of governmental activities *even* in countries that are ideologically opposed to this extension?' This is an empirical question, and we do not need to go into the interdependence of everything. It is an example of the type of question which requires explanation, and which means a stepping back from certain ideological assumptions. Why is it that in a country like America, which is severely opposed ideologically to the extension of government activities, such activities are in fact constantly growing? This is a problem which cannot be answered merely on the economic or the political level; you have to have an overall sociological model for configurational developments of this kind in order to answer such questions.

23

THE SCIENCES

The early 1970s were a prolific period for Elias. After seeing to the publication of three books in German, he now published within half a decade more articles than he had done in all previous years together. All those articles were in English, which he used as a matter of course at his home in Leicester as well as during his frequent visits to Holland. While he continued to deal with a wide range of subjects, his publications in this period concentrated on two fields: sport, often in collaboration with Eric Dunning, and knowledge and science.

Elias never lost touch with his original training in the natural sciences. He kept abreast with current developments by reading such journals as *The New Scientist*, *Nature* and *The Scientific American*. This gave him the confidence to criticize philosophers and sociologists for sticking to an ideal model of science that had in fact become long obsolete. The following article gives a fair summary of his views on that subject.

Lawlike theories represent men's aim at penetrating behind that which happens in time and space to something beyond them that is unchanging and timeless. Like human beings and landscapes painted on a two-dimensional canvas, they are projections of a four-dimensional nexus into a two-dimensional plane. They are symbolic representations of universal and eternal regularities of connections which are expected to repeat themselves regardless of any particular position in time and space. In many cases, time and space themselves are symbolically reduced to quantities included together with other named quantities in mathematical formulas.

Models of structure, stationary or dynamic, are abstractions of a different type. They include the spatial dimensions and, in the case of models of dynamic structures, of process models, also the time dimension. They are symbolic representations of three- or four-dimensional configurations or, in other words, synchronic and diachronic stereo-models. The rise of their discovery to the position of the central aim of a number of sciences and the corresponding relegation of the discovery to timeless laws and of the use of unchanging universals to a subordinate and auxiliary position in these sciences has far-reaching consequences for the theory of sciences, of which more will have to be said later. One can best illustrate at least some of them with the help of specific examples from sciences where shifts of emphasis from lawlike to structure and process models have actually occurred.

Sciences can be arranged in accordance with the degree of integration or of structuredness of the units which they explore. A comparative study of different sciences along these lines is instructive. At the one end of the scale are to be found sciences concerned with composite units, nexus, fields or whatever one likes to call them whose component parts are so loosely connected with each other that their functional interdependence approaches the zero point. Processes of integration and disintegration of such composite units, therefore, are reversible. The constituent parts can be separated and reassembled in the same manner. The structuredness of such composite units is minimal. The properties characteristic of their component parts even if they are studied in isolation outweigh those of their configuration, of the pattern of their interdependence as determinant of the properties of the composite unit. Nearer to the other pole of the scale are composite units such as organisms which grow and decay, which have not only a static but a dynamic structure. In their case, processes of integration and disintegration, in the last resort, are irreversible. It is not only that the constituent parts which belong to the same level of integration as the composite unit itself cannot be reintegrated with each other after the disintegration of the latter. The structuredness of composite units of this type or, in other words, the interdependence of the constituent parts is so high that the independence of these parts, though not entirely lacking, is very small. Hence, the properties of their configuration, of their functional interdependence, or, in other words, of the structure of the composite unit outweigh by far those of their component parts considered in isolation as determinants of the properties of the composite unit. A somewhat different picture emerges if one examines integration and disintegration processes of human societies. But that can wait. It need not be done here. All that is needed at the moment is a preliminary picture of the configuration of sciences that emerges if they are arranged in accordance with the degree of structuredness, with the balance between relative independence and relative interdependence of the constituent parts, characteristic of the composite units which they set out to explore.

An example of a scientific specialism devoted to the exploration of units with a very low degree of structuredness is the chemical study of gases. For a gas is a composite unit whose component parts are comparatively loosely connected with each other. Except in the case of collisions, the component molecules move as nearly as possible independently of each other and whatever interdependence there is diminishes as the pressure of the gas is reduced. The more that is the case, the looser becomes the connection between the molecular movements, the greater becomes the approximation of the characteristics of a gas to the ideal of atomism. The more appropriate too becomes in that case the conceptualization of regularities of the behaviour of a gas in the form of a general law. Boyle's Law[1] about the behaviour of gases, one of the best known classical chemical laws, illustrates the point. Observable gases do not strictly behave in accordance with this and other 'gas laws'. Their behaviour approximates more closely to the 'law' as the pressure of the gas is reduced. The more that is the case the more appropriate it is to regard a gas as an assembly of independently moving particles and the better does the behaviour of a gas agree with Boyle's Law. The law in other words is set for what is technically called a 'perfect' or an 'ideal' gas. The 'perfect' gas, in other words, is the gas which most closely agrees with the ideal of atomism. Like many other symbolic representations of regularities of connections between observable events in the form of a natural law, Boyle's Law is an archetypal abstraction, an ideal type construct. The fit of a lawlike, an ideal type representation of the connection of part-events of a nexus, one might say, increases or diminishes in inverse ratio to the degree of integration of the nexus. The higher its integration or, in other words, the greater the functional interdependence of its parts, the less well fitting are lawlike ideal type models, the more appropriate are other types of abstractions such as configurational or structure models, either synchronic or diachronic, as symbolic representations of connections and their regularities.

It may be useful to add that lawlike representations can have other than purely cognitive functions. They often simply have didactic functions. They help in the preliminary exposition of a problem. That is the task of the lawlike formula concerning the fit of lawlike representations. It draws attention to the task of the examples from a number of sciences which will be used here and of which that of Boyle's Law is the first.

One further general observation may be useful. It concerns the concept of order as a characteristic of a nexus of events which sciences explore, e.g. the order of nature or the order of society. According to my knowledge, whenever this problem has been discussed, it has been assumed, implicitly or not, that 'order' is the opposite of 'disorder' and that whenever any 'order' is scientifically explored, disorder and chaos can be expected as its antithesis.

It is usually not made sufficiently clear that the term 'order' can be used in two distinctively different senses. In the first sense, it expresses what people experience as order in contrast to what they experience as disorder. That is especially clear in men's experience of society where the term 'order' is closely linked to the term law. What is experienced as order or disorder in that sense depends on the I- or We-perspective of specific persons or groups. Many people, though not all, may regard, in that sense, wars and revolutions as social disorders; they may, in that sense, regard an earthquake, the flooding of a river valley or the outbreak of a volcano as a disorder of nature. This use of the term order as the antithesis of disorder, in other words, is an expression of a specific subject-centred value scale. Seen independently of any particular group and in that sense 'objectively' neither the term order of nature, nor the order of society has its counterpart in any disorder or chaos. In terms of a scientific, an object-orientated inquiry neither the dissolution of a galaxy, nor the destructive eruption of a volcano is a disorder of nature. They form part of exactly the same 'order' of nature as the course of the planets around the sun or a rich field of bearded wheat swaying in a breeze. The term 'chaos' applied to nature is meaningless. So is therefore the philosophical question how to account for the 'order of nature', the fact that natural events follow 'laws'. The wasteland of the moon, the birth of a monster, pestilence, flood and hurricanes, senseless, chaotic and contrary to what men may regard as order, are as much part of the order of nature as the eternal laws of heavens, admired by Kant and likened by him to the moral laws in our breast. To some extent one can say the same if the term 'order' is applied to society. In terms of a scientific, an object-orientated inquiry, neither war, nor revolution, neither murder nor concentration camp and genocide is a disorder of society. They form part of the same order as the division of labour in a hospital or a game of football or chess. Only when seen from the I- or We-perspective of specific groups can 'social order' appear as an antithesis to 'social disorder' and 'chaos' or co-operation as antithesis to conflict. If one is concerned with the explanation of nature or society as an order of a specific type, as one level of the multi-levelled universe, one is confronted with a nexus of events that includes anything which men according to their subject-centred value scheme may classify as disorder or chaos. It would be better to standardize two different terms for 'order', namely 'order' in a factual sense and 'order' as an expression of what specific groups or persons experience and evaluate as such in relation to themselves. Using the conventional terms, one might speak of 'subjective order' and 'objective order'. Only if used in the former sense is order the antithesis to disorder. In the second it-centred sense, 'order' cannot be used as antonym to 'disorder'. In terms of the explanation potential, there is no chaos, apart from the fact that men themselves experience and evaluate certain conditions of nature and society as chaos and disorder. Many pseudo-problems could be discarded if this distinction was clear.

The term 'order' used in a factual sense, means nothing more than that every observable event is part of a nexus of events. It means that the connections of events with each other can be explored, discovered and explained by men and that the structure and regularities of connections, the position and function of particular events within a nexus of events, can be determined and symbolically represented by concepts, models and theories whose fit is open to tests and improvements. This concept of 'objective order' is based on the present fund of human knowledge. According to that fund of knowledge, no event occurs totally and absolutely unconnected with others. No event, in other words, is unexplainable. Sciences are based on the experience of previous generations and accordingly on the expectation that whenever at a given stage of knowledge the connections of events with the already known nexus of events are unknown, such connections exist and can be discovered by men. That and nothing else is meant by 'order' in the object-centred sense of the word. It it is possible to find evidence for the occurrence of totally unconnected events, one will have to reconsider the matter. That would demonstrate the occurrence of disorder and chaos in the object-centred sense of the words. As long as that is not the case, it is useful to keep in mind that the development of the natural and to a lesser extent that of the social universe, under prevailing conditions, is indifferent to the distinction made subjectively, i.e. from the first-person perspective of particular human beings, between order and disorder.

At first, it may be hard to face the fact that the course of nature and, under so far existing conditions, also the development of human society, of the commonwealth of men, are neither ordered nor disordered in the subject-centred sense of the words, neither inherently benevolent nor malevolent, but merely blind and indifferent to the fate and feelings of men. Much of the present conceptual equipment including metaphors like 'the laws of nature' still bears the imprint of men's dream of a world which is basically ordered for their best, either by superhuman beings or by personified abstractions such as benevolent nature. Law and order in nature, thus, appears as the prototype of law and order in society. In actual fact, the social ideal is primary; lawful and well-ordered nature is its projection. Both are ideals disguised as facts. The scientific discovery of laws has been frequently misunderstood as the supreme ability of scientists to reveal the pre-ordained orderliness of nature, of reason or of society.

Thus, the reference to a particular law may help to clear away, at the same time, some of the misapprehensions surrounding the functions of sciences and the nature of general laws.

Boyle's Law can serve as a simple example of both senses. A jarful of gas is a relatively loose composite unit. It would rank relatively low on a scale on which units explored by sciences are arranged according to the degree of interdependence of their component parts or, in other words, to the degree of their structuredness. In that respect, as one saw, it approximates to the atomistic ideal. The immediate component parts of a gas, the molecular movements, have a relatively high degree of independence in relation to each other. Compared with solids or liquids, gases, in the language of involvement, represent a condition of greater disorder or chaos. The more it approaches that condition, the better its properties agree with the prescriptions of Boyle's Law; the more it assumes the characteristics of a perfect or ideal gas. One might say that in this, as in a number of other cases, the greater the disorder the better the fit of the law.

If one aims at a theory not of science, but of sciences – if, in other words, high theoretical significance is attributed to the fact that sciences have diversified – the problem of the reasons for the emergence and development of different groups of sciences and of the relationship between them moves into the centre of one's attention. It should not be forgotten that men like Comte and Spencer in the first half of the nineteenth century already raised such problems. Comte, as far as I know, was the first to formulate them clearly and to attempt an answer. He tried to explain the difference and the relationship between the main groups of sciences in terms of the growing complexity of their field of research. It was not a bad guess. In fact, one can say that this explanation still stands. But, the advances which sciences have made since that time make it possible to go further. We are now able to link the scale of increasing complexity to that of increasing structuredness. What has been said before about the relative lack of structure of gases has prepared the way.

The difference becomes very much apparent if one takes as example one or two of the problems which one has encountered in studying the structure of molecules. Even relatively small and simple molecules present problems of integration, of the manner in which the immediate constituent parts of molecules, their atoms are held together. The first step on this road was the solution of the problem: what elements, what kind of atoms form together the molecules of a particular substance and in what proportions, in which quantities? This stage has found its representation in the quantitative, the so-called 'empirical' formulae of particular substances, such as H_2O for water, indicating that a water molecule consists of two hydrogen and one oxygen atoms. At the next stage, one discovered that it was not enough to know which kind of atoms and how many of them form a particular molecule. This knowledge alone, it was found, was not enough to explain the properties of the molecule. One discovered that in order to solve this problem one had to determine the actual position and the interdependence of the constituent atoms of a molecule. It was found necessary, in other words, to develop the purely quantitative law-like formula which abstracted from all references to spatial dimensions, which represented the atoms of a molecule as if they were all situated in the same plane, into a three-dimensional representation of a molecule indicating exactly how the constituent atoms were placed and bonded in relation to each other. In terms of a theory of sciences, this transition from lawlike and purely additive to three-dimensional representations of molecules, to models of their structure has the crucial significance of a signpost. It is one of the earliest indications that the physical sciences themselves, even when dealing with atoms in practice though not necessarily in their self-understanding, are developing beyond atomism towards what has been called 'structuralism' – a term now much abused. In fact, it is only if one pays attention to the comparative development of sciences, that the meaning of the term 'structure' and the reason why this concept, together with that of process, has come to take in many sciences the place formerly held by the concept of 'law', can become clear.

One can illustrate, at this level, the science-theoretical relevance of the transition from a lawlike symbolic representations which abstract from spatial interdependencies to structure models which include them, by reconstructing briefly one of the problems that induced representatives of chemistry and physics to move in that direction – the problem of isomers. They became aware of the fact that substances whose molecules consist of exactly the same kind of atoms in exactly the same quantities can have different properties which means that they are to all intents and purposes different substances. The observation contradicted one of the basic assumptions of an atomistic belief system – the assumption that the same component parts in the same proportions result in identical composite units, in units with the same properties.

Take, for instance, a monosaccharide called hexose, a sugar with six carbon atoms whose quantitative or 'empirical' formula is $C_6H_{12}O_6$; it consists of six carbon atoms, twelve hydrogen atoms and six oxygen atoms. This is the formula for glucose, the sugar present in the blood. But fifteen other sugars, among them fructose and galactose, have the same quantitative formula; they have the same component parts in the same quantities although they differ with regard to their solubility, their sweetness, their organic functions and in other respects. They are recognizably different substances. The problem is to explain how it is possible that different substances can have the same atomic composition. The solution, as has been found, lies in the different structure of the molecules. The manner in which the atoms are bonded to each other, their spatial configuration is different in each of the fifteen substances. Although they can be represented by the same quantitative formula, their representation in the form of a three-dimensional model showing the spatial arrangements of the atoms is different.

The solution of the problem of isomers is by now well established as a fairly elementary piece of physico-chemical knowledge. Three-dimensional models of their structure have been worked out for larger and increasingly complex molecules with a high degree of fitness to the relevant evidence. The explanatory functions of such models have become particularly well known in connection with the discovery of the structure and composition of some very large molecules of the deoxyribose type of nucleic acid or, in short, of the DNA molecule. The context problem is that of the high intergenerational stablity and constancy of all kinds of living things in spite of their great diversity and variability. The basic structures which make it possible that a new organism forms itself in accordance with the models of the parent organisms appear to be the same in all living things. For some of the evidence for these structures comes from some of the simplest living things at present known, such as bacteriophages. The more specific problem was: how is it possible that large molecules of the same chemical composition which one can discover in the chromosomes of all the higher organisms and which, as one already knew, contain the 'substance' of heredity, can store the enormous quantity of information required for the controlled process, for the build up and the organized growth of a living thing, and in fact for the great variety and variability of living things. An answer to this specific problem which fitted most of the existing observational data was worked out as the culmination and synthesis of a vast amount of work done by many people (I think my 'culmination and synthesis' thesis fits the facts here better than Kuhn's thesis of a revolution), by J. D. Watson and F. H. C. Crick who produced in 1953 a model of the DNA molecule which fitted both the observational data and the functional requirements. The model has become known as the double helix because the two sugar-phosphate chains of the DNA model held together by hydrogen bonds between these bases are twisted around each other like a spiral staircase whose base to base attachments represent the series of steps. While it was indispensible to know what kind and what groups of atoms formed such a molecule, again, the crucial question was their spatial arrangement, the way they were bonded to each other, their configuration or, in other words, the structure of the molecule. For the atomic composition alone could not provide the answer to the problem. One had to know their specific configuration in order to explain the function of such molecules as intergenerational coding devices for a vast number of different organisms. The model of the configuration, of the structure of the DNA molecule worked out by Watson and Crick, appears to satisfy this requirement because the possibilities for variations in the sequence of the bases is practically limitless.

The solution of the problem of isomers and that of the DNA molecule are only two examples of the development and knowledge about the structure of molecules and of the related knowledge of the connection between structure and function. It is a development which is likely to continue. The culminating innovatory synthesis representing the solution of a critical problem in the pathway of a group of sciences opens the way for the work on a new generation of problems which prior to the solution of the antecedent generation could not be attacked and often enough not even clearly perceived and set.

In its home sciences the present knowledge of the structure of molecules commands a very wide measure of acceptance. But, the impact which this development, and a number of parallel developments in other sciences, have made on the theory of sciences is negligible. The science-theorectical innovations implied in these developments have not been brought to light. In fact even those men whose scientific imagination, whose capacity for intellectual synthesis of a vast array of details, contributed most to the innovatory solution of critical problems in their special scientific field, quite often fail to see the science-theoretical innovations inherent in their own work. In terms of a theory of sciences, they tend to interpret their own innovatory achievements in conventional terms. In this as in other cases the recognition of the innovatory science-theoretical significance of innovations in specific sciences was, and still is, apparently blocked by a whole complex of factors. Among them questions of status and prestige differentials between different sciences play no less a part than the wide ramifications of the atomistic belief system which underlies much of the present thinking about the nature of sciences, not only in philosophy, but also in the physical, biological and social sciences and in society at large. The innovatory breakthrough, when it comes, may well be regarded as 'revolutionary' in that sense of the word which most closely resembles its non-figurative meaning, namely explosive because a development long overdue is held up and blocked by an existing power structure. There is abundant evidence for a science-theoretical synthesis, for a scientific theory of sciences which sooner or later will take the place of philosophical theories of science. But even those people who go some steps in that direction usually still do so very hesistantly, perhaps because they are afraid that any development beyond the traditional atomistic and mechanistic belief system can only lead into metaphysical vitalism and transcendentalism.

An example of this reticence may help illuminate the point. In his paper 'Atomism, structure and form', Lancelot L. Whyte summed up some of these trends in the development of the natural sciences in the following manner:

It seems that the method of treating the properties of ultimate small units as fundamental only works well when a rather small number of variables – say less than five or ten – is adequate for some purpose, as in simple molecules and homogenous fluids. When it comes to complex partly ordered systems rich in structure and form, this classical method is very clumsy if we are interested in ultra-structure and its changes. Nature seems to be saying with all possible emphasis: The Laws of complex systems are not written in terms of quantitative properties of localized constituents but in terms of . . . ?[22]

The answer to this question, in the light of the examples that have been given here, is quite straightforward. It is no longer a question of finding laws. 'Complex systems', as they are called in this quotation, are units which, on an ascending scale, are determined not only by their composition, but increasingly by the configuration of their constituent parts or, in other words, by their structure. I cannot show here that this is increasingly the case as one moves from large molecules to more and more highly integrated units with more and more levels of integration. For the time being, the science-theoretical lesson to be drawn from scientific inquiries into the structure of large molecules must be enough. If one examines the science-theoretical implications provided by the discovery of the structure of very large molecules with a specific biological function, such as that of the DNA molecule, the conclusions are these. Its structure as well as its functions have been explained with the help of (a) an analysis of its component parts, (b) a synthesis in the form of a testable three-dimensional model showing, in the light of the available evidence, the configuration of the component parts, (c) an examination of the way in which composition and configuration, i.e. the structure of the molecule accounts for its function. Traditional theories of science tended to concentrate attention on analysis alone. Synthesis and integration of theoretical constructs as the counterpart of studies of 'wholes', 'systems', patterns, forms or however one has called them have long been suspect as symptons of extra-scientific speculation, of a metaphysical frame of mind and, more often than not, the suspicion was justified. The actual development of sciences, of which that of crystallography and biochemistry are only some examples, very clearly indicate that this need not be the case. Men who stand in the hardened tradition of atomism may continue to believe in the exclusivity of analysis of the component parts of a composite unit as the key to a scientific inquiry. It is this tradition which has surrounded inquiries into the integration of constituent parts, into the structure of a composite unit and the building up of three-dimensional or in other cases of four-dimensional models, as distinct from planar lawlike theories, with the odour of a non-scientific occupation. The procedure adopted at the level of intramolecular structures, paradoxically enough, is in that respect symptomatic. It heralds the break with the traditional atomism. It shows that anlysis, i.e. the determination of the properties and proportions of the component parts of a composite unit, though indispensable, is not enough. Like the quest for lawlike connections, analysis plays increasingly the part of an auxiliary operation in relation to synthesis and the working out of structure – and process – theories, as one moves from the investigation of loosely integrated units at one and the same level to the investigation of more and more highly integrated units with more and more levels of integration.

To use once more the examples of the DNA molecule, one could not have worked out a well-fitting model without a full knowledge of the chemical composition of the various bases, sugars and nucleotides forming a DNA molecule. One had to determine, for instance, the stuff composing the bases. One had to know that they contained purines, namely adenine and thymine, and pyramidines, namely guanine and cytosine, both composed of carbon and nitrogen in varying numbers. One needed a clear understanding of what the component parts actually do, both on the atomic level and on the level of small molecules; one had to know what properties they have and how they behave. But all the knowledge of the behaviour of parts which one could gain by means of a chemical analysis was by itself quite insufficient. Analysis was an indispensible auxiliary procedure in relation to the main task – the building up of an integrating model. One had to find out not only that in a DNA model many thousands and perhaps even millions of nucleotides are joined together. One had to discover above all how the component units were arranged within the long polynucleotide strands in order to explain the biological function of these giant molecules as templates for the building up of another generation of living things.

Thus, analysis stood here in the service of synthesis. One had to know the characteristics of the component parts, but one could not from this knowledge alone deduce either their configuration or the properties of the composite unit. The consequences of the fact that in the case of studies of more highly integrated units the reduction of the unit, its dissection into component parts by itself is quite insufficient as a scientific procedure – its consequences for a theory of sciences are far reaching. It means in essence that sciences concerned with the study of more highly integrated units cannot fulfil their task without the knowledge provided by the scientific specialists concerned with the study of the lower level component parts, but they cannot be reduced to the lower level sciences. The practitioners of the latter cannot on their own explore and determine the configuration of the component units, the structure of the composite unit; they cannot determine the specific properties of this unit for which the type of integration of the component parts or, in other words, the structure of the composite unit provides the explanation.

At this point, one may begin to see the answer to the question raised earlier, to the question of the reason why sciences of different types have developed in course of time. As one ascends from studies of simpler and loosely integrated to that of more and more complex and more firmly integrated units with a growing number of superimposed levels of integration, the instruments of research which one has developed in order to explore the relatively simple and loosely-knit units, among them purely analytic procedures or the concept of general laws, lose the exclusiveness and primacy which they possess on their own level, and different concepts, such as integration and disintegration or structure and process, and different procedures, such as the building of integrating, configurational models, gain the ascendency. The notion, which still lingers on, that all sciences may eventually work in accordance with the models of physics or may even transform themselves into a kind of physics, is a mistake. One cannot adequately study and explain units at a higher level of integration in terms which have been worked out and which have been found reasonably adequate for the study of units representing a lower level of integration. Nor can one expect that a method of research which has been found adequate for scientific studies of units at the lower levels will automatically prove equally adequate for the study of units which represent higher levels of integration. As one can observe them, the method of sciences are far more differentiated than the popular expression 'the scientific method' suggests. To put it at its simplest, there are considerable differences between the methods to be adopted in order to accumulate data with the expectation of discovering laws or lawlike regularities and the methods required for working out and for testing three-dimensional models, such as that of the DNA molecule, whose structure has not only to fit a vast number of measurements, but also specific biological functions. Like science in the singular, 'scientific method' is an ideal type construct. The common task of sciences is that of solving problems in a testable manner and of setting problems in such a way that they can be solved in that manner. The tendency to regard one particular type of method, of theories, of concepts or of abstractions, as 'scientific' to the exclusion of others accounts for many difficulties which one can observe in the past development of sciences. It creates analogous difficulties today.

Perhaps an example may help to illustrate the point. It may supplement the examples given before because it is taken from a much higher level of integration and can indicate how many new problems may come within our grasp if we do not proceed on the assumption that a a theory of sciences can be reduced to a theory of science. If one studies the scientific development leading up to Darwin's theory of evolution it is noticeable that this, too, was a case in which the crowning innovatory theory represented not so much a revolution – the counter-forces were strong, but by no means able to block the innovatory trend for a considerable time – but the consummation and synthesis of a fairly long preceding development on both the theoretical and empirical levels. Darwin's theory was one of the first process theories which has shown a very high degree of fitness. In terms of a theory of sciences it represented, like that of Marx, the transition to a new type of theory. Structure theories, in contrast to lawlike theories, embody the spatial dimensions. They have, as one saw, the character of three-dimensional models. Process theories have the character of four-dimensional models. In contrast to lawlike theories, they do not abstract from either the spatial or the time dimension. If one looks at the seminal conflict within which the first biological process theories developed – Darwin was not the only man who at the time worked out a biological process theory, but only the most successful – one may notice that many of his opponents differed from him not simply with regard to the details of their arguments, but also with regard to the type of theory which they put forward. They persisted in working out lawlike theories. They tried to find the eternal laws of animals, or lawlike regularities which specific types of animals had in common. I have already alluded to the fact that the transition from lawlike to structure and process theories involves a re-orientation of the whole manner of thinking. One can see it here. Among the main opponents of an evolutionary theory of living things were Georges Cuvier and Richard Owen. Cuvier, as comparative anatomist and palaeontologist, had a number of important scientific advances to his credit but he remained in his whole outlook fixated to the idea that the scientists' task is the discovery of that which is unchanging in all the variety of changeable living things. He, therefore, aimed at a type of abstraction indicating what all animals have in common. He tried to show by means of a once famous principle of the correlation of parts that the structural and functional aspects of anatomy can be regarded as part of a single universal law which is applicable to all animals. He also tried to formulate laws of correlation which showed what was common to specific types of animals (1795). An example is: 'All the animals with white blood who have a heart have bronchi or a clearly circumscribed respiratory organ. All those who do not have a heart, have no bronchi. Wherever heart and bronchi exist, there is a liver; wherever they lack, the liver is lacking.' Lamarck, who prior to Darwin was perhaps the most prominent proponent of a biological process-theory, shortly afterwards suggested abandoning the use of the blood colour as determinant of the classification of lower animals and introduced in his *Système des animaux sans vertèbres* (1801) the division of animals into vertebrates and invertebrates which has shown its greater object-adequacy by its continued use up to our own time. But he combined the quest for type criteria with the knowledge that the types are fluid, that they are phases or stages of a process. Cuvier, on the other hand, persisted in thinking of different classes or types of animals as eternally set in the same mould. He, therefore, aimed at discovering behind the manifoldness of observable data a lawlike ideal type of different classes of animals. This style of thinking was equally pronounced in the theories of his English counterpart and admirer, Richard Owen, who worked out a theoretical model by means of which he was able to reduce all the various vertebrate classes to a single archtype representing the universals of the vertebrate skeleton.

The example may help to show how similar the conceptual problems are which one encounters in the transition from lawlike to process models, even though in substance the processes which one tries to explore may be very different. The process of biological evolution is very different from the non-biological process of social development and, as part of it, the process of scientific development. Each has a distinct pattern of its own. But, in all these cases the seminal conflict between representatives of lawlike theories and of process theories show certain common structural features. The quest for the common characteristics of animals or of specific classes of animals, in short, for the universals of animals, was not unfounded. But, as the problem of the development of living things moved into the centre of the attention of biologists, the problem of the universal, of the ideal type animal, without losing its function entirely, became a subordinate problem compared with that of the evolution of the process of living things. A similar change can be expected in the theory of societies and of sciences. So far, the problem of the archetypal science has dominated the theory of science. So has the notion that one has found it in a kind of ideal-type physics and in the implied assumption that all sciences can, will or should be reduced to the model of that ideal science. By implication, advances in scientific research, of which I have given some examples, indicate why this reduction is bound to fail. But the implications of these advances for a theory of sciences have been largely neglected and obscured. Some of them have been shown here. The key to the puzzle is the discovery that the configuration of part-units as determinant of the properties of a composite unit is irreducible. In course of time this discovery will require the abandonment of the atomistic and reductionist theories of science in the singular. With the increasing diversification of sciences they have become fossilized relics of a former age. Today one requires a theory of the scale of sciences symbolically representing the scale of the universe which sciences explore. For at each level of that scale one encounters types of connections, of structures and processes not to be found at the lower levels. To some extent, therefore, different symbolic representations and different procedures are needed for the exploration of different levels of that scale.

24

ON THE CONCEPT OF EVERYDAY LIFE

In the second half of the 1970s, Elias gradually moved away from England. His star began simultaneously to rise on the European mainland. His books were translated into French, and were very well received, especially among the French historians of the *Annales* school. A German reprint of *The Civilizing Process*, issued as a two-volume paperback in 1976, became a bestseller for several years. On his eightieth birthday in 1977, Elias was presented with a *Festschrift, Human Figurations* (Gleichmann, Goudsblom and Korte, 1977), a collection of personal recollections and essays in English and German, published in the Netherlands. Later that same year, he received the prestigious Adorno Prize of the City of Frankfurt. In the following years several German universities in succession invited him for Visiting Professorships. From 1978 to 1984 he was a Fellow at the Centre for Interdisciplinary Research at Bielefeld.

As he found himself for increasingly longer spells living in Germany, he more and more resumed writing in his native German. Sometimes he was prompted to do so for a specific occasion, as when the editors of a German sociological journal asked him to contribute to a special issue on 'everyday life', published in 1978. He seized upon the chance to distance himself from some fashionable trends in sociology, and to chastise the tendency among some of his colleagues to insulate themselves behind 'philosophoidal' barriers.

> Not so long ago, the concept of everyday life could be used in an ordinary, everyday way. One could talk in all innocence of: 'the way things happen in everyday life' without pausing to wonder what 'everyday life' might actually

mean. But now the concept of the everyday has become anything but everyday: it is loaded with the freight of theoretical reflection, and in this form it has become a key concept for a number of schools of contemporary sociology.

No doubt, there are good reasons for this. But it is actually not quite clear what is providing the impetus for this preoccupation with the 'everyday' or 'mundane' among contemporary sociologists. As it is used in sociology today, this concept is anything but homogeneous. It shimmers with many colours, has numerous meanings with a whole spectrum of undertones, especially undertones of a polemical kind; but they, too, usually remain implicit, are not spelled out. Very rarely is it stated what is really meant by the 'not-everyday'. Any opponent with whom one is in dispute, and against whom an everyday term is used as a weapon, remains partly out of reach. Is it possible that even in the minds of the various theoreticians of the everyday, the common ground denoted by this multifarious concept lies rather in the negative, in what they are turning away from, than in the positive meanings they associate with the term? There is, indeed, much reason to believe that the apparent uniformity in the use of the concept of 'everyday-ness' is based on a common rejection of previously dominant theoretical constructs, rather than on constructing a new, unified theory or even attempting to do so.

For example, the representatives of a not insignificant group of sociological theorists of the everyday, including ethnomethodologists and phenomenologically-orientated sociologists, seem agreed, above all, in their common rejection of all theoretical and empirical sociological research which, in selecting the problems to be addressed, focuses attention on the object-like, not to say objective, aspects of the communal, social life of human beings. What unites them, it seems, is a common reaction against previously dominant and still highly influential types of sociological theory, and therefore, above all, against the system theories of the structural functionalists, and their opponents at the other end of the spectrum, the exponents of the Marxian type of sociological theory. In opposition to them, it seems, sociological schools concerned with the 'everyday' concentrate their attention more on subjective aspects of human communal life. They focus on the meaning of these aspects for the people involved, on the way the people themselves experience aspects of society, and especially the unofficial, non-public aspects, or at any rate those which are not solidly institutionalized.

If this is so, Erving Goffman, the master of empirical detail-work among sociologists, may prove exemplary regarding the possible fruitfulness of this kind of research. In relation to the older sociological establishment, Goffman was an outsider and a loner; no bridge could connect their theoretical approach to his type of research, based closely on the empirical. In relation to the younger establishment, to which many sociologists of the everyday belong, Goffman seems like a pioneer. But he has remained a very lonely pioneer. In him, personal sensitivity, the fineness of his powers of practical observation, his unerring eye, made up for the original lack of theoretical reference. Most of those who are attempting to proceed in a similar direction today are crushed by the weight of their theoretical reflections. Their observations lose their freshness, and are apt to ossify into formalistic constructs under the pressure of the need to force what is observable here and now into the straitjacket of some universal, axiomatic scheme. This scheme is seldom formulated clearly and unambiguously enough to convince anyone outside the circle of converts and initiates. The attempt to correct the one-sidedness of objectivist tendencies in sociology – whose representatives, even when invoking Max Weber, fail to respect his insistence on the subjective meaning of social events – is, of course, understandable. But here, as so often in the advance of scholarly work, a younger generation is reacting against an excessive swing of the pendulum in one direction by no less an exaggerated swing in the other.

There is no good reason to suppose that the investigation of structures of social life (which, if done one-sidedly, can certainly be called 'objectivistic'), and the investigation of the meanings of the various aspects of social life as experienced by the people concerned (which, if done one-sidedly, can very well be called 'subjectivistic'), are incompatible. The investigation of the experiential dimension, the way in which, in the context of their experience of social structures, people contribute both to their reproduction and to their change, is no less indispensable than that of the long-term, unplanned, blind interweaving-mechanisms which are at work in the transformation of these structures. This is especially true if one is concerned with the *process* of the transformation of social structures.

Perhaps it would be useful for me to say a few words here about how I came to be concerned with the concept of the everyday. The kind request of the editor of this special issue that I should write a contribution on this subject drew my attention to a matter about which I had felt occasional uneasiness earlier, without making any special effort to get to the bottom of it. Now there was a certain necessity to make good this omission. I had myself sometimes been counted among those who had concerned themselves with problems of the 'everyday' in the more recent, technical sense of the word. I was aware that this idea was based on a misunderstanding. As it seems to be a widespread misunderstanding, I hope it will not be taken amiss if I try to clear it up. Perhaps, at the same time, I shall succeed in making some contribution to clarifying this concept of everyday life.

In two of my books, *The Court Society* and the first volume of *The Civilizing Process*, I deal, among other things, with problems which could easily be classified as concerning everyday life in the technical sense of the word which I have just mentioned. One example is my discussion of the structure of the houses of the court aristocrats. I try to show how exactly this structure reflects the structure of the whole network of interrelationships of the people living in them. If the way in which people reside together is understood as an aspect of their everyday life, it emerged here with particular clarity that the structure of everyday life is not a more-or-less autonomous structure in its own right, but is an integral component of the structure of this social stratum and, since this stratum cannot be considered in isolation, of the power structure of society as a whole.

The same applies to the problems in Volume One of *The Civilizing Process*, which might possibly be understood as problems of the everyday. The book deals, among other things, with changes in the social code which regulates the behaviour and feelings of people of certain strata at mealtimes, on going to bed, when blowing their noses, performing their bodily functions and carrying out other similarly basic actions. My concern with these themes, too, has clearly been understood sometimes as a concern with aspects of everyday life. That, as I have said, is a misunderstanding. The concept of the everyday, as generally used today as a sociological *terminus technicus*, tacitly includes the idea that there are peculiarities of everyday life which are different to those of other areas of social life and may even be opposed to them. I myself had used my concern with what is classified by others as everyday life in precisely the opposite sense, to make clear a change in the civilizing code which is indissolubly bound up with other structural changes in society, such as the increasing division of functions or processes of state formation.

Investigations of changes in the code of behaviour and sensibility in a civilizing direction make possible something which has not been properly attempted up to now and has, perhaps, been regarded as not feasible. They allow us to make reliable comparisons between the behaviour and feelings of people in different phases of a social development. The importance of such investigations into changes in what, it seems to me, is currently classified as the 'everyday' and which I myself attempted to grasp conceptually as a change in the personality structure or in the standards of emotion management, lay precisely in the fact that changes in the personality structure could be correlated in this way with changes in the social structure as one of its aspects. They were correlated, for example, with the enlargement of social differentiation, with the lengthening of chains of interdependence, with the tighter centralization of the state and social organization, that is, with other changes which were also demonstrated and verified by means of detailed investigations. In this way the theoretical model of long-term processes of civilization and state formation to which these studies gave rise was developed through strict correlation with detailed empirical work, and *vice versa*, in a dialectical process by which knowledge advances on two levels. Such a process is one of the basic conditions for the verifiability of scientific results.

Without this twin-track method, the knowledge-value of sociological as of other scholarly investigations remains questionable. Purely empirical investigations – that is, investigations without a theoretical framework – are like sea voyages without a map or a compass. One sometimes chances on a harbour, but the risk of shipwreck is high. Theoretical investigations without an empirical base are usually, at bottom, elaborations of preconceived dogmatic notions; the dogmas are enshrined as a matter of faith, and cannot be refuted or corrected by any empirical proofs or detailed investigations. At most, an attempt is made to buttress them *a posteriori* with a few empirically-related arguments. In this way, one or two felicitous ideas are sometimes to be found floating like blobs of fat on a thin philosophical soup.

Some, though certainly not all, attempts to turn the notion of everyday life into a useful sociological concept seem to me to be of this kind. If not exactly philosophical, they are philosophoidal in character. It is often difficult to understand why they put themselves forward as sociological investigations. Others are empirically descriptive studies, straightforward and sometimes highly informative, with a wealth of detail, but without any theoretical reference and thus slightly rudderless.

To gain an overview of the diverse new uses of the concept of everyday life, I have compiled a provisional list (figure 24.1) of a number of types of usage which are encountered predominantly, if not exclusively, in the literature which purports to be sociological. This short selection also points to two circumstances which are revealing with regard to this usage and deserve to be mentioned here.

As a rule the fashionable concept of everyday life is used in a partisan way, either for or against something which is not everyday life. But what this something is must usually be guessed; with a few exceptions, there is no clear definition of the non-everyday entity which is to be denigrated or praised, opposed or supported by what one has to say about everyday life as its antithesis. The list which follows therefore gives a preliminary indication of what is implied by the 'not-everyday'. Without this antithesis we can never really understand what the various accounts of 'everyday life', and also of 'everyday consciousness' and 'everyday culture', refer to.

The second circumstance I should like to point to in advance is the almost complete absence of attempts to discern the unity underlying the multiplicity of shades of meaning in the contemporary use of the concept of the everyday, as revealed by the following list. This is bound up with the lack of communication between representatives of different meanings of the concept, to which I shall return later.

Figure 24.1 is anything but comprehensive. It is intended to stimulate thought about this multiplicity of mostly quite unrelated, randomly juxtaposed uses of the same term. Many readers will be able to add to the list from their own experience. There are mixtures and overlaps between the different meanings. Leaving aside the first type, everyday versus feast day, the

Figure 24.1   Types of Contemporary Concept of the Everyday with the Implied
Antitheses

	– A Selection –		
1	Everyday	⟷	holiday (feast day)
2	Everyday = routine	⟷	extraordinary areas of society not subject to routine
3	Everyday = working day (especially for working class)	⟷	bourgeois sphere, i.e. that of people living on profits and in luxury, without really working
4	Everyday = life of the masses	⟷	life of the privileged and powerful (kings, princes and princesses, presidents, members of government, party leaders, members of parliament, business leaders)
5	Everyday = sphere of mundane events	⟷	everything regarded by traditional political historiography as the only relevant or 'great' event in history, i.e. the centre-stage of history
6	Everyday = private life (family, love, children)	⟷	public or occupational life
7	Everyday = sphere of natural, spontaneous, unreflecting, genuine experience and thinking	⟷	sphere of reflective, artificial, unspontaneous, especially scientific experience and thinking
8	Everyday (everyday consciousness) = ideological, naïve, superficial and false experience and thinking	⟷	correct, genuine, true

antithesis which gives the term 'everyday' its special connotation is, as I have mentioned, only dimly intimated in the sociological use of the term. Hardly ever does one find it unequivocally stated what the non-everyday reality is to which the aspect of life characterized as everyday is contrasted as different or antithetical. But without a fairly clear picture of this implied, sometimes praised, sometimes hated non-everyday sphere, one can never really understand in what sense the term 'everyday' is being used in a given instance. That is why it has been made explicit in the list.

It is also true that in many cases bodies of ideas in which the term 'everyday' functions as a key concept employ a type of abstraction which makes it difficult, if not impossible, to guess which observable data these discussions refer to. It cannot be denied that many versions of the contemporary concept of everyday-ness, which purport to be sociological and whose authors identify themselves professionally as sociologists, originate in philosophy, especially that of Husserl. These versions of the concept of the everyday are an example of the unreflecting use of philosophical models – which, through their very origin, can elude verification by experiments and other forms of empirical reference – as a substitute for a sociological theory which cannot escape such verification. What often emerge as a result are peculiar hybrids – neither philosophy nor sociology, neither fish nor fowl.

This tendency to indulge in philosophical reflections without empirical foundation in the sphere of sociology is made possible and reinforced by an unplanned consequence of academic organization, which favours the development of esoteric abstractions in the human sciences and particularly in sociology. Some elaborations on the 'everyday', because of their total lack of empirical reference, are perhaps comprehensible to the members of the small academic circles in which they are cultivated. For them, they may have a meaning as contributions to the sect's internal debate. For non-members they are often virtually incomprehensible. Moreover, the members of such circles may often be primarily concerned, in their writings and discussions, with the internal consensus within their group. They make hardly any effort to expound their insights and viewpoints in a language which non-members can understand – and this, despite the fact that sociology in particular is failing in its task if its research cannot be made fruitful for other disciplines.

The strong tendency towards the formation of sects in the contemporary human sciences, and especially in sociology after the collapse of the great American attempt to create a comprehensive central theory, explains, among other things, the multiplicity of concepts of the everyday to which the above list bears witness. There is really no discussion between the groups which use the term 'everyday' in different senses, and still less with those who reject it. Not only among specialists in 'everyday-ness' but among sociological specialists in general, there is an increasing tendency to develop systems of argumentation internal to the group, which seem wholly watertight to the members of the sect but which do not have to prove their worth in a continuing friendly debate with other scholars who do not belong to the circle, as is the case in other areas of research.

It thus comes about that the concept of the everyday is sometimes used simultaneously with two almost antithetical meanings, as in the case of items 7 and 8 in figure 24.1. This example is revealing; for the difference in the meanings with which the term 'everyday' is used here is not based on verifiable results but on the divergence between preconceived axiomatic basic convictions which are not susceptible to testing by systematic research. The meaning of 'everyday' listed as item 7 is symbolic of a romantic belief whose exponents, although themselves representing through their whole personality structure a high level of reflection and a considerable ability to restrain spontaneous impulses, at the same time entertain a longing for a sphere of life in which the oppressive weight of scholarly work, especially the work of thinking, vanishes, and in which people are able to experience the world spontaneously and unhindered by the burden of thought. The concept of everyday life here becomes a symbol for this wish-dream. As such it has a certain kinship with the dream of 'community' which was very widespread in sociology at one time – the dream of the warm, friendly, spontaneous, harmonious kind of communal life, not clouded by too much self-consciousness, enjoyed by people in earlier times, which has now given way to the hard, cold, soulless life of urbanized industrial societies. The concept of 'everyday-ness' now replaces that of community, while 'society' gives way to 'science', 'reason', and so on.

In item 8 in figure 24.1 the meaning of 'everyday life' is reversed, becoming the receptacle for everything which people find negative: false consciousness, the myths and lies of everyday life, to which they doubtless tacitly oppose the vague image of a 'true consciousness'. It is, indeed, not easy to imagine how, given this use of concepts which have meanings based on different articles of faith, a discussion between their representatives can come about.

Perhaps what I have said in the foregoing may help to make such discussions possible. Should that be the case, I should like to offer those who make use of this far from everyday concept of the everyday two further points for consideration, which, it seems to me, need to be cleared in any discussion relating to this subject. The first concerns the character of 'everyday life' as a social datum. Does this term, and therefore its counterpart, the 'non-everyday', refer to distinguishable spheres, sectors or regions of human societies? The question one needs to address is whether such a special sphere, with its own structure and a certain autonomy, actually exists. Most current discussions of everyday life, everyday consciousness, everyday culture, and so on, presuppose the existence of a special sphere of this kind. But one might consider whether one is not simply referring here, with the aid of an esoteric abstraction, to peculiarities of the present working and professional societies, which could be denoted just as well by terms such as leisure, the private sphere and related concepts. These peculiarities are undoubtedly given their special stamp by the overall structure, and therefore by the power relationships, of industrial state societies.

This gives rise to a second question which needs to be discussed in this context. At present the term 'everyday' is used extensively, even among sociologists, as a universal concept. That is all part of the term's philosophical inheritance. It appears as if the 'everyday life' referred to in contemporary sociological publications were a universal category, an eternal and immutable peculiarity of all possible human societies. The question is whether what we read in books and articles on 'everyday life' today is really applicable to societies in all times and places. Does it apply to Vietnamese peasants, to the cattle-rearing Masai nomads of Kenya, to the savage, armoured knights of the early Middle Ages, to Chinese mandarins and to the non-working upper strata of Athens and Rome, just as well as to members of present-day industrial societies, or are we dealing here simply with a piece of speculation inflated to universal proportions from the church-steeple perspective of the present?

25

THE RETREAT OF SOCIOLOGISTS INTO THE PRESENT

By the 1980s, Elias had become a major figure in German sociology. He was revered as one of the last representatives of the last generation of sociologists of the Weimar Republic. He, for his part, while enjoying the respect paid to him, did not hesitate to speak his mind about what he considered deplorable trends in the discipline. He knew that some younger sociologists, such as Peter Gleichmann and Hermann Korte, were strongly influenced by his ideas; but the profession as a whole suffered, in his opinion, from severe short-sightedness. He engaged in a sharp polemic with adherents of rational choice theory, and, in another article, criticized the tendency among sociologists in general to disregard long-term processes. When, a few years later, the latter article was translated into English, Elias could not resist the temptation he so often felt when confronted with a text he had written earlier to add several new sections (Elias 1987a). Although valuable in their own right, those additions are not included here.

I

Not much attention has been paid to the retreat of sociologists into the present. This retreat, their flight from the past, became the dominant trend in the development of sociology after the Second World War and, like this development itself, was essentially unplanned.

That it was a retreat can become clearly visible if one considers that many of the earlier sociologists sought to illuminate problems of human societies, including those of their own time, with the help of a wide knowledge of their own societies' past and of earlier phases of other societies. The approach of Marx and Weber to sociological problems can serve as example. Marx tried to throw into better relief what he regarded as the most urgent problem of his time by presenting his own time as a stage between the past and possible futures. Weber again and again tried to clarify general sociological problems by means of evidence from past ages and from societies at an earlier stage of development.

II

The narrowing of the sociologists' focus of attention and interest to the immediate present, in some respects, undoubtedly represents progress in the development of the discipline. Sociologists are now much better able than before to study and in some cases solve short-term problems of their own society in a resonably reliable manner. Concentration on present issues has found a striking expression in an almost explosive profusion of empirical sociological investigations, partly but by no means only of the statistical variety.[1]

III

The immediate present into which sociologists are retreating, however, constitutes just one small momentary phase within the vast stream of humanity's development, which, coming from the past, debouches into the present and thrusts ahead toward possible futures. It is not surprising, therefore, that the recent abundance of empirical sociological inquiries went hand in hand with an improverishment in other respects. One of its symptoms was the pronounced cleavage between the great majority of these empirical inquiries and the inquiries now presented as sociological theory. This cleavage is already foreshadowed in the work of Max Weber, whose action theory, which is set out in the early parts of *Economy and Society*, is often hardly noticeable in his empirical work. For a time the theoretical work of Talcott Parsons and, as its counterpart, that of neo-Marxist sociologists, held the centre of the theory stage. But the theoretical eminence of these two schools of thought has not been matched by a rich harvest of empirical work inspired by these two types of theories and at the same time capable of testing their cognitive value. The real significance of the split into two camps, Parsonians and neo-Marxists, which with some transitions and fusions has determined much of the teaching of sociological theories in the universities of this world for quite a while, is political rather than scientific. The two types of theories represent a projection into the social sciences of the political division in society at large between conservatives and liberals on the one hand and socialists and communists on the other. No wonder that in sociology much empirical work is done without reference to theory and that many theoretical discussions proceed without any reference to empirical work. It is as if scientific researchers in the field of physics were divided into followers of a conservative or liberal and socialist or communist theory of physics. There is obviously something very wrong with a scientific discipline if its leading representatives allow political sentiment to dominate their scientific work. In sociology one can observe again and again that what seems at first to be a serious scientific and learned discussion conducted on a very high level of abstraction reveals itself on closer inspection as a complex superstructure erected in order to attack or give support to specific positions on the contemporary spectrum of social ideals and beliefs. Scientific detachment in such cases can hardly disguise the partisanship underneath; nor can the façade of a scientific theory conceal the underlying extra-scientific commitment, although the latter can often only be recognized if one is able to penetrate the blur of an idiosyncratic terminology.

Thus Parsonianism and neo-Marxism, as the two most prominent schools of theoretical thought in sociology, fought out an attenuated version of the class struggle within the setting of an academic discipline. The intellectual edifice of these two schools of thought did not really represent scientific theories in the sense in which this word is used in the older sciences. Though it may now be forgotten, physics and biology too had to fight a long battle of emancipation from extra-scientific beliefs. Galileo is still remembered as an exponent of the struggle of physics for autonomy from powerful extra-scientific ideals, in that case particularly of the religious type. As far as can be seen, representatives of sociological theories, and indeed of theories in the human sciences generally, are as yet hardly aware that an analogous struggle for autonomy still lies ahead of them. But in their case the principal fight for emancipation has the character of a struggle for autonomy from the political and social ideals of the day.

IV

The human population has undergone an unplanned process of growth, in more than purely numerical terms and in spite of all fluctuations. Throughtout history, it has been divided into different groups, into survival units of one kind or another. These survival units have also grown in size. From small bands of twenty-five to fifty members, perhaps living in caves, humans coalesced into tribes of several hundred or several thousand members, and nowadays more and more into states of millions of people. Their changing size has changed the structure of these social units. The means

of control – of external control as well as of self-control – required for the
survival and integrity of a social unit of thirty people are different from
the means of control required for the survival and integrity of a social unit
formed by millions of people. The whole way of life of humans has changed
in the course of this process. One can see here in a nutshell, as it were, why a
theory of society prompted by different political ideals of twentieth-century
industrial societies and presented as a universal theory of human societies can
have only very limited cognitive value. Transitions from smaller to larger
units of integration occur today under our very eyes. I do not think that sociological theories without a developmental framework can be of much help in
elucidating the sociological problems presented by such changes, either on the
theoretical or the empirical level. As long as theories prevail that abstract from
the diachronic as well as from the dynamic character of societies, it will not be
possible to close the great gap that exists today between this kind of theoretical design and empirical sociological research.

The understanding of human societies requires, it seems to me, testable
theoretical models which can help to determine and to explain the structure
and direction of long-term social processes – i.e. in the last resort, the development of humanity. I do not think, moreover, that theories of this type can
be of use only in the field of sociology. A unifying developmental frame of
reference without ideological encrustations, without, for instance, any built-
in postulate of a necessarily better future, could also be of use in the other
human sciences. The range of explanations is unduly narrowed if inquiries are
focused on contemporary problems. One cannot ignore the fact that every
present society has grown out of earlier societies and points beyond itself to a
diversity of possible futures. If we immure sociological problems in static
typologies and static concepts of structure and function, we neglect the
intrinsic dynamics of human societies.

V

A number of universal concepts that indicate the properties common to all
societies are also required for the construction of process models, that is,
models of the development of humanity. Where the investigation of processes
as such constitutes the focus of the research task, however, the universals
acquire a different cognitive status and value than is the case where timeless
law-like regularities stand in the centre. In the latter case, the discovery of
universals is the highest research aim, while in the case of process models it
constitutes only an auxiliary tool for the construction of process models.
Moreover, in the case of process universals, the researchers must be certain
that they are genuine universals, that they refer to the least differentiated as
well as to the most differentiated societies. General law-like regularities or

typologies abstracted from the researcher's observations of his own society and presented as universals are in that case not of much use.

VI

It might be useful to discuss an example of the type of universals that play a central role in the construction of process models. In all possible societies, people who belong to a group with regard to which they say 'we' have to fulfil a specific set of elementary functions for each other and for the group as a whole if they are to survive as a group. I need not consider here all these elementary functions but shall give a few examples. Usually interwoven and certainly interdependent, they are often conceptualized as strands or spheres of social development. In many cases, one of them is presented as the sole motive force of social development. Ideas as the driving force, class struggle as the driving force are obvious examples. Multifunctional and, in that sense, nonreductive process models are still to come. I cannot and need not in this context give a fuller account of the variegated patterns of their interrelationship. Nor do I need to argue here with the assumption that this interrelationship, throughout this development, is always the same. What I shall do is give a short diagnostic summary of some of the elementary functions and then some examples which, I hope, will bring them to life.

It was Karl Marx who identified the first of these elementary functions which members of a group have to perform satisfactorily if they are to survive as a group. Traditionally it was called the 'economic' function. And it is perhaps not necessary to break with this tradition, but there can be no doubt that the term 'economic' is imprecise. If a long-term development is the frame of reference, one has to distinguish very clearly between a stage of development in which economic functions are performed by groups of economic specialists and a stage of lesser differentiation where everyone must fulfil economic functions in a nonspecialized way. To put it at its simplest, one can say that one of the elementary universals of human groups is the provision of food and other basic wherewithals of life.

The second of these survival functions is that of control of violence or, in a somewhat wider sense, the function of conflict management in its two aspects: control of violence within a group and control of violence in the relationship between different survival groups. Both in the case of economic functions and in that of violence control functions one has to distinguish between stages of social development where the same persons who perform economic functions also perform violence control functions – where, in other words, these functions are not yet performed by specialists – and stages of development where economic functions on the one hand and conflict management functions on the other are performed by different persons, i.e. by specialists. There are, of course, many transitional stages. By and large, however, one can say that the condition in which specialists are entirely set free from the performance of other vital functions, among them that of food production, and where their central social function is confined to that of violence control and conflict management within and between groups, is identical with the social formation we call a 'state'. Perhaps it needs to be added that I am not concerned with the question whether it is good or bad that such a specialization emerged. I am simply concerned with the clarification of a demonstrable fact. The emergence of social specialists for violence control is a good example of the interwoveness of the changing patterns of the way in which these vital functions are performed in human societies.

Specialists in violence control can emerge in a society only if its members produce more food than is needed for the survival of the food producers and their families. However, in the long run, the regular production of surplus food requires a comparatively high level of physical security for the producers of food. It requires the effective protection of whatever it is – livestock, fertile acres, rich fishing grounds – against marauders. In their development, advances toward specialization of economic and of violence control functions are reciprocal.[2]

The excavations of Sumerian towns offer a number of clues to the stages that led to the development of permanent monopolies of violence. Presumably, this occurred in conjunction with the parallel development, quite indispensable in that case, of a monopoly of taxes. Excavations indicate, for example, that, from a certain period on, Sumerian settlements were surrounded by solid and undoubtedly also very expensive walls.[3] Viewed together with other evidence, this fact indicates that here – and possible for the first time – human societies attained the organizational stage of city-states. They produced enough food not only to support those building and guarding the walls, but also to feed the priests in their temples, the monopolistic specialists controlling the basic funds of knowledge of a group, especially knowledge of the ways of the spirit world,[4] as well as the monopolistic controllers of violence, the princes in their palaces and the warriors, the controlled specialists in the use of violence. Among other tasks, the latter guarded and coordinated the labourers in the fields, the building and maintenance of the vulnerable irrigation canals and of the city walls, the palaces, and the temples. From smaller settlements, perhaps with the character of village-states centred on a temple, the settlements we now know as Sumerian grew into the first type of large-scale organization, with a greater differentiation of specialized functions. They grew into walled city-states, each with a large temple and a palace organization. These Sumerian city-states, like the Greek city-states of a later age, fought with each other for centuries an indecisive struggle for hegemony until they all were conquered by, and to some extent subjected to the rule of, a stronger state from outside.

In the more advanced societies of our own age, groups of economic specialists are among the most powerful groups and, in some cases, the most powerful groups of all. The prevalence of specialized economic activities in many contemporary societies has given rise to a sociological theory according to which the specialized economic sphere is at all times the only basic sphere of society. All other aspects of society, it seems, can be explained in terms of their economic development. Conflicts between groups of economic specialists, according to this theory, are to be considered as the universal driving force of the development of humanity, and monopolization of economic functions, of the means of production, can be regarded universally as the main source of social power.

This would suggest that throughout the development of humanity, as in more recent times, economic specialists monopolizing the means of production constitute the most powerful, the actual ruling groups of society. However, whether or not that is a correct diagnosis of the distribution of power chances in contemporary industrial societies, it most certainly is not a correct diagnosis of the distribution of power in earlier state-societies. There, with very few exceptions, the principal ruling groups were warriors and priests. In one guise or another these groups of specialists, as allies or as rivals, formed the ruling groups of state-societies for the greater part of their development. Economic specialists, such as merchants, usually ranked lower than nobles and priests and could until very recently rarely match the power and wealth of their leading groups such as kings or popes (in countries such as Russia, Germany and Austria, not until 1914). One cannot help asking which structural characteristics of human societies are responsible for the long-lasting dominance in most state-societies of these two groups of specialists, of warriors and priests. It certainly suggests that the attempt at presenting a universal theory of society, if one's vision is foreshortened by preoccupation with short-term, present-day causes, increases the risk of failure. The discovery of the economic conditions of social change was a great advance, the reduction of all social changes to economic conditions a great impediment to further advance. With regard to the distribution of power in a society one can say that monopolization of the means of violence or of the means of orientation, that is of knowledge and particularly of magic-mythical knowledge, plays no less a part as a source of power than the monopolization of the means of production. Neither the social function of violence management and control nor that of knowledge transmission and acquisition can be simply reduced to, and explained in terms of, the economic functions of a society. All three, and a number of others which need not be considered here, are equally basic and irreducible.

A word about knowledge may be of some use here. Knowledge in particular has never quite recovered from the curse put on it by Marx, who attributed to it the ontological status of a mere superstructure. To perceive its basic role in human societies one need only think of a 'knowledgeless' group – that is, a group to which no knowledge has been transmitted from previous generations – in order to recognize the basic social function of knowledge. The idea of such a group evidently is an unrealizable thought experiment, but it demonstrates quite clearly that human groups, which certainly cannot survive without food or protection from physical violence, also cannot survive without knowledge. Nonhuman organisms, to a greater or lesser extent, are capable of finding their food 'instinctively', that is, with the assistance of innate steering mechanisms, and perhaps in conjunction with a comparatively small degree of learned knowledge. Human beings, on the other hand, are entirely incapable of orienting themselves without learned knowledge: except at the infant stage, they cannot find the right food or even any food at all without transmitted knowledge. The human need for knowledge, in other words, is as elementary as the need for food. Like the means of satisfying other elementary needs, those of satisfying other people's requirements of knowledge can be monopolized. In the form of a monopoly, the means of orientation, the appropriation of the means of satisfying the human requirements for knowledge can serve as a basis for power inequalities.

One further elementary function should be mentioned. Other social organisms occasionally possess innate self-control that make it possible for them to live together in groups without destroying themselves or each other. Human beings, however, have no such inborn restraints. They must acquire the patterns of self-restraint indispensable for social life through learning while living with others. Accordingly, individual learning of a social pattern of self-restraint or a civilizing process of sorts is also one of the universal elementary survival functions which one encounters in every human group. One of the social institutions that performs this function can be found in the initiation rites of less complex human groups. They represent an early form of civilizing individual group members. Group pressure toward the exercise of self-constraint, like all the other elementary functions I have mentioned, can also be monopolized and utilized as a source of power and status differentials, and thus as a means of domination and exploitation. Initiation rites, for example, are not only a means of producing a specific pattern of self-constraint, but also important episodes in the concealed or overt power struggle between the generations. This elementary function too is irreducible. The learning of self-constraint is certainly not possible without simultaneous fulfilment of the other functions mentioned before, including the control of violence. However, they in turn require individual patterns of self-control.

These four elementary functions do not constitute the entire range of possible functions. There are others. Those I have mentioned provide, nonetheless, examples of universals of social development that can be empirically tested and, if necessary, corrected.

VII

I would like to illustrate by means of an example the cognitive value of the concept of basic social functions. Marx attempted to understand the whole dynamic of social development theoretically by reference to a single common denominator. He considered the monopolization of the means of production – for instance, the means of satisfying hunger – as the source of social inequalities and as the root of all other inequalities. He regarded the conflicts arising from this monopolization of chances to satisfy 'economic' needs as the primary and perhaps even as the exclusive driving force of social development.

As a result, he perceived a ruling class of feudal warriors as a stratum more or less of the same type as a ruling class of commercial or industrial entrepreneurs. He did not attach great relevance to the difference between those who owed their 'economic' power to their class and those who owed it to their capital. Yet, the French slogan *nul terre sans seigneur* was really a class slogan. It meant that no one who did not belong to the warrior nobility, and thus was skilled in the use of physical violence in order to enforce obedience, had the right to own land. In a number of cases, custom reinforced by class solidarity denied peasants and other nonprivileged groups the possession and use of the weapons of the upper classes.

The recognition of the role of structural conflicts as a motor of change was a gain for the diagnostic capacity of social scientists, the restriction to intrastate conflicts of an economic nature an impediment.

Marx saw more clearly what feudal and entrepreneurial groups had in common than he saw the structural differences. He noted that, since both could monopolise the economic means of production, both acquired power chances that allowed them to exploit other groups. Yet he failed to ask, and therefore found no reason to explain, why those in possession of power monopolies consisted of a nobility of warriors in the one case and relatively pacified merchants in the other.

Sociologists defeat their own ends if they neglect such differences, if they omit, for instance, to ask why classes of economic specialists did not always play the same central part in the power structure of their society that they play today. It is easy to see that the social characteristics of those groups which formed the most highly placed establishment in a state-society and which therefore presumably possessed the greatest power resources has changed in a highly specific manner since the days when, probably in ancient Sumer, societies with the distinguishing characteristics of a state first emerged from pre-state societies. Since that time, between five and six thousand years ago until fairly recent times, two groups of social functionaries, with relatively few exceptions, held the position as the highest ranking, most powerful, and often as the richest groups in the status hierarchy of state-societies. These two main establishements were, broadly speaking, groups of priests and groups of warriors; those who ruled the temple and those who ruled the palace (the princes, kings, and emperors at the head of their courts in conjunction with, and sometimes deposed by, oligarchic groups of warrior nobles).

There were exceptions. One of them was the city-state. The Phoenician, Greek, and, later, the Italian and Dutch city-states are examples. Sea-states, that is, states whose principal military establishment was based on ships, generally had ruling groups with different social characteristics from those of the ruling groups of land-states, that is, states whose principal military forces were land armies. England since the time of Henry VIII as well as the Netherlands are obvious examples. The development in China also followed a different course. The officials of the civil administration at the imperial court, and throughout the country, a class of land owners with administrative functions, succeeded relatively early in wresting power from the warriors. Sometimes called 'gentry', sometimes 'mandarins', they formed throughout the vast country a fairly closely knit hierarchical network with a unified cultural tradition and a strong sense of their own superiority in relation to all other groups. Thus, in China a non-military social formation, which for the maintenance of its high power ratio and its high status required from its members a fairly high level of self-control, replaced for hundreds of years the warriors who, wherever they formed the ruling establishment, ruled more directly and also were ruled more directly by means of pressures from without. Moreover, during the period roughly corresponding to the Middle Ages of the West, the ruling officials of China developed what was probably the most advanced state organization of the time, which then slowly rigidified and declined.

In the majority of states, however, the greatest power and status chances, in some cases well into the twentieth century, were in the hands of either warriors or priests, or of both as allies *and* rivals. The relationship between these two establishments, throughout the long years of their supremacy, was basically ambivalent and varied a great deal. At times they competed for power, as in ancient Egypt and in the medieval West, where the struggle between emperor and pope offers a telling example. More recently, the conflict between the Shah and the mullahs in Iran offers another. In other cases they became allied in their endeavour to ensure law and order through the obedience of other groups. Compared with the status of princes, nobles, and high priests, the status of merchants in the past rarely surpassed the second or third rank. This fact in itself can serve as a fairly reliable indication that their power chances too were generally smaller than those of warriors and priests.

In the course of the nineteenth and twentieth centuries, two groups of economic specialists, first the middle-class entrepreneurs and managers and later, to a lesser extent, representatives of the organized working classes, in a growing number of state-societies, gained ascendancy over the two traditional ruling establishments. Before that time one or other of the latter (or both) had usually held a dominant position in the estate assemblies wherever they existed. Now representatives of the groups of economic specialists, organized in the form of mass parties, gained the ascendancy in the state assemblies, which changed their character: estate assemblies gave way to parliaments. One should perhaps not close too soon the question of which structural changes are reflected in this development from state-societies – where for a long time warriors or priests (or both) contributed the most powerful and the highest ranking establishments – to more recent state-societies – where nobles and priests lost their privileged status and two antagonistic, yet interdependent economic classes gained the ascendancy.

Moreover, a new development has occurred in very recent times. Yet another social formation with different social characteristics now frequently exceeds in power and status the establishments of the two groups of economic specialists, while often remaining in a latent condition of competition with them. I am referring to men and women who are professional politicians and members of a party establishment. Both in one-party and in multiparty states, career politicians (i.e. political specialists) possess at the present time in many state-societies a better chance of gaining access to the state's central monopolies and to the concomitant power chances than do military, priestly or economic specialists. The latter groups, wherever they are organized and powerful enough, are competing for power chances with party politicians.

26

Renate Rubinstein

Elias may well be described as an incurable sociologist, who was always ready to regard human activities *sub specie sociologiae*. Still, his interests were by no means confined to sociology in any narrow sense. He could be equally enticed by sports, music, art, politics, and literature. Throughout his life he was an avid reader of novels as well as poetry; and he also wrote poetry himself. In 1987, his German publisher Suhrkamp brought out a collection of his poems, mostly written in German. That volume was dedicated 'to Renate, in pain and joy'.

Renate Rubinstein was one of his close friends in Amsterdam. Since his first visiting professorship in 1969, Elias had built up a circle of friends in the Netherlands, all many years younger than he, whose company he enjoyed. To this circle belonged some sociologists such as Bram van Stolk and Cas Wouters, but also other people. In 1984 Elias left Bielefeld and settled in Amsterdam, where he had decided to spend the remaining years of his life. One reason for that choice was that he found the city congenial, with a cosmopolitan atmosphere and convenient means of transport by train and plane to other parts of the world. At least as important, however, was the vicinity of people who knew and appreciated his work and with whom he maintained close and affectionate relationships.

The following text is the introduction that Elias wrote to the first book by Renate Rubinstein to be translated into German. Typically, he combined a character-ization of Renate's own work with a brief discussion of a more general issue: the difficulties encountered by writers from small language communities in the context of the larger and more dominant European nations.

One of Renate Rubinstein's special gifts is her ability to write about problems which move her deeply in such a way that everyone is moved by them. To achieve this she has developed her own style: biting, irreverent, tender and direct, and her own form: the short essay – sometimes only a vignette – which shines a spotlight on a particular issue. There are also, from time to time, landscape descriptions, evocations of atmospheres, prose poems. But from the many short pieces, which sometimes seem to wander back and forth without a central theme, people emerge, people in a story and, most sharply of all, Renate Rubinstein herself.

That many of these pieces were originally written for her weekly column in a large-circulation Dutch newspaper may seem curious to German readers. Journalists – especially female ones – seldom write week-in, week-out about problems that happen to concern them personally. On the contrary, the person usually disappears behind what is written. Not to allow this to happen, and nevertheless to address a very wide circle of readers, is Renate Rubinstein's special art. From the mosaic of short pieces, a picture of a woman after a divorce emerges with a rare force and directness – a personal fate which finds resonance in our mobile world, where many people face the task of coming to terms with separation from a person they love. In the original language – Dutch – the impression is probably stronger. But much of the urgency, the intensity of the experience, doubtless comes through in the German. We can also see that the taboo threshold has a different pattern in Dutch than in German. This is not the only reason why it is fruitful to make what is unique to one culture area of Europe accessible to people in another.

Part of what is recorded in this book could be called a love story. But if one wants to use that rather stale term, one has to add that it is a story bearing the stamp of the late twentieth century. In the age of Freud, and with a further advance of women's emancipation in full swing, such a relationship has, in some respects, a different character than it had in earlier times. The elemental force of the feelings has not diminished; nor has the suffering. But the Romantic aura has vanished. The man is neither a hero nor a monster, nor is the woman a heroine – when the pain becomes too great she goes to a psychiatrist. Curiously, this does not mean that the poetry has been dispelled – from time to time it surfaces again, as in the mood of a dune landscape in which the woman has lost her spectacles and must search for them *alone*.

The singular art which is presented to us here is the art of an inspired journalist, the great essayist of a small country. Her parents were German, her, father Jewish. Fleeing from Germany, she herself lived for a short time in England, then, still a young girl, moved with her parents to Holland – a flight, as she writes, in the wrong direction. She is now wholly rooted in Dutch culture while enjoying the rank of a European writer or, in the literal sense, of a *femme du monde*. One can imagine that her name would have been widely known today, had her parents moved on westwards from England.

In the long years I have known her I have often thought about the problem which such a situation entails. The language of a small country restricts access to its writers and poets. What happens when highly-gifted people are tied to the cultural traditions of a small country? To be sure, Europeans are striving towards unity. Customs barriers have been lowered and relaxed, but the cultural barriers are as high as ever. This particularly affects the smaller countries. The large countries do exchange cultural assets – though still to a very limited extent. Holland has at present a very lively literature. Relatively little of it finds its way outside.

Perhaps one ought to think somewhat more about the problems which result from the fact that it is far more difficult for the cultural assets of smaller countries, being bound to their languages, to breach the cultural barriers of other nations, than it is for those of the larger nations. Paradoxically, the educated people of a small country like Holland are generally far better informed about what is going on in the large cultural centres. That can be felt in this book. English phrases, allusions to French plays, can clearly be presented to Dutch readers as a matter of course. And the greater freedom of a woman who can speak publicly about her personal problems seems to be a part of the Dutch climate. But that is precisely the enrichment one can enjoy by exchanging cultural assets across national frontiers. Literature, too, is often bound to national patterns of repression, of which one may perhaps become aware only through seeing that there are other patterns. This book gives many opportunities to reflect on such differences – especially as the common humanity underlying them emerges no less clearly.

27

THE CIVILIZING OF PARENTS

In Germany during the 1980s, Elias played a public role extending far beyond the field of professional sociology. His works were widely read and referred to by historians, art historians, and students of literature. He was also in demand as a guest speaker at conferences on topical issues. Thus he gave several lectures on ageing and dying, published in book form as *The Loneliness of the Dying*, which went through several editions and was soon translated into English (1985a). Another lecture, about changes in the relationships between parents and children, demonstrated his keen eye not only for age but also for gender relationships. At the same time, it showed his ability to apply the theory of the civilizing process to contemporary trends in a way that could appeal to a general public. And it gave him an opportunity to show that the contradictory views of the history of childhood by Philippe Ariès and Lloyd de Mause sprang from their biased reading of the evidence: both men let their own value judgements prevail over a more dispassionate analysis in sociogenetic terms.

I

In the course of the twentieth century we have seen the acceleration of a transformation in the relationship between parents and children which can be traced back to the early Middle Ages. In his thoughtful and empirically rich book, *Centuries of Childhood*, Philippe Ariès devoted a chapter to the discovery of childhood, and identified the period of this discovery as lying between the fourteenth and sixteenth centuries. When one looks at it more closely, it is easy to see that it concerns a long process – a process which is continuing. We are ourselves standing in the middle of it. This is not just because children individually are often a mystery to their parents, since to a certain extent they have to be discovered by them, but above all because the social state of knowledge about the problems of children is, even today, still quite incomplete. Despite a growing literature, in many respects we do not completely understand how we can help children enter into such a complex and unchildish society as ours, one which demands a high degree of foresight and self-control; how we can help them survive the inescapable individual civilizing process of becoming adult, without stunting their chances for pleasure and joy. However, this discovery of childhood most certainly concerns not just an advance in knowledge about children and understanding of children, but also something else. We could perhaps characterize it as the necessity for children to live their own lives, a type of life which in many respects is distinct from that of adults, even though the two are interdependent. The discovery of childhood is ultimately the discovery of its relative autonomy, in other words, the discovery that children are not little adults, but only gradually become adult in the course of an individual social civilizing process which differs according to the developmental state of the society's pattern of civilization.

Events such as the Year of the Child are actually the recognition of this right of children, to have their particular identity as children respected and understood. This, too, is a human right. However, new attempts to do justice to this right are accompanied by particular difficulties. When one speaks of the human rights of oppressed human groups, one usually has clear boundaries in view – the groups are distinct from each other. But with children it concerns a group of a completely different sort, an age group – it concerns children of parents, little people who are completely dependent on adults but are on the road to independence. This is also a social group. The behaviour of parents and children in their relations with each other is a form of group behaviour, which is always co-determined by a specific, socially-determined code, and cannot be understood simply in terms of individual roles. In the case of children, it concerns a group of human beings whose behaviour, rights and obligations are always brought under normative social control. Initially these human beings are completely dependent on adults, at least on their parents. The Year of the Child symbolizes the fact that in today's societies children, despite their dependency, are recognized as having, to a very high degree, their own unique character as a particular group of members of this society.

II

This is not only something relatively new in the history of humanity in general and children in particular, it also generates specific, new problems for the relations between parents and children. It demands of parents, who have far greater power chances than children, a degree of caution and restraint, of civilization, if we may express it so, which far exceeds the degree of self-control and restraint socially required of parents in earlier epochs – if such restraint was ever expected of parents at all. Since, in addition, there is usually a high degree of emotional engagement at play in relations between parents and children, the social proscription to allow children a considerable degree of autonomy leads to a peculiar paradox and a situation which is not at all easy to manage. In earlier times, and often still up to the present day, the relationship between parents and children was a clear authority relation; it was a relationship between a person giving orders and one obeying them. As such, it was subject to social norms, and to a large extent it was also understood as such by the participants themselves. As an authority relation with a decidedly unequal distribution of power chances between parents and children, the modes of behaviour which the realization of this relation demanded of the participating people were relatively simple and unambiguous. Parents were not only actually responsible for the decisions on their children's activities, it was at the same time also ordained as a social norm that this distribution of the power ratio – commands to the parents, obedience to the children – was good, correct and desirable, and not only from the standpoint of the parents, but also, so people saw it, from the standpoint of the children themselves. Today we are thoroughly sceptical about the notion that the unconditional authority of parents and the unconditional obedience of children is also the best, healthiest, most productive social arrangement from the standpoint of the children themselves. We grant children, to a far greater degree than before, a greater decision-making field, a greater degree of autonomy. In other words, developmental trends in this direction make themselves more strongly felt than ever before, even though in practice they have certainly often maintained the absolute authority of parents; and the same goes for the notion that this is the norm. In brief: we find ourselves in a transition period, in which older, strictly authoritarian, and newer, more egalitarian parent–child relations exist alongside each other, and which often coexist in one and the same family. The transition from a more authoritarian to a more egalitarian parent–child relationship produces, for both groups, a series of specific problems and, all in all, a rather high degree of uncertainty. I will say something more about these problems later.

But we cannot properly understand its character and its peculiarity if we concentrate our attention, with a more or less narrow intellectual horizon, exclusively on the current problematic of the parent–child relationship. This current problematic is something emergent in the course of social development. We cannot understand it, let alone explain it, if we do not have a vivid picture of how different the form taken by the current parent–child relationship is, in many respects, from that of previous periods.

III

Accordingly, I would like to reconstruct, as far as possible in the limited space, the broad contours of the civilizing process of the parent–child relationship. Only when one has a picture of this developmental trend in view does one gain a more vivid understanding of the particularity and the problems of the parent–child figuration in the developed industrial nations of our time. In reconstructing this aspect of the civilizing process, I will make use, as I have already done in other cases,[1] of a series of snapshots. In themselves, each of them can be misunderstood as a description of a state. But if one sees them as 'stills' in a movie, as fragments of a process, then with their help it is not difficult to see the broad line of the development.

Today the treatment of children in earlier times, especially infants, is in many respects difficult to imagine. There is an abundance of evidence for it, but the facts which it refers to are unwelcome today. Our feelings bristle, our consciences resist the insight. At first glance the facts can also appear contradictory. One sees no order in them; and this is also how they are usually written about, as if it concerns a heap of facts without their own order.

Nevertheless, there is a clear order in the sequence. The model of the civilizing process can serve as a guide. What is decisive is how one conceives the functions children have for parents. There are social relations in which it is an advantage for parents to have many children. For farmers with sufficient land, for example, children usually represent cheap labour power. In such cases, they often begin early to help with work, and they may produce more than they consume.

Particularly in urban societies, although not only in these, simple families often have no use for more and more children. Everywhere in the history of urban societies, from antiquity to the European eighteenth century, and perhaps still further, we thus encounter accepted methods of infanticide. Children came, they cried, they generated work, and the parents had no use for them, often enough no food. Eliminating little children is easy. In ancient Greece and Rome we hear time and time again of infants thrown onto dungheaps or in rivers. Exposing children was part of everyday life. People were used to it. Until the late nineteenth century there was no law against infanticide. Public opinion in antiquity also regarded the killing of infants or the sale of children – if they were pretty, to brothels, otherwise as slaves – as self-evident. The threshold of sensibility among people in antiquity – like those of Europeans in the Middle Ages and the early modern period – was quite different from that of the present day, particularly in relation to the use of physical violence. People assumed that they were violent to each other, they were attuned to it. No one noticed that children required special treatment. In a recent study it was said:

Infanticide during antiquity has usually been played down despite literally hundreds of clear references by ancient writers that it was an accepted, everyday occurrence. Children were thrown into rivers, flung into dung-heaps and cess trenches, 'potted' in jars to starve to death, and exposed on every hill and roadside, 'a prey for birds, food for wilds beasts to rend' (Euripides, *Ion*, 504). To begin with, any child that was not perfect in shape and size, or cried too little or too much, or was otherwise than is described in the gynaecological writings on 'How to Recognize the Newborn that is Worth Rearing,' was generally killed. Beyond this, the first-born was usually allowed to live, especially if it was a boy. Girls were, of course, valued little, and the instructions of Hilarion to his wife Alis (1 BC) are typical of the way these things were discussed: 'If, as may well happen, you give birth to a child, if it is a boy let it live, if it is a girl, expose it.' The result was a large imbalance of males over females which was typical of the West until well into the Middle Ages . . . [2]

It was similar regarding the role of drives in the relations between parents and children. Whether it concerned feelings of love or hate, tenderness or aggression, they all used to play a far greater and more open role in interactions between parents and children, they were far more untamed and spontaneous, not only on the part of children, but also that of parents – corresponding to the prevailing standard of civilization – than is the case today.

Today it can happen that a mother experiences a sort of shock – a baby shock – when she finds herself confronted by the untamed animalism of her young child. Only the child's smallness and relative weakness conceals the intensity of infants' greed and the strength of their desire from parents. The fact that children have quite strong instinctual needs, prefigurative forms of sexuality, was only brought to adult consciousness in the twentieth century through Freud's scientific discoveries. For many people this has remained an unwelcome message to the present day. The preceding great spurt in rationalization had largely hidden this fact from people's consciousness. Particularly in the eighteenth and nineteenth centuries, but also before that, among adults human sexuality was increasingly placed behind the scenes of social life. The growing reserve which adults had to impose on interaction with each other, worked into their interiors – it became a self-constraint, and also rose like an invisible wall between parents and children. Corresponding to this unarticulated shame among adults concerning their own sexuality, the notion spread that children are human beings who are still free of the sin of sexuality, who in this respect are as innocent as angels. Because in reality no child lived up to these ideal expectations, parents in the seclusion of their own homes always had to ask themselves why precisely their children had characteristics which did not measure up to the angelic character which was supposed to be normal for all children. Perhaps it is because of this discrepancy between a socially accepted, but completely fantastic ideal image of children and children's thoroughly non-angelic, more animalistic, at least passionate and wild nature, that the punishments which people in this period regarded as necessary disciplinary measures were particularly harsh. This sequence in the reflective shifts – the first, in the course of which adults tried to conceal the passionate and strongly animalistic character of children's nature in connection with the stronger control over their own animalistic impulses, and the second, in the course of which, with the help of scientific reflection, the particularity of children and, as an aspect of that, their initially weakly domesticated animalistic drives, was rediscovered – has to be kept in sight, if we wish to understand why in earlier epochs the relationship between parents and children in many respects took a different form from more recent times.

IV

For a long time, the relation between parents and children was determined to a large extent by traditional customs, which left a great deal of room for spontaneous drive-impulses among both parents and children. Rules which were based on scientific or scientifically-presented reflection played hardly any role in the formation of the relationship between parents and children. Today it is not entirely easy for us to put ourselves in a situation in which parents are almost completely uninfluenced by knowledge about the particular nature of their children, that is, about the differences between the personality structures of children and adults. Parents in ancient Greece and Rome, or in the Middle Ages, did not ask themselves, as is increasingly the case today: Am I making any mistakes in my relationship with my child? Will I damage them, if I do this or that? They conducted themselves spontaneously to a far greater degree, and were generally more influenced by what they felt themselves than by attempts to empathize with children, more influenced by what children meant to them than by thoughts on what they and their actions meant to children.

In this situation a circumstance came to light, which today is often concealed from view, namely the fact that the relation between parents and children is a relation of domination, one with a highly unequal balance of power. Children are initially as good as completely in the power of their parents; more precisely, the parents' power chances – compared with those of their children, particularly young children – are very great. In societies like ours there is hardly any other form of relationship in which the power differential between interdependent people is as great as that in the parent–child relation. Nonetheless, in this case, too, there is a reciprocity of power chances. It is not only that parents have power over children – normally children, and even new-born children, also have power over parents. They can call their parents to their aid by crying. In many cases, the birth of a child forces parents to re-arrange their lifestyle. If one asks why it is that children have considerable power over adults, one encounters again a situation referred to earlier: children have a function for parents. They represent the fulfilment of particular parental needs and wishes. I do not want to enter here into which parental needs the presence of children fulfils. It is sufficient to pose the question: what form does the parent–child relation take when children fulfil no needs or wishes for their parents? Today, thanks to a specific technological development, parents are able to decide whether and how many children they want to have. But in earlier societies parents usually produced children blindly, without any wish or need for a child or a further child. They had children, who had no function for them. These children, accordingly, also had limited power chances in relation to their parents, all power lay with the latter.

Earlier societies were generally more set up than industrial ones so that the people composing them would try to exploit their power chances to the last, relatively unconcerned about the destiny of subordinate people. They were then prepared to accept the same when fate turned against them.

We need to keep this relatively greater harshness of social life in view if we wish to understand the structure of the parent–child relation in societies like ancient Greece and Rome or the Middle Ages. What strike us as atrocities and inhumanity in the relations between parents and children in earlier times does not exclude the presence of parental love and affection for their children. But today a legend has become established which makes it look as if parental love and affection for their children is something more or less natural and, beyond that, an always stable, permanent and life-long feeling. In this case, too, a social 'should' is transformed into the notion of a natural 'is'. The exposure and killing of infants in earlier times was basically nothing other than a barbaric form of birth control. Particularly for the poorer strata in ancient, medieval and even early-modern urban societies, a high birth rate was a great burden. No wonder that in London one still found dying infants on dungheaps in the eighteenth century. Adults also imposed fewer restraints on their own drives in relation to children than is the case today. Mothers playing with their children's sexual organs is also today in some countries a widespread custom. That children witnessed their parents' sexual activity was self-evident in the enclosed quarters of the poorer groups in the population. That sexual games, whether it be children among each other – such as siblings who slept in the same bed – or between children and adults, often occurred, just as in ancient society, is easy to understand if we consider that for a long time the state did not concern itself with such occurrences, and that the participants developed no guilty consciences because of such acts.

Contemporary historians often speak in this context of the 'abuse' of children in earlier times. But that, too, is a projection of current standards onto societies which did not have the same living conditions. Children had a strong and quite physically expressed need for love. Today we cannot establish how far children in, say, antiquity, were willing, how far unwilling partners in adults' sexual games. That they often were involved, can hardly be doubted.

By nature children are so constituted that they can awaken delight and love in adults. How chubby, how coquettish they can be, how fiery their tenderness and their displays of love! But then they often change quite suddenly. They are fickle, they cry, are filthy, refuse cuddles, thrash about and fight like little wild animals. A contemporary poet has written:

> I cried
> half dead
> the neighbours
> rang
> why
> does the child cry?
> end
> of the blows[3]

But it is doubtful whether neighbours in earlier societies were always concerned when a child cried. For a long time, too, state authorities had neither laws nor executive organs to mobilize in the protection of children. What would prevent adults from allowing children to die when they got on their nerves or when they had insufficient food to eat? I will refrain from listing all the other aspects of childhood which used to be possible and which are no longer possible today.

V

In almost all societies in earlier times the ruling authority of parents was, as I said before, far more unlimited than is the case today. Historians have until quite recently devoted little thought to parent–child relations in earlier societies. Today the number of studies on this theme is growing, bringing much new material to light. The best-known is Philippe Ariès' *Centuries of Childhood*. The collection of articles edited by Lloyd de Mause, *The History of Childhood*, also contributes much to our knowledge of the parent–child relationship. Of the many German books on this theme I would like above all to mention Katharina Rutschky's *Schwarze Pedagogik* (Ullstein-Buch 1977). She lets the German pedagogues and philosophers of the late seventeenth century to the early twentieth century speak for themselves. Much of what they had to say is shocking and gruesome for the sensibilities of people living today. In her instructive introduction, she also points out the significance of a theory of civilization for an explanation of the transformations which have taken place in the parent–child relationship.

In fact, historical research on the change in the parent–child relations remains insecure, it remains impossible to understand or explain as long as one does not have the conceptual framework of a theory of the civilizing process in view. Without it, instead of seeking an explanation of the distinctiveness of earlier and current standards, it is difficult to resist the temptation to give free rein to one's feelings. Depending on the partiality of one's own sensitivities, one then gives priority either to the past over the present, or to the latter over the former. In this respect, Ariès and de Mause stand on opposite sides. Ariès works, to his detriment, with hardly any theoretical framework. De Mause limits himself to a purely psychogenetic theory, which he presents as absolutely autonomous. But how should the simultaneous transformation of the personality structure of many people be explained without reference to the society, the network of relations which many people form with each other? How can one make long-term psychic changes comprehensible and explain them without recourse to the associated long-term social changes? We are indebted to the authors of these two books for the material which they have made accessible; but in contrast to the heteronomous evaluations included in both cases, a word of warning and critique is in order. Ariès trusts in a better past, de Mause rages against those who tried to conceal the awful past, including Ariès. But in principle this is not the issue.

Even so, we can learn from such mistakes. Ariès sees, albeit in the light of his romantic bias, a side of the problem which emerged slowly in the civilizing spurt in the parent–child relation of the sixteenth and seventeenth centuries. I myself made this clear back in the 1930s, in *The Civilizing Process*. In medieval society, as well as in all earlier societies, children were part of the adult world. Nothing was kept hidden from them by parents or teachers. Parents had no secrets from children. Perhaps only the very richest could manage to give children their own beds. Children usually slept in their parents' bed. Occasionally we hear some complaint that children soiled their parents' bed, but most were used to it. Adult standards of regulating natural needs were certainly not identical with those of little children. But the distance between them was not as great as it is today. People also did not think of isolating them from adults by reserving their own room for them. We sometimes encounter children's rooms in the homes of the wealthy from around the sixteenth or seventeenth centuries.

As always, changes in the use of living space symbolized, in a very visible way, changes in human relationships, in this case the relationships between parents and children. Slowly during the early modern period, children were removed from the adult world and their lives isolated on their own island of youth within society. Children's rooms, schools, youth movements and not least student life are among their most salient symbols. *The Civilizing Process* includes some material which can serve an understanding of the growing distance between children and adults in the early modern period. Ariès perceived these changes. But he regarded them with a certain resentment:

> Henceforth it was recognized that the child was not ready for life, and that he had to be subjected to a special treatment, a sort of quarantine, before he was allowed to join the adults.
> This new concern about education would gradually install itself in the heart of society and transform it from top to bottom. The family ceased to be simply an institution for the transmission of a name and an estate – it assumed a moral and spiritual function, it moulded bodies and souls . . . Parents were no longer content with setting up only a few of their children and neglecting the others. The ethics of the time ordered them to give all their children, and not just the eldest – and in the late seventeenth century even the girls – a training for life. It was understood that this training would be provided by the school, an utterly transformed school, an instrument of strict discipline, protected by the law-courts and the police-courts . . . 'Those parents,' states a text of 1602, 'who take an interest in their children's education [*liberos erudiendos*] are more worthy of respect than those who just bring them into the world.' . . . Family and school together removed the child from adult society. The school shut up a childhood which had hitherto been free within an increasingly severe disciplinary system, which culminated in the eighteenth and nineteenth centuries in the total claustration of the boarding-school. The solicitude of family, Church, moralists and administrators deprived the child of the freedom he had hitherto enjoyed among adults.[4]

As is so often the case the romantic orientations, Ariès also sees above all what was good in the past, which can be set against what is bad in one's own time, and forgets the connections between these good aspects and that which even people at the time regarded as unbearably bad, if one perceives it. Medieval societies were – compared with our own – very violent. Apart from the periods of plague, in medieval societies there were children, like the able-bodied poor, in abundance. Parents left children more readily to their own devices and thus to their own fate.

They were societies full of contradictions, in which there was certainly no lack of acts of compassion and goodwill, but also in which many people – not least children – starved to death, beggars and cripples were a normal part of the landscape, and the ill and the aged were left to die. De Mause argues against Ariès:

> Ariès's central thesis is the opposite of mine: he argues that while the traditional child was happy because he was free to mix with many classes and ages, a special condition known as childhood was 'invented' in the early modern period, resulting in a tyrannical concept of the family which destroyed friendship and sociability and deprived children of freedom, inflicting upon them for the first time the birch and the prison cell.[5]

De Mause's own theory is, as he puts it himself, a psychogenetic theory of history. It does not lack in interesting references. But psychogenetic studies alone, without the closest connection with sociogenetic studies, are hardly suitable for revealing the structures of social processes. This is only possible with a theory of civilization which links psychogenetic and sociogenetic aspects to each other. It is not entirely easy to summarize briefly what the theory of civilization contributes to a clarification of the changes which over time have taken place in the relations between parents and children. Even the simple fact that in earlier times the authority of parents over children was much less circumscribed has civilizing implications.

VI

We can see some of the changes in the relations between parents and children quite well in the particular changes in housing conditions. I refer here to one of the studies in this area by Peter Gleichmann on 'The domestication of bodily functions'.[6] In earlier times it was possible, to a far greater extent than is the case today, to give free play to natural needs even in public. People were less ashamed of being seen engaged in these activities by other people.[7] Gleichmann illustrates the advances in thresholds of shame and embarrassment in this area with changes in living arrangements. To an increasing extent, these activities were removed from the view of other people. One step in this direction was their removal from courtyards and streets into the home. More and more, separate toilets, often in connection with a separate bathroom, became part of the normal fittings of a home, even in the homes of the poorer strata.

In the first shift, the sociogenetic feelings in this area were limited to the feelings of shame and embarrassment which people experienced when they were within sight, hearing and smell of people who were not part of their family.[8] Gradually it also became embarrassing for people to deal with their natural needs even within the perception of members of their own family. This possibly applied first for the older children within the perception of their parents; today it applies more and more also for parents within the perception of their children – in fact it applies to every individual person with the perception of every other person. This, too, is a sympton of a social transformation towards a reduction of inequalities, that is, a process of functional democratization.

Every little child, however, chafes unwillingly at these high thresholds of shame and embarrassment among adults. Without knowing it, they assail adults' taboos. They have to be taught that they have to be ashamed when they do not restrict their natural needs exclusively to those specialized places in the home where the individual is isolated. This civilizing process of the single child, the training in a quite high degree of individual self-regulation, usually lasts a number of years. In a society where the demands for individual self-regulation in relation to natural needs – and certainly not only in relation to these – are as high as in today's developed industrial societies, it lasts considerably longer than in simple peasant societies, where there is no complicated sewerage system to remove human excrement from people's sight and smell.

VII

In simpler societies the process of drive-transformation, in the course of which young children are brought from their free expression of drives to the level of drive regulation required by adult society, requires less time – the individual civilizing process is shorter; it is less difficult and less deep-rooted. The deeper and more fixed the isolating regulation of individuals' natural needs – and other elementary needs – is anchored in adults, the more frequently one encounters among them problems in adjusting to the unrestrained way in which young children give free play to their needs. The increase in the distance between the socially-demanded adult level of individual drive-regulation, and the animalistic spontaneity of young children's expression of their drives, produces changes in the relations between parents and children. The domestication of the natural needs, which in the developed industrial states has developed into a complete isolation of individual people engaging in these activities, is certainly only one aspect of a far more comprehensive civilizing process. But it illustrates quite graphically the fact that many problems of current parent–child relations are problems of civilization.

VIII

In the areas of other, more animalistic aspects of human life one encounters, in the course of this change, even within the family, this tendency to increasing isolation of the individual. Think of the change in the socially-given domestic sleeping arrangements. In the Middle Ages and long after, it was quite self-evident for the majority of people that they shared their sleeping quarters with other people, naked, and that there was no specialized night clothing. Children and parents often slept together. One can separately trace – I have tried to show it in my book on civilization – how the shame about too-close bodily contact with people gradually grew. At the same time, the increase in social wealth made it possible to create living arrangements which corresponded to these sensibilities. It became possible, and in the course of time became regarded as normal, that every person had their own bed, first in well-off and then in all families. We can see in this process, in relatively simple form, the more comprehensive and not at all simple shift in individualization of more recent times. The development then went a step further in the same direction. In accordance with this sensibility, it became gradually necessary and economically possible for more and more families to consider a separate space for children as a normal part of a family home. In this way children were removed not only from their parents' bed, but also their bedroom. In well-off communities if finally became more accepted that each child should have not only their own bed, but also their own room. The unplanned development in this direction then generated specific problems. The early isolation of children, the distancing of children from close physical contact with parents, may have a certain function as preparation for the high degree of individualization which one expects today from adults in industrial societies; but young children have a very strong animalistic need for physical contact with other people than is generally accepted, which then gradually develops a more sexually-tinted character as they grow up. Adults' reserve about such contact – adults among whom awareness of the sexual colouring of close physical contact is fully developed – easily leads to the young child being weaned from such contact too early. I have already said that it is not very easy to say briefly why one cannot properly grasp the changes in the parent–child relationship without a theory of civilization. The example of changing living arrangements and associated changes in physical contact may in this respect throw some light on the significance of a linking theoretical model.

Today there is relatively little understanding of the fact that the problems of adolescents concern a combination of a biological process of maturation on the one hand, and a social process of civilization, the adaption to the current level of societal civilization on the other. People usually regard problems of growing up and in the parent–child relation, which have their origin in the changing combination of this biological and this individual–social process, simply as biological problems; in a word, people treat them as immutable and natural facts. This immediately deprives one of the possibility of finding a means of dealing with the difficulties which emerge for parents and children in the course of the long process of civilization. Human social life in the form of urban-industrial national states encloses each individual person in a complex network of longer, more differentiated chains of interdependence. In order to claim to be an adult in societies with such a structure, in order to be able to fulfil an adult's function in a way which is as meaningful for the individual is as it is for the society, it is necessary to have a very high degree of foresight, restraint of momentary impulses, for the sake of long-term goals and gratifications. It requires a degree of restraint which corresponds to the length and complexity of the chains of interdependence which, as an individual, one forms with other people. It requires, in other words, a high degree of self-regulating restraint of drives and affects. By nature, however, people possess only the biological potential for such restraint. They possess a biological apparatus which makes a control of drives and affects *possible*. The pattern and extent of this control, however, is in no way naturally given. They unfold in the development of the child in and through relations with other people. The biological potential is actualized in the course of an individual process of civilization, and according to the pattern and extent of socially-given drive- and affect-regulation. This is how the 'uncivilized' child becomes a more or less 'civilized' adult.

IX

The more complex and differentiated adult society becomes, the more complex is the process of civilizatory transformation of the individual, the longer it takes. Take, for example, the example of the relation between parents and children in a relatively simple nomadic group living mainly from hunting, such as an Eskimo group in the time when Eskimos still lived undisturbed by the expanding influence of industrial societies. Think of the transformation of young Eskimo boys and girls required to prepare them for their specific adult existence, and to secure the continued existence of the group. As little children Eskimo boys learn, during their play, all the skills they require to survive as adult hunters. They get little bows and arrows, and learn from an early age to help in the construction of boats or snow shoes and to maintain them. Girls learn to treat skins; they help from an early age to repair clothes and tents, on which the survival of the group depends no less than on the hunting catches. There is, then, a direct developmental line from children's games to adult practices. The structure of drives and affects which one requires for adult activity is not as far from that of children as is the case in the scientific industrial societies, the individual civilizing transformation of the person is less deep-rooted and temporally shorter. When our children play 'cowboys and Indians', it has hardly any direct significance for their future adult activity. It is a manifestation of the relative autonomy of childhood in our society. When Indian children play 'cowboys and Indians', if that were to happen, it would correspond to a very high degree with adult reality. At this level of social development the structure and pattern of self-control which a person requires as an adult – and the adult life of the simplest hunter–gatherer peoples most certainly requires a specific pattern of self-control – is less distant from children's play behaviour than the structure of self-control of our adult occupations is from the play behaviour of our children.

Similarly for the medieval warrior societies. The education of a knight in the twelfth or thirteenth centuries led far more directly from children's games to adult activity. Only in this way can we understand that we sometimes hear of a twelve-year-old Prince commanding an army. To a certain degree, a very young warrior could compensate for what he lacked in physical strength with agility and dexterity. When, then, a historian like Ariès complains about the fact that in our society children are no longer, as was earlier the case, perceived and treated as little adults, then he speaks without understanding of the changes in social structures which have taken place since the Middle Ages. He presents the view as if it were in principle possible to send children in urban-industrial states forth into the adult activities which dominate these societies in the same way as the medieval agrarian states dominated by priests and warriors. We can argue about whether or not today's pattern of school and university education is well suited to prepare young people for the specific adult existence, and thus also for the occupational activity which they antici-pate engaging in as adults in our society. Indeed, in many respects it is not. But one can hardly doubt that a much broader knowledge-horizon and a very differentiated capacity for self-control and regulation of drives and affects is necessary to maintain oneself as an adult in societies of this sort, and to be able to fulfil functions for oneself as well as for others. To attain this knowledge-horizon, this specialized ability and the corresponding level of self-control, requires a learning process lasting many years, which would certainly be senseless and useless if it did not go hand in hand with an extraordinary lengthening of individual life. In this respect it is irrelevant whether it concerns capitalist or communist industrial societies. What is said here applies to both.

Naturally it is possible for a limited number of people to drop out of these societies. They can set out travelling and manage one way or another. But ulti-mately this is only possible because the social product of these countries is so great, or, in other words, because these societies – as societies – are so rich, that they can maintain, directly or indirectly, a considerable number of non-working people, including in the form of unemployment benefits. In their habitus, drop-outs are also formed by the society from which they are seeking to escape, particularly by the civilizing transformation to which people maturing in these societies have been exposed in their families, school and university. Just the learning of reading, writing and arithmetic requires a considerably high degree of civilizing drive- and affect-regulation; it takes, even in its most elementary form, at least two to three years of childhood and mostly demands some activity in the context of a special institution outside the family – in a school, a symptom of the partial defunctionalization of parents.

X

Today one constantly encounters a series of stereotypical misunderstandings when one speaks, as is being done here, of long-term social processes, of which the introduction of an ever-longer preparatory period between childhood and adulthood is one example among many. One of these misunderstandings is the notion that the social change in this direction was brought about in a more or less planned and conscious way, perhaps on the basis of the ideas of some great men. I would like to call this the *voluntaristic misunderstanding*. Another is the notion that this change took place with the necessity of a naturally lawful progression, and thus had the character of a predetermined natural process. This is the *naturalistic misunderstanding*. The process model which can take place of this portrait of voluntaristic and naturalistic concepts of social processes can here only be indicated in brief. The process model which I have in mind rests on two premises: first, on the insight that social compulsions differ ontologically and in terms of their structure from natural compulsions; they rest primarily on the constraints which interdependent people, secondarily on the constraints which groups of people and non-human natural processes – with changing power ratios – exercise on each other. Second, the interweaving of the planned acts of many people results in a development of the social units which they form with each other, unplanned by any of the people who brought them about. But the people who are thus bound to each other constantly act intentionally, and purposefully from within the course of developments which they have not planned, and with results that feed back into the unplanned course of development. The process model which I have in mind encompasses as its nucleus a dialectical movement between intentional and unintentional social changes.

There are clear examples. From the early eighteenth century – in the puritan sects, already earlier – a wave of repression grew which was aimed especially at human sexuality. In contrast to the clerical tendencies directed against human sexuality, such as those originating in the teaching of St. Paul, in the eighteenth and nineteenth centuries the wave of sexual repression concerned a predominantly secular social shift in repression, a sort of inner wordly asceticism. It lasted, roughly speaking, up to the end of the nineteenth century and in its effects up to World War I. The emancipatory movements of social strata – and occasionally whole peoples – often went hand in hand with accompanying self-regulative, 'puritan', tendencies; and in many European states these two centuries were very decisive for the rising third estate, the bourgeoisie, in their conflict with the aristocracy, especially with the court aristocracy and the absolutist monarchs. The code of the court aristocracy was a code of good manners. It also subordinated people's love games to a certain regulation; but they had an open place in social life. The leeway granted to open speech and action in sexual affairs under the code of manners was quite great. The rising bourgeoisie opposed the code of good manners with a different pattern of civilization, a moral code. It was this code, which surrounded the whole area of sexuality as one of the largest danger zones of human existance with a differentiated, finely-meshed fence of prohibitions, the strict observation of which was treated as the touchstone of the bourgeois respectabilitity of families as well as their individual members. The strength of status anxieties with the rise of the secular moral code – as the correlate of the social ascent of bourgeois strata – which as motors of repression now encompassed the whole area of sexuality, can be seen in one of the most remarkable phenomena of their period, the growth of anxiety about masturbation, which from about the early eighteenth century took on almost epidemic proportions. A not inconsiderable specialist literature, written in part by doctors, warned people, and especially children, of the terrible dangers which accompanied this act. What can today usually be seen as the unconscious guilt fantasies surrounding this act were presented in this literature as reality and spread throughout society in this form. According to the beliefs of this period, the consequences of masturbation, which people presented as fact, included blindness, dehydration of the spinal cord, loss of all vital energies, and madness. The burden of punishments associated with this misdeed to which children were exposed grew accordingly. They were beaten, their hands were tied, their genitals barricaded, and so on. The memory of this epidemic of masturbation anxiety is just as useful an example of the heightening of the prohibitions of sexuality in the name of the bourgeois moral code, as it is of a period of unlimited adult authority over children. This epidemic was very clearly unplanned. It was connected with more general social changes which I have only been able to outline briefly with reference to the emancipatory movement and the status anxiety of rising bourgeois strata. In the course of the twentieth century, not least in connection with the establishment of bourgeois hegemony after the two world wars of this century, there set in from various sides a fairly conscious and intentional campaign against the increased sexual taboos of the previous period and its moral code. In the course of this change, many of the prohibitions of this moral code, which had often been regarded as eternal, particularly in the area of sexuality, began to loosen. Particularly the then-younger generation of the post-war years were unwilling to accept, sight unseen, traditional civilizing principles as injunctions of the then older generation, and began, after each war to an increasing degree, to experiment with other forms of sexual relations, not so much on the basis of existing principles, but in predominantly pragmatic manner, particularly with the use of new scientific and technical knowledge.

XI

In earlier cases, such as the period we call the 'Renaissance', the phase of experimentation with new relational forms and rules merged with a phase of consolidation, under the aegis of established groups which also wished to consolidate their domination. In relation to the present, the following diagnosis must suffice; it would be mistaken to present a prognosis. In this sense, that is, purely diagnostically, we can say that today in the more developed industrial states, many small groups, individual couples and individuals are experimenting with a rejection of traditional taboos, with the management of the problems they produce and the silent development of another code. It concerns, as far as we can see, primarily a relatively limited circle, particularly students, journalists, younger academics, artists, and so on, rather than the circle of bourgeois entrepreneurs or union officials and the respectable working class.

But what is taking place in these experimenting intellectual groups is certainly not a return to the period before the great wave of repression which reached its high point in the Victorian period – that is, a return to the standard of the sixteenth and seventeenth centuries. Quite the contrary, it concerns a selective loosening of Victorian taboos which, like the taboos on premarital intimacy or childhood masturbation, were recognized as excessive, functionless and, quite often, damaging. To a certain extent people have begun to dismantle the all too rigid walls which intervened between people's bodies, and the view that allowed contact with the naked body of another person – outside the family and even within it – to appear as a danger zone. Mothers have rediscovered the courage to pick up their babies and cuddle them, as well as the joys of that experience. Young parents and their children play naked on the beaches with each other.

But when we speak of these waves of informalization,[9] it is easy to overlook the fact that they take place in highly complex societies which demand a very precise regulation of people in their relations with each other in many areas. What are disappearing are many of the symbols of authority and formal indications of respect, which in earlier times served as symbols of authority, and also as a means of securing parental authority. The slow decline of the ostentatious attitudes and symbols of respect in relations between children and parents is clearly symptomatic of the reduction of parental authority, of a lessening of inequality in relations between parents and children. This is the unplanned outcome of broader multi-faceted changes in the more developed state-societies, which I cannot discuss here. But one of the factors at play deserves to be mentioned in this regard. It indicates, with particular urgency, how little this rejection of the rules and prohibitions of Victorian morality, perceived as outdated and functionless, concerns to return to the standard of the pre-Victorian period. This is the increasing renunciation by parents of physical violence as a means of disciplining their children. Such renunciation is partly demanded by state legislation, partly self-imposed on the basis of growing sensitivity about the use of physical violence in human relations. But this precisely shows how complex the civilizatory change in our time is. A loosening of the barriers of respect in the relations between parents and children, that is, an informalization, goes hand in hand with a tightening of the prohibition of the use of physical violence in family life. And this applies not only to the relations between adults and children within the family; it also applies in the relation between adults and children in general, particularly to those of teachers and children at school.

This relatively violence-free education has far-reaching consequences for the personality structure of adolescents. They are too numerous to discuss here, but the reference to them is particularly important because the observable informalization, the relative loosening of Victorian rituals and taboos is quite often understood as a loosening of individual self-discipline. Certainly such signs of loosening exist in our times as much as in earlier days, and perhaps they are particularly prominent in a period of experimentation with new forms of social relations. But quite often we forget the fact that the developmental trend in the clearly more complex, more strictly organized and to a large degree more pacified societies of our day demands a higher degree of differentiated self-control from individuals than ever before. That the informalization of the parent–child relationship and the loosening of traditional taboos in inter-generational relations goes hand in hand with a heightening of the taboos against violence in relations between parents and children, and demands – perhaps even forces – a higher degree of self-control on both sides, is one of many examples of the complexity of the civilizing movement in our time.

XII

At the same time this indicates that the changes in the relations between people in their capacity as parents and children, or even as husbands and wives – in short, as members of a family – are quite inseparable from the changes in the relations between people as inhabitants of a city or as citizens of a state. Family relations are often presented as the foundation of all human social relations. But this is a misunderstanding. The structure of the family, the socially-given form of the relation between man, woman and child, changes in connection with, and corresponding to, the larger society it is part of. This is true not only of the structure of a farming family, where husband, wife and children may contribute collectively to the family income through their labour, but also of the different structure of an industrial working-class family where this is not the case. Distinct structural differences in the family can also be observed when one compares societies with an average of five children per family with those averaging two children. The lower a society's fertility rate, the more valuable children become, not only for their parents, but for the society concerned in general. And since the fertility rate usually drops in the course of increasing industrialization and urbanization, in the course of this change, and in connection with increasing social wealth, the social concern for children grows, as does the understanding for their particular needs. Everything points towards how little the family is an autonomous figuration within the surrounding figuration of the state society. Indeed, throughout this century the latter has acquired more and more social functions which used to fall to family units. Man, woman and children used to work not only as farmers, but also as artisans in the context of family units. Today they largely earn their incomes outside this unit. The education of children among the majority of the population used to take place in the context of the family, today more and more outside it. Care for the sick and elderly, good and bad, used to lie primarily in the hands of the family. Today public institutions, particularly state insurance companies and hospitals, have taken on a good proportion of these functions. The development of the welfare state has also reinforced the relative independence of adolescents from their parents. Even in times of unemployment, unemployment benefits are for many young people a bulwark against the worst; the state, no longer the family, forms the bulwark against the most extreme need.

Today the family has lost to other institutions, especially the state, many functions which helped determine its character and especially its authority structure. All the stronger, then, appear those functions left to it today, above all the affective and emotional functions of the people composing families for each other. In optimal cases the family represents a stable focus for the continual satisfaction of drives and the need for affection, the reliable social location of people's social anchoring, and wherever this is the case, one can really speak of a civilizing of family relations. If one wants, one can also speak of a democratization, for today the power balances between men and women, like those between parents and children, are, if not equal, still more equal than they used to be. The 'discovery of childhood', the 'Year of the Child' are indications of this transfer of power. Parents, teachers and occasionally even state officials, have greater regard for the particularity of children than ever before. Adults have ceased seeing themselves in children, as if they were only little adults. They know that the needs of people as children are different from their own. These childhood needs are usually passionate, intense and satisfied in fantasy to a far greater degree than those of civilized adults. In many cases parents are rather helpless in the face of the passion of children's desires. We cannot say that today they already understand the nature of the civilizing process which children must go through before they can reach the adult level of civilization, although they themselves, the parents, contribute decisively to this process. But currently it has come to be socially accepted that it is not simply an 'evil will', 'disobedience' or 'naughtiness' which brings children to do what is forbidden to adults. Parents themselves accordingly curb their initially violent superiority over children. Such a modified authority relation, however, now really demands of parents, as we can see, a relatively very high degree of self-control, which as a model and a means of education then rebounds to impose a high degree of self-constraint on children in their turn.

XIII

At the same time, however, in our societies there are conditions which work against the success of such a civilized relation between parents and children. They include, above all, the increasing individualization and autonomization of all the people taking part in the construction of a family. Not only men, but also women are to an increasing extent absorbed by paid work outside the home. More than ever before, all family members tend to live a life for themselves as individuals, to take on tasks and develop human relationships independently of other members of the family. Adolescent children also attempt, as soon as they can, to go their own way. And, at least in the large cities, it is relatively easy to find the opportunities to do so. We are perhaps even inclined to stigmatize children who do not become autonomous early enough. The more ageing parents need their children's emotional affection and perhaps their assistance, the more children are concerned with their own affairs.

The unplanned social process, in the course of which, *inter alia*, people's family relationships have experienced a profound transformation, raises many unresolved problems. But we are barely conscious of them as *our* problems, as the shared problems of a series of generations in the course of a broader social development. The social reality of this problem as a symptom of a particular developmental phase, and thus also the opportunity to manage it better, is today largely concealed from people's consciousness because a number of traditional clichés, conjuring up a completely unrealistic ideal image of the family, still generally dominate human thought. While sober observation shows that the dominant characteristic of human family relations, in contrast to the corresponding relations of many other living creatures, is precisely their extraordinary plasticity, these traditional clichés propagate the notion of the human family as a simply unchangeable and eternally identical human figuration. The idealistic character of this cliché then also contributes to the fact that people in every single family group are a long way from recognizing that their difficulties are, at least in part, the normal difficulties of the

family relationships of our time; they are far more inclined to see the difficulties as something which only happens to them. Not only religious, but also
a whole series of secular traditions, including especially the conception of an
unchanging nuclear family put forward by sociologists and anthropologists,
contribute to the continuation of a fantasy image of the family in society at
large. In a US Supreme Court decision on a child's committal to a psychiatric
institution, the Judge appealed, *inter alia*, to the notion 'that the traditional
presumption that the parents act in the best interests of their child should
apply'.[10] In his judgement, one of the judges, Chief Justice Warren Burger,
spoke additionally of law's 'family concept' which, he wrote, recognizes that
the parents' 'natural bonds of affection lead parents to act in the best interests
of their children'. Here, then, we encounter legal decisions based on an
obvious fiction. It is actually unclear why judges need such idealistic fictions
for their decisions, at a time when it has at least become possible to call upon
more reality-adequate sociological studies.

XIV

The anachronistic insistence on an idealistic conception of the parent–child
relation, like that of family relations in general, is one of the greatest obstacles
standing in the way of a more object-adequate management of contemporary
family problems. In conclusion, I should like to provide at least a broad indication of why this is so. As always, in every society in which the power-ratio
between the people forming families is very uneven, the relation between
parent and children, like that of men and women, tends to be formalized to a
large extent. It has, in other words, a socially sanctioned, relatively fixed form.
Certainly this form allows some room for individual variations, but the
patterns of superordination and subordination, command and obedience are
unavoidable. The room for variation is only great for the superordinate and
the commanding; relatively limited for the subordinate and the obedient.
When the power imbalance in families, and even the power imbalance
between parents and children, decreases – and that is the developmental trend
of our time – the situation changes. The people making up families are then
tied to previously existing forms to a lesser degree than before, they are
compelled to a greater degree than before to work out a *modus vivendi* with
each other through their own efforts, that is, more purposively. By presenting
family relations as something which is more or less given by nature, and so
normally well-functioning of its own accord, one blocks perception of the fact
that – under the current conditions of the non-authoritarian family more than
ever – the success of the relationship, its functioning for its participants in a
more or less satisfactory way, is a task which the people bound to each other
in this way may or may not take upon themselves. One can assume that the

chances of success are greater when they are conscious of this task as such, and work on it together. In addition, every family relationship is a process. The relationships are ever-changing, and the task always poses itself anew. For human beings, the need to work consciously at our relationships with each other never ends.

28

TECHNIZATION AND CIVILIZATION

Elias's public performances in Germany in the 1980s included several interviews on television. He also appeared more or less regularly in the pages of such general weeklies as *Die Zeit* and *Der Spiegel*. His fame was not confined to Germany, however. *The Civilizing Process* and other books were translated into many languages, including English, French, Spanish, Dutch, Polish, Hungarian, and Japanese.

When, in 1978, the English translation of Volume One of *The Civilizing Process* appeared, a conference on 'Rationalization and Civilization' was held in New York, chaired by the sociologist Richard Sennett. Elias himself attended, but the conference did not arouse an enduring interest in his work. It was only after some time that some American sociologists came to recognize it as important. Elias's most ardent admirer in the United States became the sociologist Thomas Scheff, who discovered him only after his death (cf. Scheff 1994).

In Europe recognition came earlier, especially among historians and sociologists, including such prominent figures as Roger Chartier and Pierre Bourdieu in France. A great deal of attention was paid to Elias by the prestigious British journal *Theory, Culture and Society*. After devoting a special issue to his work in 1987, *TCS* published posthumously the English translation of a paper Elias delivered at a meeting of the German Sociological Association in Hamburg in 1986. The following text consists of two sections from that paper.

. . . The tiny word *and* in the title 'Technization and Civilization' can be easily misunderstood. Present-day habits of thought lead all too easily to the conclusion that one of these two processes will prove to be the leading one, with the other one following on, the one acting as cause, the other as effect. It may also be thought that a process such as economic development plays the leading role and that both processes under consideration constitute the dependent effects of this leading process. But I find that the evidence does not correspond with this simple cause–effect model. The interaction of the different part-processes is complex and has no beginning. I cannot offer you, with the best will in the world, a new fundamental process that would satisfy the ideological need for causes, only the development of humankind itself. The progression in the technization of transport in the nineteenth and twentieth centuries is certainly impressive, and there is no doubt that the use of these means of transport demanded high discipline among the participants, a uniform and moderate self-regulation. This applies not only to the engine driver, the motorist, the aircraft pilot and mechanic, but also to the passengers. In many of the advanced countries trains depart punctually to the minute, perhaps even to the second. I have already pointed out elsewhere[1] the extent to which self-regulation to social time becomes second nature to people in the more advanced countries. This is not to say, however, that technization is the cause and civilizing self-regulation the effect. One can also read this the other way round.

In order to get under way and keep going, technization already demanded a relatively high degree of civilizing self-regulation. In the search for a better understanding of the stage of preliminary experiments in the nineteenth century – which ultimately came to fruition in the form of the practicable motor vehicle and a little later the practicable aircraft – there was one observation which particularly impressed me. In some respects the better known nineteenth-century inventors who shared in the experiments to develop the motor car and aeroplane resemble one another. Take Gehlen, the clockmaker, who had experimented with flying devices as early as the beginning of the nineteenth century, or Otto Lilienthal from Pomerania (and later Berlin) whose gliders came close to the design of the motor-powered plane, when he was killed in his last attempt in non-powered flight, and whose preliminary work led eventually to the breakthrough to a motor-powered plane by the brothers Wilbur and Orville Wright. Or take Karl Benz or Henry Ford. It does not matter whom one takes – the self-discipline with which they pursued their goal over many years is impressive. They could never know for certain whether this goal could be reached. They all started without funds, or with very few; such finance as they had was, in any case, probably borrowed. They all constructed their first machine – and quite often the engines – by hand in their small workshops and, sometimes, in the kitchen. Without doubt they all had unusual gifts, particularly but not solely in the field of technology. They also had tenacity in conducting their experimental work. Henry Ford and his friends, in their efforts to build a motor-driven four-wheeled chassis, forgot that the door of the workshop was too small to get it out on the road.[2] Angrily, Ford tore out the bricks around the entrance to get the chassis out on the road for a trial run. Many of these inventors most certainly were up and coming young men. They knew that their only chance of getting on was to invent something. Let us not forget, however, that it was a characteristic of their society that it gave young people a relatively good chance of advancement if they had not only the talent but also the discipline necessary for the techno-logical invention in question.

What I am saying is, that the cause–effect concept cannot really be applied to the technization–civilization relationship. At the present time they are pressing forward, yet in some cases also moving backwards.

For the purpose of the investigation, and in order to communicate with one another, we are using different concepts that we can mentally handle sep-arately from each other. Concepts with which we can deal separately let us forget all too easily that they are always to do with people coexisting with each other. It is particularly important for sociologists, whenever they make use of objectifying concepts, not to lose sight of how these actually refer to people-in-their-groups. There are people who bring about the technization of certain aspects of their social life, use it, and, in turn, are themselves stamped by this process. There are also people-in-groups who are either – so to speak – civi-lizing themselves more, or de-civilizing themselves more. The civilizing process is a process of *human beings* civilizing *human beings*. The language handed down to us forces us often to think and speak in a way that plainly contradicts the observable facts. If one wishes to bend them, one initially strays perhaps too much to the other side and loses contact with one's fellow beings, or their goodwill. I may be going perhaps too far if I say that 'it is the same societies that become more technized and more civilized'. But it can indeed be observed that a spurt in technization and a spurt in civilization quite often go hand in hand in societies. It quite often happens that a counter-spurt also occurs at the newly-reached stage of technization, a spurt towards de-civilization.

That is just what can be observed when the process of technizing road vehi-cles moved from the start of its experimental period into the period of maturity, and into mass production. I have already pointed out that all these processes are learning processes. When such a technological innovation as the motor car has reached maturity, then people have to start learning all kinds of new experiences. They must learn to re-model their cities and road network, in order to make them suitable for the new means of transport. For they were all, of course, originally designed for horse-drawn carriages and pedestrians. The roads, covered in loose gravel, for example, had been prepared for horse-drawn coaches and now proved to be positively dangerous for motor cars. In 1903, the Paris–Madrid Grand Prix Motor Race was prematurely called off. So many drivers had crashed after being blinded by the clouds of dust that the organizers stopped the race to save the surviving drivers. The authorities had to learn. The designers had to learn. The makers of the new contraption had to learn. And this great learning process connected with the newly-reached stage in the technization of road vehicles was of particular concern to the beneficiaries of the new means of transport, the drivers themselves. It is common knowledge that, in the course of the twentieth century, particularly among the more developed industrial nations – the so-called Western group of states – the possession of one's own motor car became a normal, almost indispensable, accessory to life. This was so for the majority of families and often also for individual people, young and old. For many people the car became a part of themselves that widened the freedom of movement for everyone in a hitherto unknown way. A person gives the order and the car obeys, at least when that person has looked after it well. It gives its 'Lord and Master' a power that in former times not even people with a large retinue of servants had at their disposal. It carries them almost effortlessly at great speed across countries, gives almost unalloyed pleasure, but sometimes also trouble. All in all, it has raised the quality of life at a tolerable cost.

Something that has not always received the attention it deserves, however, was the fact that the spurt of technization brought to the large mass of people a new civilizing spurt corresponding with the new spurt in technization. It was the latter that had made the motor car and, particularly, the private motor car an adjunct to one's personal life. Of course, motorized road traffic demanded a certain degree of regulation by the government. The English Highway Law of 1835 laid down a maximum speed of four miles per hour. Since then, the maximum speed laid down by law has in many cases been left to individual drivers. This is an example to show to what extent, amidst all the public regulations, motorized traffic depends on the self-regulation by the driver. This is the civilizing spurt which I mentioned before. Although a certain degree of law-enforced regulation and supervision is indispensable for the safety of motor vehicle traffic, the level of self-regulation imposed by the driver on himself is and will remain decisive for the safety of motor vehicle traffic. This is one of the most concrete examples of how technization and civilization interact. In this respect we are still in the middle of the learning process. The great advantages and pleasures that accrue from the ownership and use of motor vehicles, private as well as business ones, have led to the disadvantages being accepted. The annual rate of accidents is largely accepted almost as something unavoidable. But once confronted with the fact, one cannot deny that the motor car is accompanied not only by a civilizing spurt towards a specific form of individual self-regulation, but, at the same time, by a decivilizing spurt. It is accompanied by the regular murder of human beings and frequent physical injuries, many of them sufficiently severe to harm the people affected for the rest of their life, and to inflict more or less severe suffering.

It has been possible in the course of the years, at least in more developed countries, to lower the accident rate quite considerably. This was mainly achieved by making improvements in the materials used in the lifeless motor car itself – material changes such as safety glass and particularly the seat belt. As far as people are concerned, most countries have largely been content with regulations relating to the consumption of alcohol. The enjoyment of alcohol, however, implies only an extreme reduction in the ability for self-regulation. People sometimes say 'Conscience and intellect dissolve in alcohol'. The limits on alcohol consumption imposed on motorists are certainly quite effective. Seen as an absolute figure, however, the number of injuries and, particularly, of fatal injuries in connection with motor vehicle accidents is still frighteningly high. One can be fairly certain that action must follow once we have learned to increase the structural safety of the car as far as that is possible, and to deal more or less effectively with the decrease of individual self-regulation through alcohol in extreme cases of inebriation. Thus the question of other faults and shortcomings in individual self-regulation and, above all, the *social standard* of self-regulation is now becoming the focus of the accident problem. This is, therefore, a civilizing problem.

Differences in self-regulation can be observed not only between persons in the same national community, but also between different nations. The theory of civilizing processes suggests that individual self-regulation in less-developed societies will be less stable, less uniform and permanent than in the more highly-developed countries. Correspondingly, one would expect that the number of dead and injured as a result of car accidents, as a factor of the number of cars in a country, would be higher in less-developed than in highly-developed countries. This is indeed the case. I am fully aware of the statistical difficulties that one encounters in such comparisons. The definition of an accident is not everywhere the same. Sometimes the number of dead is taken to be the number of all those who die within thirty days following an accident. But even if one takes such considerations into account, and therefore does no more than present a hypothesis that may well be worth checking, then one can still allow oneself to be a little impressed by the enormous differences between the coefficients in the more and the less-developed countries. The suggestion that, in such differences, differences can be seen in the effectiveness of social standards of self-regulation is, in my opinion, worthy of further research. This must include adequate consideration being given to the effectiveness of legally enforced regulation. The theory of civilizing processes offers the possibility of an explanation, in a context where statistical figures are usually recorded side by side without any explanation. Table 28.1, reproduced from Billian, gives a list of countries in rank order for the year 1974.[3] This table cannot claim to be reliable in every detail. But it is a stimulus to thought. The regularity with which the coefficient in the more developed countries is comparatively low, and that in the less developed countries comparatively high, does not fit

Table 28.1 Road deaths: statistics by Continent, 1974

Continent	Inhabitants	Registered Vehicles	Number of Deaths	Coefficient
Europe	537,457,000	98,122,777	73,598	7.50
America	426,536,000	151,354,858	82,834	5.47
Asia	2,365,451,000	33,323,688	47,978	14.39
Africa	281,668,000	5,902,457	21,404	36.26
Oceania	17,915,000	7,186,700	4,462	6.20
	3,629,054,000	295,890,000	230,276	7.78

Sources: Official statistics published by particular countries, and the World Road Statistics 1975
(International Road Federation).
Population statistics for each country are from statistics published by the International Postal Union,
aggregated into continents.

too badly with the idea that differences between societies in the stability and
evenness of individual self-control – and, in that sense, in the level of civilization – play a role in the differences in the coefficients.

Jan-Willem Gerritsen and I can claim a somewhat greater reliability for
tables 28.2 and 28.3 which we drew up ourselves, based on sources that can
be considered reliable. Durkheim may perhaps be recognized as the force
behind this.[4] We attempted to discover whether a certain coefficient (the ratio
of the number of persons affected by car accidents to the number of registered
cars) shows the same differences year in year out, when comparisons are
drawn between different countries, not only for a single year, but for more
than two decades. We calculated a coefficient on the basis of the number of
injured and, separately, people killed per 10,000 vehicles (private cars and
taxis). As can be seen, the differences between different countries really do
show quite considerable constancy over the years. Some people will be
inclined to interpret such constancies in terms of diverse national characteristics. Let me try to put this notion in more concrete terms by interpreting
them as national variations in the level, and perhaps also in the pattern, of
personal self-regulation.

Statistical data on motor car accidents are very often interpreted as data on
impersonal factors. This appears to me to be inadequate. It is difficult to overlook that the principal part in motor car accidents is played by the people
involved, that is, mainly by the drivers themselves. Controlling the car
(including maintaining it) is nothing but an extension of the driver's self-
control or self-regulation. The pattern of self-regulation by a driver at the
wheel of his car, however, is determined to a large extent by the social standard that society in every country has developed for the individual
self-regulation of the men and women who drive cars. All kinds of regulations
are included in this social standard of individual self-regulation by drivers.
Legal regulations, perhaps regarding maximum speeds, can be part of it, as

Table 28.2   Road deaths as an index of the Effectiveness of social standards of self-regulation

	1955	1960	1965	1970	1975	1980	1982
Denmark	27.9	18.0	13.6	10.0	6.0	4.7	4.6
France	26.7	15.0	12.7	12.2	9.1	7.1	6.5
Germany	55.0	33.2	17.6	13.7	8.3	5.6	4.8
Great Britain	15.6	12.9	8.5	6.4	4.8	4.0	3.8
Italy	65.4	41.0	16.4	10.0	6.8	5.2	4.2
Netherlands	57.9	37.6	19.5	12.9	6.8	4.4	3.7
Norway	17.5	13.8	9.1	8.1	5.6	2.9	3.0
Sweden	14.2	8.7	7.3	5.7	4.3	2.9	2.6
Greece	na	na	73.2	41.0	27.0	15.9	17.5
Portugal	53.4	40.8	32.4	24.4	37.1	23.2	20.5
Spain	117.4	58.7	34.7	22.9	12.1	8.6	7.0
Turkey	371.1	339.1	298.1	325.2	158.9	64.7	73.0
United States	na	na	6.5	5.9	4.2	4.2	3.6
Japan	na	na	64.4	24.8	8.1	5.0	4.8

Number of persons killed per 10,000 cars (private cars and taxis) in different countries [provisional findings].
Sources: Statistical Report on Road Accidents in 1983, ECMT, 1985; Statistics of Road Traffic Accidents in Europe 1980, UN, 1981.

well as local police enforcement. A further component may be the unrecorded code of driving behaviour that, tacitly, may have already formed among drivers in one country, and perhaps as a common standard in Europe among drivers of a whole group of countries. It may, for instance, happen that a speed limit of sixty miles per hour on a motorway is obligatory in one country, whilst in practice a speed of seventy to eighty miles per hour is usual and can be considered as standard. It is decisive for understanding what the coefficient aims to determine that all standard regulations, and all norms in motor vehicle traffic, in the end relate to the individual self-regulation by the driver. Standard rules in his or her society may have become a habit, second nature with the individual driver. A newcomer to these rules may need to be consciously recollecting them, with an occasional nudge to his memory. In whatever way he responds, the social standard of regulation is ineffective if it is not translated into individual self-regulation. Furthermore, individual self-regulation by the driver, the regulation of his or her own behaviour in relation to other people, remains undirected and dangerous if it is not orientated towards socially standard regulations which all drivers share. An individual driver who fails to regulate him or herself within the terms of the common standard is a danger to all others.

At first glance the concept 'social standard of self-regulation' may sound

Table 28.3 Road deaths as an index of the effectiveness of social standards of self-regulation in some Asian and African countries

	1965	1966	1967	1968	1969
Asia					
India	196.0	190.5	204.0	xx	xx
Indonesia	106.4	98.2	xx	115.4	108.6
Iraq	171.0	165.8	143.0	115.0	26.4
Japan	64.4	55.2	39.9	30.8	26.4
Africa					
Cameroon	52.9	42.1	43.6	xx	xx
Ethiopia	225.7	214.8	182.7	149.5	xx
Ivory Coast	61.3	55.0	52.6	77.2	xx
Kenya	124.3	121.6	124.2	136.1	140.3
Uganda	183.5	183.8	174.2	xx	xx

Number of persons killed per 10,000 cars (private cars and taxis) [provisional findings].
Source: *World Road Statistics 1965–69*, IRF, 1970.

somewhat complicated. It may need a little patience to recognize its productiveness. It corresponds exactly to the theoretical postulates of the theory of civilizing processes. The examples of changes in manners that are embodied in books on good manners in various decades or centuries do not simply relate to changes in the patterns of individual self-control, but to changes in the social standard of self-regulation. The same is true, for example, of speaking. An individual speaker who wants to be understood has to follow the rules in his mind of a common standard language, and may sometimes perhaps consult a reference book such as the *Oxford English Dictionary* to confirm that he or she is doing it right.

Theories about 'action' and 'behaviour' create the impression that a human being is a composite consisting of a multiplicity of atom-sized single actions. That is to say, they seem to impute that single bodily actions are all that one human being can perceive in another one. Perhaps they still retain something of the behaviourist eggshells. The link to a person as a unit of integrated single actions is missing.

The concept of self-regulation, as can be seen, belongs to a different image of humanity. It is sufficient for now simply to draw attention to it. I have suggested that the results in tables 28.2 and 28.3 should be interpreted as indicators of the effectiveness of the social standard of individual self-regulation in different countries. The regularities that can be observed in this and also in the preceding table make this interpretation of the theory of civilizing processes more obvious. What a closer inspection of the table 28.3 immediately reveals is the persistence with which the number of fatal car accidents is, and remains, higher in the less developed than in the more developed countries. The same is also true of the less developed countries – Greece, Portugal and Turkey – among the European countries in table 28.2. The constantly recurring attempt to interpret social statistics as impersonal, almost given-by-nature, units of measurement occasionally obscures the view even in this case. Sometimes people try to explain the larger number of people killed in the less developed countries by pointing to their substandard roads. But roads as such do not kill. Certainly, worse roads demand greater caution from the driver. The large number of people killed in the less developed countries is thus not due to the state of the roads, but to the fact that the self-regulation of the driver is not, or only to an insufficient extent, adapted to the state of the roads.

The figures for the more developed countries (table 28.2) provide certain indications as to how development can be continued through improving the road network, as well as through self-regulation by drivers in accordance with the demands of the improved network. From the viewpoint of a process theory what is interesting is *the interweaving of an unplanned process and human planning*. The still higher figures for road deaths in the 1950s, even in the more developed countries, bear witness to an unplanned process. The level of fatal car accidents was most decidedly unplanned. It was then that there began planning in order to reduce the chances of death in motor traffic. This was, to a certain extent, successful. But the unplanned aspect of motor traffic proved to be persistent. In not one of the countries was it possible to reduce the number of fatal accidents below a certain figure. In an absolute sense, the number of deaths in motor traffic is still quite considerable. It is certainly greater than the number of people killed by terrorists in these countries.

The figures for the more developed countries provide certain indications of this. The level of road deaths in the 1950s, even in the more developed countries, bears witness to a process which the manufacturers and users of motor vehicles had certainly not planned. One can unequivocally tell from these figures the effect of a learning process. All participants – authorities, manufacturers and, not least, drivers – methodically learn to increase the safety of driving and to reduce the risk of death to the driver. The effectiveness of the standard of self-regulation increases. The coefficients, at least in all more developed European countries, increase very considerably.

One sees this process with some clarity only when one is not content with a short-term perspective, that is, with coefficients for one or two years. When one follows the curve for the process over twenty-seven years, then comparisons between different countries provide an informative picture. Differing structural characteristics in the sample countries suddenly emerge more clearly when considered on a long-term basis.

(a) Throughout, the coefficients for the less developed countries – Greece, Portugal, Turkey and to a lesser extent Spain – in table 28.2 are significantly higher than those in the more developed ones. And, although they fall noticeably in the course of the twenty-seven years in all four of the less developed

European countries that are recorded here, they remain at the same time noticeably higher than the equally falling coefficients in the more developed countries.

(b) Some regularities also stand out in the more developed countries (table 28.2). The figures show more clearly and more reliably significant differences in the data columns for the different countries. There is a striking similarity in the column representing the three countries that suffered defeat in the Second World War: Germany, Italy and Japan. In the case of Germany and Italy the coefficients for 1955 are 55 and 65, and they gradually reduce to 5.6 in the Federal Republic, and to 5.2 in Italy. Japan's coefficient in 1965 is 64.4 and then rapidly drops to 4.8 in 1982. One would expect that Japan's rise into the class of highly developed countries would bring with it that standard pattern of self-regulation – that is, mainly greater stability and evenness of self-regulation – that is indispensable to a highly technological society in competition with other similar societies. In table 28.3, the astonishing feature of the data in the Japanese column becomes particularly evident in comparison with the data on three other Asian countries. These are all 'developing' countries – that is, in less apologetic language, less developed and correspondingly poorer countries. The data on them is in line with what the theory of civilizing processes predicts, that the evenness, stability and all-roundness of individual self-regulation is lower in such societies. A comparative sample survey of the African group of countries shows a similar picture. Further experimental sampling that we carried out showed significant differences between the anglophone and francophone countries of Africa. The coefficient is remarkably lower in the majority of francophone countries than in the anglophone ones – though significantly higher than the coefficients in the more developed European countries.

It would perhaps be a little risky to speak of a coefficient of civilization. What I am presenting here certainly are differences in the social disposition of members of highly developed and those of less developed societies. Please note: differences in *social* disposition, not biological differences. Japan is a good example of the fact that such differences in self-regulation can change in the course of social development.

When people in the less developed countries drive in such a way that they cause death and injuries, then it is the fault of the people and, in particular, of their own defective steering, not of the roads as such, nor of the vehicles that are being steered by them. People in the less developed countries apparently just career along without any consideration for bad driving conditions. And this is exactly what I want to say when I speak of a lower social level of standards in steering *oneself.* Indeed this is just the point to which I would like to draw attention. Poverty brutalizes people. This is not to be interpreted as a statement regarding individual people, but societies. When one meets a higher level of civilization, a code of behaviour and feeling that encourages a more uniform and stable self-regulation, it is not because the people concerned are, so to speak, more civilized by nature. The higher standard in the stability and steadiness of their self-control is not innate in them. This standard is an integral part and, at the same time, a condition and consequence of the higher stage of development, and thus also of the greater wealth, of their society. The wide motorways, well-built, well-signposted and very well-planned, cost a lot of money. They are designed for good-tempered drivers. Conversely the comparatively worse road network in many less developed countries and the relatively greater lack of consideration shown by the driver are not in a cause and effect relationship. Both are symptoms of people living together socially at an earlier stage of social development.

I am not afraid of speaking of societies at different stages of development and certainly not of poorer and wealthier societies. But some people are afraid to recognize what is well-known to the attentive observer, that different stages of development go hand in hand with different personality structures.

A brief reference to the astonishingly fast transformation of the Japanese can perhaps help to illustrate the problem that I have in mind. Laurens van der Post, the South African writer resident in England, in a recent radio talk, called the Japanese national character semi-medieval. He thought Japan had been a proud, courtly, feudal nation of warriors that looked upon itself, on its unconquered islands, as the centre of the world. For having been forced to give up its isolation and for allowing itself to be pulled into the wider family of peoples, continued Van der Post, this nation was now revenging itself by its rapid rise to economic and technological superiority. A remark concerning the Second World War should be enough to highlight the traditional method of Japanese self-regulation:

Civilized troops showed a pronounced tendency for preferring to surrender, when they were surrounded, to continuing a hopeless resistance; the 'less civilized Japanese' presented a difficult problem by not being prepared to surrender, whatever the circumstances.[5]

The traditional warrior code of the Japanese made being captured alive appear an unforgivable humiliation. It thus bred an extreme form of self-control, a fanaticism that did not allow any adjustment to changing circumstances. It resulted in a boundless contempt for the Allied Forces who had let themselves be captured when resistance was hopeless. The counterpart to the extremely high degree of self-control shown by the Japanese in certain respects was, for instance, the extreme capacity for acting out sadistic pleasures on their prisoners. It is possible that only the Japanese Emperor was in a position to bring about a break with this code by laying down the Japanese arms after the first American atom bombs had been dropped. From then onwards there has been a gradual change in the personality structure of the Japanese. It is among the peculiarities of such civilizing changes in personality structure, and changes especially in the social standards of self-regulation, that they follow other social changes, perhaps economic and technological ones, usually only after a lapse of time. In table 28.2 the row of figures representing the Japanese – which indeed differ very considerably from those of all other more developed countries – shows the Japanese pattern of self-regulation on an upward curve. The pattern of self-control demanded by motor vehicle traffic is, of course, quite different from the code of a courtier or a warrior. As can be seen, in 1970 the Japanese coefficient indicated a lower self-regulation than the German one, became higher in 1974 and has been approximately the same since 1981. It remains to be investigated whether this change in the standard of self-regulation in modern states that are based on a high degree of autonomous self-control by the individual, arises more in constraints enforced by the state and the police, or more from self-constraint. (In modern states based on a high degree of automatic self-regulation by the individual, these are distinguishable but not separable.) For the moment, however, this is unimportant for our purposes.

Conclusion

I have attempted to point out that the development of new means of transport, mainly the motor car and the aeroplane, is not an airy project, but must be understood as an unplanned process derived from the development of European and American society in the nineteenth and twentieth centuries. However, the revolutionary transformation of transport that was set in train in this way reacts in turn upon the society which had produced it. For example, the aeroplane without being – as is often said – the *cause* of a sociologically highly important social transformation which began in the nineteenth century but came into affect mainly in the twentieth has, without doubt, had a very considerable share in it. I refer to the rapidly increasing integration of humankind, the fast-growing interdependence of all hitherto independent subgroups of humankind. Growing air traffic brought people together, irrespective of all global obstacles, despite all the oceans and mountains, all the deserts and snowy wastes. It brought all groups of people swiftly into contact with one another, and achieved this with a comparatively high degree of safety. In the eighteenth century the word 'humanity' was associated with a beautiful but unrealizable dream.[6] Today humanity has become a unit to a greater degree than ever before and, if I may say so, a social reality. Not only the aeroplane, but also the telephone, radio and, in particular, television have brought people across the globe into a greater proximity to one another. One can find American films in African homesteads. South American guerrillas appear 'live' on European TV screens. Indians in their homes watch battles in Northern Ireland, It is, however, doubtful whether Sikhs and Hindus, Tamils and Singhalese, Basques and Spaniards, Catholic and Protestant Irishmen recognize themselves when television brings them in their own home pictures of their counterparts. The advance in technization has brought people all over the globe closer together. But the development of the human habitus is not keeping up with the development of technization and its consequences. Technization encourages humankind to move closer together and to unify. The more this happens, the more will the differences in human groups become apparent to human awareness. The growing integration of humankind, the rapidly rising dependence of all subgroups of humankind on each other is expressed not only in a whole series of global institutions such as the World Bank or the United Nations, but also in specific tensions and conflicts arising from the integration. In Africa, tribes merge into states under pressure of the powerful spurt of integration in which we find ourselves. Here it can be very clearly recognized how the traditional habitus of people, a habitus initially based on their identity with the tribe, comes into conflict with the necessity for joining together into larger units, states. An analogous process on a different level can be observed in Europe. The pressure to unify within a larger European framework is unmistakable. But people's habitus, the dominant pattern of their self-regulation, is focused on identification with sovereign states.

In the early days of the human species' existence – which are indeed not easy to visualize – there was possibly no more than a handful of human beings on this earth akin to our genus. The present time is perhaps the only other time since then that human beings have collectively formed a real social unit, not simply as a beautiful ideal, but as a social reality. Even now the fact is not fully understood that the increasingly more active human integration process is proceeding in the direction of the regional interdependence of humankind and their internal pacification, as well as levelling off the differences in wealth. This is not easy to understand, because the overall process moving in that direction carries with it, as always in such cases, powerful forces of an opposing process. And the latter, in view of the human misery that can accompany them, are more clearly in people's minds than the former.

Besides, people are still rather unaccustomed to this 'Let us come closer' tendency. It is one of the immovable features in the accelerating pace of change that people's whole outlook on life continues to be psychologically tied to yesterday's social reality, although today's and tomorrow's reality already differs greatly from yesterday's.

Today, the aeroplane has brought Berlin, Washington and Moscow closer together in space and time than the capitals of continental Europe were in the nineteenth century. But the emotional attitude of the Europeans towards each other and to the people of Russia and America continues in many respects to adhere to the pattern of the past. And the same is certainly also true of the attitude of the Americans and Russians themselves. Emotionally, they are as far apart from all the others as they were in the nineteenth century.

I explained as far back as the 1930s, that is about fifty years ago – helped by theoretical–empirical investigations – that a theory of interdependence is indispensable for sociologists, and that its central function in the investigation of societies can in no way be met by the theories of action and interaction prevalent at that time. The triumphant advance of the aeroplane, as a medium for global traffic in peace and war, has decisively contributed to the growing interdependence of all states on the globe and, at the same time, is also its product. It has an enormous civilizing influence, by bringing people from all regions closer to each other. This is particularly, though not solely, because it aids people of all colours to begin to get used to the fact that they have to live with one another, however different their patterns of self-regulation may be. Growing interdependencies, however, are accompanied with great regularity by specific tensions and conflicts. No group of people is pleased when it realizes that it is now more dependent on others than before. I have called such tensions 'integration and disintegration tensions'. They dominate the social figuration of states in the late twentieth century. Here, too, the civilizing thrust in the direction of a more united humankind is joined by a decivilizing counter thrust. The tensions and conflicts which the growing interdependence brings with it are – so far – only of secondary importance. Let us hope that this will never change.

A brief example can perhaps help to clarify the contribution made by technological development in this thrust towards interdependence with its civilizing potential and its decivilizing potential. Remember that in the nineteeth century a somewhat impecunious Russian Czar sold Alaska to the United States of America. Russia and America were then so far away from each other that no one, obviously not even the Czar and his advisers, thought that the two countries could possibly become military rivals and pose a mutual threat to their security.[7] The aeroplane has contributed to some extent to this having changed. But let us not make the mistake of placing the process of technization, so to speak, at the very beginning. Like many other processes contributing towards the development of humankind, technization has an immanent momentum which continually receives new impetus from the rivalry between individuals and groups of people. But other contributory processes also continually receive new impetus – just like technization itself. They receive it from the prevailing overall composition of humankind, from the dynamic of the development of humankind and the various survival units – from the tribes and states which they form over time. The immanent momentum of part-processes such as scientification, technization, economic development, or state-formation, always has only a limited autonomy within the framework of the total development of humankind. The overall process may be steered in one or other direction, or can even be stopped or reversed, through the rivalries and the power struggles between groups of people and their individual representatives.

I should not like to give the impression that I want to attribute to technical development – or in an even narrower sense, the transport revolution – the role of initiator, of 'first cause' in this integration movement. For me, the explanation lies in the intrinsic dynamic of humankind itself, of which I have already formulated one example in the model of monopolization processes in the second volume of my book *The Civilizing Process*.[8] Here I have given another schematic representation of this dynamic. It is the intrinsic dynamic of humankind from which the ultimately successful striving for ever faster means of transport, motor cars, aeroplanes and spacecraft derived its force. It can, however, equally be said that at the same time the level of integration of humanity, which fluctuates to and fro but is now being propelled forward by its own dynamic, would – had it not been for this kind of technizing spurt – have been unattainable in the face of the ever-present risk of disintegration. It used sometimes to be imagined that technological development, cultural development, and perhaps even economic and social development were, so to speak, self-governing events, each independently charting its own course. One could then argue it out whether the movement along each of these channels had its own momentum, or whether one of these subsidiary movements was providing the prime mover for all the others. But within the given facts of nature – at any rate if enormous natural changes such as the coming and the passing of the Ice Ages are set aside – one would look in vain for explanations of changes in humankind that lie outside humankind itself. One then reaches the limits of causal explanations. It then needs a period of readjustment to recognize that explanations for changes in the structure of humankind have to be sought in the structure of humankind itself, in their intrinsic dynamics, and not outside it or in one or another 'subsystem'.

Technological developments, such as the aeroplane or television, increased the pressure towards growing interdependence and, correspondingly, towards greater institutional integration. They have thus presented people with a civilizing task – and that is difficult. It cannot be said in advance whether they can handle this situation or not. But the civilizing task is clear in itself. People's self-regulation is (in accordance with their origin and, therefore, understandably) geared to the identification with small sub-units of humankind, tribes or states. Compared with the emotional importance of one's own tribe, one's own folk, one's own nation, the concept of humankind is an empty word. It is indeed to a large extent, but not solely, because of technological developments that people now find themselves in the position of having to be prepared in the long run either to live in peace with one another or to perish in further wars with one another. This is a learning process. One cannot know how it will end. It is, like so many other processes among which we live, an unfinished social process.

I have tried to give, through a discussion of the relationship between two partial processes, the process of technization and the civilizing process, an example of a way of doing sociological research which strives consistently to avoid reducing social processes to something static. This is achieved by presenting *as* social processes those social processes that can actually be observed as such in the investigation and not reducing them to states or to laws, to something eternal, on the model perhaps of classical physics.[9] The model of the transport revolution of the nineteeth and twentieth centuries, from the steam engine, through the motor car and the aeroplane to the space-craft, is an ideal example of an unplanned and – as can be seen – also an unfinished process. I have often wondered why it is so difficult for a process-sociology to make headway, why it is so difficult for many people to perceive changes in human societies – and particularly long-term changes – as struc-tured processes, and to investigate them as such. It is, apparently, easier and probably more satisfying for most people, and very likely also for most soci-ologists, to imagine the world as basically unchanging, fundamentally ever-constant. This is also the picture cultivated by scientists from Newton to Einstein and beyond. But the influence of thinking in terms of processes has begun to affect even contemporary physics, though at first marginally, only at the periphery. The concept of a constantly changing universe, and thus thinking of the universe as a process, somewhat contradicts the received conception of an unchanging nature. It seems to me that there are sound reasons why the concept of a constantly changing world is not found emotion-ally desirable, nor particularly satisfying. If one imagines the world, or a society, as a process, then one is inescapably reminded of a fact one would like to avoid recalling. One is reminded that after one's own death the future society of people will most likely be quite different in many respects from the present world in which we now live. The present world, the world of the twen-tieth century, will appear to people in the next century to have been rather old-fashioned and superseded in many ways – probably to the same extent as we see the world of the stage coach, or the world in which experiments were made with motor cars at four miles per hour and in which attempts were made to fly with wings made from 10,000 goose quills, as Clement Adie did. The kind of research prevalent among most sociologists concentrates on the search for something that appears to be a constant state and perhaps even eternal – something which, if it does not have external existence, then is at least endowed with eternal validity in the philosophical sense. There is apparently only one alternative to this eternalism, and that is the historicism of the researching historian. Faced with a world which is caught up in endless change, the historians generally represent it as continually changing without any order, without any direction or structure. If one takes the historicism of historians seriously, then it basically states that whatever is happening in the twentieth century could equally well have happened two hundred or even two thousand years ago. And conversely, the events of the Ancient World could equally happen today or tomorrow. The great shortcomings of the historical historian is the lack of a clear undogmatic conception of the development of human societies. Originally, the concept of a development was thrown out of the history books because it was a specific theory of development that became the creed of Marxism. They quite simply threw out the baby with the bath water. Because Marx's theory of development had been tied to a prophecy of the future state of humankind, the concept of long-term development was altogether thrown out of the history books. The development that led from the stage coach, by way of the railway, the motor car and the aeroplane to experiments with spacecraft is a small example of a social process in a definite direction, but quite certainly without aim and not involving any prophecy as to where all this might lead.

The concept of development is not essential only when one is striving to investigate technological change. Imagine there are no aeroplanes and you find yourself also politically in a different world. Let us not forget how the Russian Czar sold Alaska to the United States in the nineteenth century. At that time, Russia and America were so far apart, that they did not present a military threat to each other. As we all know, this subsequently changed.

No one can know when or whether spacecraft will be developed beyond the experimental stage in which they now are, whether a breakthrough to a stage of fruition will be possible, so that spacecraft become regular means of human transportation. The world in which we live is an emergent world, it is humankind on the move. We obscure our view of the process that we as humankind experience, if instead of accepting the world as it really is, we judge it as if it were an eternally unchanging world, or as if it represented a final stage. That is what one does when one presents the world as bad or as good, as civilized or as barbaric. Humanity is in a great collective learning process. We do not know what kind of future faces humankind. We can be fairly certain of only one point: the humanity of the future will look quite different in many respects from the humanity of today. I sometimes have the feeling that this is an area of knowledge which I would like to get across to people. They want to know as little as possible about the fact that the process of which they themselves are part will perhaps develop insights or institutions for which they actually pave the way, but that will remain unknown and fundamentally inconceivable to them. The difficulties people seem to have when they are asked to perceive the world, and thus also human society – and, not least, themselves – as processes in the making, are possibly connected with the difficulty of seeing themselves as precursors of an unknown and, in part, inconceivable future. It seems to me that they seek to protect themselves from it by letting academics reduce processes to states, or even distil out eternities from a short-term present by means of powerful abstraction. In order to do process-sociology, one has to be satisfied with a somewhat more modest starting point. The social processes of which one seeks to construct a model, are not only unplanned, but also unfinished. By working on the social processes that have led to the present time one helps the living to obtain a better orientation in the world. At the same time, one prepares the way for future generations who – helped by the preliminary work carried out at present – can have a more comprehensive and more secure knowledge than we have now. We can see today that the task that lies before us is to work towards the pacification and organized unification of humankind. Let us not be discouraged in this work by the knowledge that this task will not in our lifetime progress to fruition from the experimental period in which it is now. It is certainly worthwhile and highly meaningful to set to work in an unfinished world that will go on beyond oneself.

29

THE SOCIETY OF
INDIVIDUALS – III

When he was almost ninety years old, Elias turned once again to the problem about which he had written essays twice before: the relationship between 'individual' and 'society' (see above, pp. 68–74 and 92–5. The gist of his argument remained unchanged; but he now was able to express it with greater directness, while at the same time putting his ideas in a larger evolutionary perspective. As in the early 1960s, he enriched his original approach with new concepts and formulations, speaking of changes in the 'we–I balance', and pointing out how pointless it is to regard individuals merely as 'we–less I's'.

The nature and degree of self-detachment change in the course of social development. I should like to suggest that one way to track down changes in the position of individual people within their societies, and the changes in self-perception that go hand in hand with social changes, would be to investigate the development of languages, and especially the way in which pronoun functions are symbolically represented at different stages of language development. When, in a medieval French epic, the palace gatekeeper sometimes still says 'thou' and sometimes already 'you', one might suppose that the splitting of the form of address between a 'thou' and a 'you' is the symbolic representation of an increasing social distance. When, in a peasant's letter from the past, the words 'we' and 'us' appear more often than 'I' and 'me' – or, more exactly, more often than one would expect of an urban letter-writer of that time – one can assume that the balance of we-and I-identity tilted more to the side of we-identity in the case of the peasant, and more towards I-identity in that of the urban correspondent.

Since the European Middle Ages the balance between we- and I-identity has undergone a noticeable change, that can be characterized briefly as follows: earlier the balance of we- and I-identity was heavily weighted towards the former. From the Renaissance on, the balance tilted more and more towards I-identity. More and more frequent became the cases of people whose we-identity was so weakened that they appeared to themselves as we-less I's. Whereas previously people had belonged, whether from birth or from a certain point in their lives, to a certain group for ever, so that their I-identity was permanently bound to their we-identity and often overshadowed by it, in the course of time the pendulum swung to the opposite extreme. The we-identity of people, though it certainly always remained present, was now often overshadowed or concealed in consciousness by their I-identity.

When Descartes wrote his famous sentence *Cogito, ergo sum*, he was the pioneer of a growing shift of emphasis in the human self-image, a shift from the then established overlaying of the I-identity by we-identity to the converse. At Descartes's time most members of a society were still permanently assigned, often by heredity, i.e. their family origin, to a certain group. The princes, kings and emperors, as individuals, owed their high position in society, and the wealth that went with it, to their birth as members of a family privileged by heredity, a dynasty. In the same way nobles, considered as individuals, owed their positions to the family into which they were born. Their identification with their ancestral groups, as shown in their family trees, largely determined their individual identity. Citizens belonged to guilds, which also often had an hereditary character. The peasants, the great majority of the population, were tied to the land. An exception was formed by members of the church. They were not hereditarily bound to the church when they made their vows, but only for life, i.e. individually. Naturally, there were always individuals who withdrew from their group bond and wandered the world, like the itinerant scholars, as groupless persons. But in a society where group membership – often hereditary – had decisive importance for an individual's position and prospects, groupless people had less scope to rise in society. The humanists were one of the earliest groups of people whose personal achievements and character traits gave them opportunities to rise to respected social positions, particularly as state and municipal officials. The shift towards individualization that they represented was certainly a sign of a change in the social structure.

Descartes's *Cogito*, with its accent on the I, was also a sign of this change in the position of the individual person in his society. While thinking, Descartes could forget all the we-relations of his person. He could forget that he had acquired a French mother tongue and Latin as the language of educated people, that every thought he formulated, including his *Cogito, ergo sum*, was conditioned by a linguistic tradition that had been learned, and not least that he was encoding his ideas somewhat for fear of the ever-alert church Inquisition. While working on the *Meditations* he heard of Galileo's arrest. While thinking, he forgot that he was communicating with other people. He forgot other people in their role as we, you or they. They were *de facto* always present in the philosopher's consciousness as he sent his triumphant 'I' out into the world. But the group he belonged to, the society to which he owed his language and knowledge, disappeared as he thought. In his consciousness the isolated I stepped out of the shadow of social allegiances, and the we–I pendulum swung in the opposite direction. The isolated thinker perceived himself – or more precisely, his own thought, his 'reason' – as the only real, indubitable thing. All else might possibly be an illusion conjured up by the Devil, but not this, not his own existence as thinker. This form of I-identity, the perception of one's own person as a we-less I, has spread wide and deep since then.

A great part of the philosophical theory of knowledge – one might say the whole tradition of its classical representatives from Descartes through Berkeley and his thesis *Esse est percipi* (to be is to be perceived) or Kant, who found it impossible to say that objects of the outer world were not within the subject himself, to Husserl's wrestling with solipsism – rests on the idea that the human being who tries to acquire knowledge is an isolated being who must remain for ever in doubt whether objects, and therefore persons, actually exist outside himself.[1] If it were just that of a single person who felt like a totally isolated being was plagued by constant doubt whether anything or anyone existed outside himself, one might perhaps diagnose this as a somewhat eccentric mental state, a kind of sickness. But the situation is that from the early modern period – especially but doubtless not only in philosophical writing – this basic problem shows an extraordinary persistence transcending individual persons over a number of centuries. It is the problem of the person who perceives himself as standing totally alone and who cannot resist doubting the existence of anything or anyone outside himself. A whole flood of writings from the second half of the twentieth century presents the reading public with one version after another of the same basic figure of the isolated person, in the form of the *homo clausus* or the we-less I, in his voluntary or involuntary loneliness. And the wide resonance achieved by such writings, the lasting nature of their success, shows that the image of the isolated human being and the fundamental experience that gives him his strength, is not an isolated phenomenon.

There are passages in Sartre's well-known novel *Nausea* of which one could almost say that Descartes has been resurrected. But in Descartes the individual's doubt of the existence of the outside world and the idea that doubt, i.e. thinking, was the only guarantee of his own existence, were something new. The joy of discovery and the whole climate of rising modernity in France and especially in the Netherlands, where Descartes had found a second home, counteracted the possibility that the doubt might lead to despair. And the verb *esse* took on a new gravity through being transformed into the verb 'to exist', and often enough gained an existence of its own, a reification, through the philosophical use of the associated noun 'existence':

> . . . this sort of painful rumination: *I exist*, I am the one who keeps it up. I. The body lives by itself once it has begun. But thought – *I* am the one who continues it, unrolls it. I exist. How serpentine is this feeling of existing – I unwind it, slowly . . . If I could keep myself from thinking! I try, and succeed: my head seems to fill with smoke . . . and then it starts again: 'Smoke . . . not to think . . . don't want to think . . . I think I don't want to think. I mustn't think that I don't want to think. Because that's still a thought.' Will there never be an end to it?
>
> My thought is *me*: that's why I can't stop. I exist because I think . . . and I can't stop myself from thinking.[2]

We find another example of a we-less or almost we-less I in Camus's *The Outsider*. One of the peculiarities of the lonely man that the hero of this book appears to be is a curious confusion of the emotions. He kills someone, but the corresponding feelings, whether of hate or remorse, are lacking. His mother dies, but he feels, actually, nothing. The feelings of grief or being left behind alone do not arise. Isolation, abandonment are the permanent underlying feelings. They are not associated with people. The I is alone, without any real relation to other people, without the feelings that the we-relation makes possible. This theme occurs again and again in literature, and each time it strikes a chord. To give only one other example, there is the almost we-less hero of a novel entitled *La salle de bain*. Throughout the book the hero repeatedly withdraws from other people into the bathroom. When his girlfriend asks him why he has left the capital and her, he cannot answer. He suffers from solitude, but does not know why he is alone. He suffers, and thinks suffering the last proof that he exists: 'La souffrance était l'ultime assurance de mon existence, la seule.'[3] Suffering, he withdraws constantly to the bathroom. What is he suffering from?

The we-less I that Descartes presents to us as the subject of knowledge already feels to a certain extent imprisoned in his own thought, in what one could reifyingly call his 'reason'. Seen positively, one's own thought becomes the only thing in the world that is indubitable. For Berkeley one's own senses form the walls of the prison; the sense perceptions of the isolated person are all that one can experience of other people and other things. One cannot doubt that in all these examples we have to do with an authentic experience, a genuine mode of self-perception. The elaboration of this self-perception in the form of a theory of knowledge omits, in a curious way which is repeated with great regularity, to take account of the fact that each adult has as a child to acquire knowledge from others in a long learning process, before he or she is able to develop this knowledge individually. The philosophical image of man as a static being who exists as an adult without ever having been a child, the omission of the process in which each person is constantly engaged, is one of the reasons for the dead-end that epistemology constantly comes up against.

Another reason is a forgetting of the constant meetings of the individual with other people and the intermeshing of his life with those of others in the course of this process. That a feeling of we-lessness is one of the basic problems of this specific image of man is seen particularly clearly in the literary examples from recent times. In them we come upon a peculiar conflict of human beings that, we can be sure, is not confined to literature. The experience underlying the notion of the we-less I is clearly the conflict between the natural human need for an emotive affirmation of one's own person by others and others' need of affirmation by oneself, on one hand, and fear of fulfilment of the need and resistance to it on the other. The need to love and be loved is, to an extent, the strongest condensation of this natural human craving. It can also take the form of the giving and finding of friendship. Whatever form it takes, the emotive need for human society, a giving and receiving in affective relationships to other people, is one of the fundamental conditions of human existence. What the bearers of the human image of the we-less I appear to suffer from is the conflict between the desire for emotional relationships with other people and their own inability to satisfy this desire. The heroes of the stories mentioned are alone because a personal sorrow denies them the possibility of genuine feelings for other people, genuine emotional bonds. The chord struck by this theme, particularly in the twentieth century, suggests that we are not concerned here with an isolated, individual problem, but with a habitus problem, a basic feature of the social personality structure of people in the modern age.

These brief indications may be enough to throw the dominant direction of the sequence of stages in the development of the we–I balance into somewhat sharper relief. At the earlier stages, as I have said, the we–I balance first titled strongly towards the we. In more recent times it has often swung strongly towards the I. The question is whether the development of humanity, or the all-embracing form of human communal life, has already reached a stage, or can ever reach a stage, when a more stable equilibrium of the we–I balance will prevail.

30

INFORMALIZATION AND THE CIVILIZING PROCESS

Even after 1984, when he was living in Amsterdam, Elias continued to be very much occupied with German society: with the problem of how Germany could have become the setting for the atrocities of National Socialism, as well as with the prospects for more stable political development in the future. In collaboration with Michael Schröter he collected a number of essays, articles and papers written over a period of almost thirty years and edited these for publication in book form under the title *The Germans. Power Struggles and the Development of Habitus in the Nineteenth and Twentieth Centuries.* The collection included a revised version of his notes on the Eichmann trial, written in the early 1960s (see above, pp. 113–21). A newly written introductory chapter focused on some recent trends in the civilizing process in Europe, and in Germany in particular. One of those trends, which has become known as informalization, is the central theme in the following exerpt.

A few brief notes and comments should be enough to pave the way for the discussion of the peculiar spurt of informalization, a smaller wave of which could be observed after the First World War, and a larger and stronger wave after the Second. These comments seem to me to be particularly necessary in order to remove a difficulty standing in the way of explaining this process. From time to time, it has been claimed that the key to my theory of civilization can be found in a single sentence from a late medieval book of etiquette: loosely paraphrased, it runs 'Things that were once permitted are now forbidden'.[1] The question then understandably arises immediately of whether the direction of change has not been revised since the 1930s, and whether we should not rather say nowadays, 'Things that were once forbidden are now permitted'. And if that were so, would that not mean that we were living in a time of regression in civilization, or rebarbarization?[2] This question, however, is I think based on an inadequate understanding of the theory of civilizing processes.

If one wanted to try to reduce the key problem of any civilizing process to its simplest formula, then it could be said to be the problem of how people can manage to satisfy their elementary animalic needs in their life together, without reciprocally destroying, frustrating, demeaning or in other ways harming each other time and time again in their search for this satisfaction – in other words, without fulfilment of the elementary needs of one person or group of people being achieved at the cost of those of another person or group. At earlier levels of social development, people took their own way of life, their own social conventions, entirely for granted. Only very late in the development of humanity, and particularly in our own times when people became increasingly conscious that patterns of human life are highly diverse and changeable, did this become a problem. Only then moreover, could people attempt to explain and examine at a higher level of reflection the unplanned changes in these social patterns and to try to plan future long-term changes.

Central to my approach to the problems of humanity, and accordingly to the problem of civilization, is an examination of the constraints to which people are exposed. Roughly speaking, four types can be distinguished:

(a)   The constraints imposed on people by the characteristics of their animal nature. The imperatives of hunger or the sexual drive are the most obvious examples of this sort of constraint. But the constraints of ageing, being old and dying, of longing for affection and love, or even the constraints of hatred and enmity, and many more that arise in people spontaneously equally belong to this category.

(b)   The constraints arising from dependence upon non-human natural circumstances, especially the constraint imposed by the need to seek food, or the need for protection from the harshness of the weather, to name only two.

(c)   The constraints which people exercise over each other in the course of their social lives. These are often conceptualized as 'social constraints'. But it is useful to be clear that everything we describe as social constraints, or possibly as economic constraints, are constraints which people exercise over each other because of their interdependence. I will call them 'external constraints' for the moment, but they are literally 'constraints by other people' (*Fremdzwänge*). Such external constraints are to be found in every two- or three-person relationship. Every person who lives together with others, who is dependent on others – and we all are – is subject to these constraints because of this very dependence. But we are also subjected to external constraints when we live with fifty million people; for example, we have to pay taxes.

(d)   From those constraints based on the animal nature of humans, and in particular on the nature of their drives, a second type of individual constraint is to be distinguished, which we denote by such concepts as 'self-control' (*Selbstzwänge*). Even what we call 'reason' is, among other things, an apparatus for self-control, as is 'conscience'. I term this type of constraint 'self-constraints'. It differs from the first category of constraints derived from natural drives, because we are endowed biologically with only a potential for the acquisition of self-constraint. When this potential is not actualized through learning and experience, then it remains latent. The degree and pattern of its activation depend on the society in which a person grows up, and they change in specific ways in the continuing process of human development.

The theory of civilizing processes fits in at this point. The constellation of constraints, that is the interplay between the four types, changes. The elementary constraints of human nature – the first category – are the same, with relatively few variations, at all phases of human development, and are thus the same for all branches of our species *Homo sapiens*. However, the patterns of self-constraints which develop as a result of differing experiences are highly dissimilar. This holds in particular for the relationship between external and self-constraints in societies at different stages of development, and to a lesser extent also in different societies at the same stage.

As far as I know, there is no human society in which the restraint of people's elementary animal impulses rests only on external constraint – that is, on the fear of others or on the pressure of others. In all the human societies that we know, a pattern of self-constraints is formed through external constraints in early childhood upbringing. But in simpler societies, and in fact in agrarian societies throughout the world, the apparatus of self-control is relatively weak and, if I may for once so phrase it, full of holes compared with that developed in highly differentiated, and especially in multi-party, industrial states. This means that for self-restraint, members of the former kinds of society require a very great deal of reinforcement through the fear created and pressure exerted by others. The pressure can come from other people, such as a chief, or from imaginary figures such as ancestors, ghosts or deities. Whatever the form, in this case a very considerable external constraint is required to strengthen the framework of people's self-constraint which is necessary for their own integrity and indeed for their survival as persons – and for the integrity and survival of the people with whom they have to live.

The hallmark of civilizing processes, as my researches have revealed, is a change in the relation between external social constraints and individual self-constraints. Although this is just one of several criteria, I shall concentrate on it here since it permits relatively simple access to the far from simple problems of the contemporary trend towards informalization.

Let us consider a child who is often hit by its angry father whenever, in his view, it has been naughty. Such a child will learn to avoid disapproved behaviour out of fear of its father. But its self-constraint apparatus will in this respect develop only partially. In order to be able to restrain itself, it remains dependent on others' threats. Its capacity to restrain itself could develop more strongly if the father were to make the child avoid the disapproved behaviour of its own accord, through persuasion, reasoning, and signs of caring. But the child who is often hit does not learn to restrain itself independently of an external constraint, without the threat of paternal punishment, and is accordingly also to a great extent at the mercy of its own impulses of hatred and hostility. It is highly probable that such a child will in turn become a beater, taking the father as a model without knowing it.

This example can be carried over to political systems without difficulty. Members of a state society which has long been absolutist – ruled from above in the form of what we would call a police state – develop quite analogous personality structures, in which their ability to exercise self-constraint remains dependent on an external constraint, on a strong force which threatens them with punishment from outside. A non-absolutist, multi-party regime requires a far stronger and firmer apparatus of self-constraint. It corresponds to the model of upbringing which builds up such an apparatus in individual people, not through the use of the stick nor through the threat of punishment but rather through persuasion and conviction. This is one of the reasons why – even though participation and opinion formation by the ruled is still quite severely limited in today's type of multi-party rule – the transition from an absolutist, dictatorial regime (or from a regime of chiefs) to a multi-party regime is so arduous. In terms of personality structure, even this small claim on opinion formation and self-control by each voter is enormously difficult for people who have lived under a system of chiefs or despots; this holds especially for the emotionally controlled election campaign and the curbing of passions it demands. These difficulties are so great that it usually takes three, four or even five generations for personality structures to adapt successfully to the non-violent form of party contest.

Put briefly, in the course of a civilizing process the self-constraint apparatus becomes stronger relative to external constraints. In addition, it becomes more even and all-embracing. An example of the latter is that in societies with very unequal power ratios a self-control apparatus develops for the establishment – those in power, those higher in rank – mostly with regard to their equals. In dealing with those lower down the social scale, they do not need to restrain themselves, they can 'let themselves go'. Andreas Capellanus, who wrote about the rules of behaviour between men and women in the twelfth century, described in detail how a nobleman should conduct himself with a woman of higher rank, one of equal rank, and also with a 'plebeian' woman. When he comes to speak of behaviour towards a peasant girl, he as good as says, 'You can do what you want'.[3] A lady of the court in the eighteenth century allows her footman to wait on her while she is bathing: for her, he is not a man, not a person in front of whom she needs feel shame in her nakedness.[4] Compared with these earlier societies, in ours an all-embracing feeling of shame is cultivated. Social differences are certainly still fairly great, but in the course of the process of democratization, the power differentials have lessened. Correspondingly, we have had to develop a relatively high degree of self-restraint in dealings with *all* people, including social subordinates.

*   *   *

Now let me turn to the current spurt of informalization which is central to these reflections. I would like to limit myself to two areas of relationships in which it can be observed particularly clearly: the relationship between men and women, and between older and younger generations.

How the thrust towards informalization is manifested in the relationship between men and women can perhaps best be demonstrated by comparing the code governing relations between the sexes which was prevalent amongst students in Germany before the First World War, with that which is developing today. Before the First World War, the majority of German students came from the well-to-do middle classes. They generally belonged to a student society, often a fighting fraternity, were entitled to give and demand satisfaction and thus trained to duel. For them, there was a clear distinction between two types of women. On the one hand, there were women from the same social class – women one could marry. They were absolutely untouchable. The conventions of good society applied to them: one bowed, kissed their hand, danced with them in the prescribed way, kissed them when they allowed it, called, when necessary, on the parents – in short, contact with them was ruled by a quite well-established, strictly formalized code of behaviour. On the other hand, there were girls of another social class, either prostitutes in a brothel or girls from the lower-middle or working class, with whom one could have an affair.

It can be seen how very much things have changed in this field. Prostitution and affairs with lower-class girls have, as far as I know, as good as disappeared completely from the horizons of the students. Rituals such as addressing a young woman as '*Gnädiges Fräulein*' ('gracious young lady'), and even the distancing use of '*Sie*' (the formal 'you') have become obsolete in relations between the sexes at universities, and certainly not just there. Men and women students, like other members of the same age group, use '*Du*' (the informal form of 'you') to each other as a matter of course, even from the very beginning when they are not previously acquainted with each other at all.

This provides a simple example of an informalizing trend; but it poses obvious problems. In the generations of the early twentieth century about which we were speaking, there were pretty precisely fixed courtship rituals between young men and women. The young student fraternity member, the 'crass fox',[5] in the unlikely event of not having been taught these rules at home, would very soon have been taught the rules of good behaviour towards the young ladies of the social circle in which the fraternity moved and towards other marriageable young girls by his older fraternity 'patron', just as he would have been taught the ceremonials of the pub or of duelling. All this, although it is certainly part of German history, is apparently not considered worth studying by the writers of conventional history. For sociologists, by contrast, it is of the greatest significance, but not to denigrate or praise the past, nor to set up a 'cultural history' approach in opposition to 'political history' – such categories are no longer useful. How could one separate social changes in universities from changes in the state societies of which they form a part? The task at hand is first to make the broad outline of behavioural changes comprehensible, and, through comparison with the structures of an earlier phase, to shed new light on what is problematic about the current phase.

Clearly the emancipation of a previously less powerful group, women, opened the universities to girls as people with approximately the same rights. In this situation, the very peculiar conventional ritual which regulated relationships between men and women in European societies lost a great deal of its function. It is now observed only in very rudimentary form. But this ritual did give men and women a certain amount of support in their relationships with each other. It served as an external constraint, on to which a person with a relatively weak apparatus of self-contraint could cling. The ceremonial of student associations in many ways had the same function. Through it, members grew accustomed to an externally controlled discipline exactly as in the military.

Emancipation from this socially inherited apparatus of external constraint, which in some but not all cases took the form of a deliberate revolt, means that young people at university (and of course outside) find themselves faced with a predicament in which society now offers little guidance. In the process of attracting a sexual partner, the entire process of forming pairs which characteristically used to be described from the man's point of view as 'courting', the participants are forced to rely on themselves more than ever before. In other words, dating and pair-formation are individualized to a greater extent. At first glance it may perhaps appear to be paradoxical that this informalization process, this emancipation from the external constraint of a preordained social ritual, makes higher demands on the self-constraint apparatus of each individual participant. It requires the partners to test themselves and each other in their dealings with each other, and in so doing they can rely on nothing and nobody except themselves, their own judgement and their own feelings.

Naturally, the beginnings of the formation of new codes of behaviour, even the beginnings of a form of group control, can also be observed in all this. It sometimes happens that friends in a circle of acquaintances will become involved when a partnership is going through problems, when one of the pair is behaving too badly towards the other according to the opinion of the group. But the main burden of shaping life together at any rate now lies on the shoulders of the individuals concerned. Thus informalization brings with it stronger demands on apparatuses of self-constraint, and, at the same time, frequent experimentation and structural insecurity; one cannot really follow existing models, one has to work out for oneself a dating strategy as well as a strategy for living together through a variety of ongoing experiments.

What I have attempted to illustrate with the example of relations between the sexes at universities also holds for the development of the relationship between men and women more broadly. The American magazine *Time* has occasionally reported on the insecurity experienced by men in whom the old customs are still deeply ingrained:

A man seated on the downtown bus might endure agonies of self-examination before offering his seat to a woman. The male has to learn to size up the female by age, education and possibly ferocity of feminism before opening a door for her: would the courtesy offend her? It makes for ambiguity: if a man studiously refuses to open a door for a woman, is he sexually liberated? Or just an ill-bred slob?[6]

And a recent American book of etiqette lays down the rule that 'Whoever happens to be in the lead, opens the door and holds it for the other.'[7] All of this points towards what is particularly relevant sociologically in this context: first the distinctive features of, and then an explanation for, the informalizing thrust which has occurred in the twentieth century. Only when the structure of this trend has been recognized and understood can one then go on to answer the question of whether or not this is the beginning of a process of rebarbarization. Is it the beginning of the end of the European civilizing movement, or is it not rather its continuation on a new level? The example of relations between the sexes shows how closely the breakdown of a traditional, older code of behaviour and feeling is connected with a change in the balance of power between the social groups whose relations were socially regulated by the code. I cannot here go into the sociogenesis of the code which regulated the conduct of men and women of the upper and lower classes to each other in European societies. It must be enough to point out that in this code, features of the social elevation of women were connected in a remarkable way with those of their subordination to men. Briefly, forms of conduct which were unambiguously characteristic of behaviour towards higher-ranking people, such as bowing or kissing the hand, were adopted towards women and integrated into a code of behaviour which was otherwise quite andrarchic.[8] The transformation of this entire, ambivalent framework of power in the direction of greater equality is illustrated in the changing standards of behaviour between the sexes.

* * *

Without a clear sociological idea of the past, one unavoidably arrives at a distorted view of social relations in the present. Just as this is true of relations between the sexes, so too is it of relations between the pre- and post-war generations. In this case, too, for the sake of brevity I can best bring out the changes in the code of behaviour and feeling by limiting myself at first to comparing university generations, in particular students.

In comparing student life in my own youth with that of today's students, the first thing which strikes me is the emphatically hierarchical form of behaviour under the Kaiser, and the no less emphatically egalitarian behaviour of the generations after the Second World War. The difference is most obvious when one remembers that in the period before the First World War, fraternity members comprised the majority of students; moreover, the student fraternities inculcated attitudes in which dominance and subordination were sharply stamped – perhaps they still do so today. The young fox was required to run all sorts of errands for his older fraternal 'patron', if not to polish his shoes daily as in the corresponding relationship at English public schools. The fraternity rules for drinking in pubs – known in German as the *Bier-Komment* – demanded that the younger person had to empty his glass every time the elder toasted him or raised his glass to him. And if he eventually felt ill, he was allowed to disappear to the toilet. Since German universities traditionally had no facilities whatsoever for the social life of their students, concentrating on their minds and hardly giving the rest of the human being a thought, the student fraternities played a complementary role which should not be under-estimated.

Furthermore, as far as I know, until the First World War the large majority of students had their fees paid by their fathers. This consequently led to a quite specific pattern of social selection. Even without statistical records it can be estimated that before the First World War 90 per cent of students in German universities came from the affluent middle classes. In contrast, consider the breakdown by father's occupation of students at a West German university in 1978:[9] worker (18.1 per cent); white-collar worker (34.6 per cent); civil servant (19.5 per cent); self-employed (20.5 per cent); other (7.2 per cent). Although this does not in fact tally with the proportions of parents' occupations in the total population, compared with 1910 it does show the trend of change in the distribution of power.

Closer examination reveals that amongst students there are certain traits which are less class-specific than generation-specific. It may be that changes are in the offing. But for the time being, there is a widespread generation-specific mistrust amongst German students towards the older generations – that is, those generations who went through the war. Without it being articulated precisely, they are blamed for all those events of the war and the Nazi era which one would really prefer to forget, and with which the younger generation cannot identify itself. The feeling that 'We didn't have anything to do with it' separates the younger generations from the older generations, and separates them more and more from those who 'did have something to do with it'. Although the latter do in fact occupy positions of authority in West Germany, my observations indicate that their authority is not acknowledged by the students.

The strongly egalitarian tendency among the up and coming generations is also expressed by the students' use of the informal 'you' ['*du*']. To a certain extent, it also extends to younger lecturers and professors. For a while, it was apparently a matter of course to address even full professors without their title, simply as 'Mr. . .' – clear signs of an informalizing tendency, and at the same time of a greater claim to power on the part of the students in relation to the professors. I do not dare prophesy how this trend will develop further. In the end, the development at the universities depends on the overall development of the Federal Republic. If authoritarian tendencies in the latter are strengthened, they will also grow stronger at the universities.

Cas Wouters, in an essay which concentrates in particular on the Netherlands, emphasizes how strongly many people of the younger generation, very conscious of the negative example of regimentation by the state, wish to 'free the individual personality totally from social constraints'. But in contrast to earlier periods, when young people strove to find a meaningful responsibility for themselves as individuals, there exists

a greater tendency among these emancipatory generations to seek individual self-fulfilment and self-realisation in groups or in social movements. In that respect the strongly individualistic tendencies which one encounters here have a very different character from that presented by political or cultural liberalism. [And therefore] . . . the restraints which life in groups or movements inevitably imposes on the individual are apt to thwart again and again the imaginary hopes for individual freedom . . . [10]

With all due caution regarding generalizations, this raises a problem very closely related to informalization. The highly formalized organizations of the early student corporations – the duelling corps, the nationalist fraternities, the gymnastic societies – and their strictly hierarchical and authoritarian structure just need to be compared with the endeavours of present-day students towards more egalitarian forms of organization. Then the difference becomes apparent; but so also do the special difficulties facing these aspirations of present-day students. The outcome of younger people joining together today to form an egalitarian group is in many cases the renewal of hierarchy. Because people living together always impose constraints on each other, any group which does not recognize this fact and attempts to realize a life free from constraints (which does not exist) inevitably (if one can so put it) leads to disappointments.

The comparison of the German student associations at the turn of the century and at the present day reveals a few other important points of difference between then and now, especially with respect to the relationships between generations. Two points are particularly striking. First, the fraternities have declined; the shift of power in favour of students who are not members of fraternities means *ipso facto* a massive impetus towards individualization, an emancipation from a formal group discipline which did not relax its hold on group members even in the easy-going atmosphere of the pub. And the more highly individualized younger generations, who also did not feel the need for the patronage of the alumnus Old Boys in their careers, demanded instead more equality with the older generations. A whole series of interwoven factors contributed to shifting the balance of power between the generations in favour of the younger. The advent of state grants for students has played an important role in this context; so did the discrediting of many of the members of the older generations through their association with National Socialism, and more generally, with the lost war. But those are only examples. In the conflict betwen the generations which never totally disappears, a whole complex of factors dealt better cards into the hands of the younger generations of the post-war period.

As is often the case in such a situation, many of the members of the younger generations felt the wind in their sails, and at the same time over-estimated their own strength. In a sometimes grandiose misjudgement of their actual power resources, they concluded that they could now achieve everything they wanted. If the older generations had formerly expressed their superior power *vis-à-vis* the younger via formal rituals of behaviour, then for a while members of the latter fought for the destruction of all these formalities – not just those used between the generations, but those used between people in general. Thinking back on this time in the 1960s and 1970s, one remembers perhaps only the excessive expectations and the bitter taste of disappointment left in the mouths of many people by the actual course of events when these expectations were not fulfilled. The futility of power struggles with over-high hopes sometimes obscures the simple fact that, once the froth and turmoil of the conflicts subsided, social development did not just fall back to the earlier stage of formalization. The dreams were not fulfilled, but the distribution of power between the generations remained most definitely less unequal than it had been before the conflict between the generations openly broke out.

One area in which this is especially evident is in the relationship between unmarried daughters and their parents, and between young women and members of the older generations in general. Of all the changes in the patterns of formalization or informalization and in the balance of power between the generations which have occurred in the course of this century, one of the most marked and significant is the growth in power of young, unmarried women. Right up to the early part of the twentieth century, the life of such women in large parts of the middle class and the aristocracy was predominantly regulated by their family. The individual scope for self-regulation which was open to the young girls of these strata was very limited. Control by older people tightly encompassed all aspects of their lives. To remain alone in a room with a young man not of the family, or even to cross the street unaccompanied, was totally outrageous. Sex before marriage damned a woman who had any self-esteem to lifelong shame. Gerhart Hauptmann's tragedy, *Rose Bernd*, portrays fairly realistically the story of a farmer's beautiful and honest daughter, pursued by men as if she were fair game, who eventually succumbed to the seductive talents of one of them, and who then broke under the shame she thus caused both herself and her family. One should not forget that this regulation of young women's behaviour and feeling by parents, church, state and the entire circle of acquaintances was a type of formalization which corresponded to the then prevalent balance of power between the generations and the sexes.

In less than one hundred years, as can be seen, a really radical change has been accomplished. If now at the end of this century a young woman gets together with a young man and becomes pregnant, then in many cases neither parents nor the young people themselves regard this as a scandal. The informalizing spurt is evident in this attitude, even though it has certainly not been adopted to an equal extent by all strata and all sectors in the more developed societies. But what has actually changed, the structure of the change, often still remains unclear in public discussions. People can frequently see nothing in these changes other than degeneration into disorder. It appears merely as an expression of a loosening of the code of behaviour and feeling, without which a society must fall into destruction. But such a view does not do justice to the facts. The change in the social code regulating the life of young unmarried women shows quite unambiguously that the burden of decision-making and regulation has now shifted to a large extent from the parents and family to the girls themselves. In the relationship between the generations, too, there is increased social pressure towards self-regulation, or, in other words, a thrust towards individualization. If such a change is regarded as decivilizing, then this is because the theory of civilizing processes has been misunderstood.

31

MOZART'S REVOLT

Among Elias's last works was a brief collection of essays on Mozart, written in German, and published posthumously as a book. Many themes from his earlier work converged in these essays: the peculiarities of court society, changing standards of shame and revulsion, established–outsiders relationships, and, of course, the social functions of art – in this case, music. In Elias's work the book on Mozart is especially interesting because here, for the first time, Elias tried his hand at the sociological interpretation of the career of an individual person – an extremely gifted person whose talents were strongly stimulated but eventually thwarted by the promises and pressures emanating from the society of his time.

The following piece is taken from an unfinished final chapter, dealing with the tragic last phase in Mozart's life, after he had broken with both his employer, the Archbishop of Salzburg, and his father.

For almost twenty years Mozart had lived with his father. For all that time his father had guided him. For the major part of this impressionable phase he was Mozart's teacher, manager, friend, doctor, travel guide and middle-man in his dealings with other people. We sometimes hear of the childish traits which Mozart retained until his death. He did indeed have such traits. Given the long reliance on his father that restricted his chance of independence to music-making and composing, that is hardly surprising.

Mozart was a perceptive observer of what went on around him – with regard to particularities and small matters. But his grasp of reality was limited, and was considerably impaired by wishes and fantasies. When he came to a new court and a prince addressed friendly words to him or one of his works was received with applause, he was seized again and again by the absolute certainty that his dream of a secure position laden with honours was about to be fulfilled. That remained the case almost throughout his life. Only very late, under the growing weight of his debts, did he realise somewhat more clearly that this hope might be an illusion, and this reality-shock did much to break him. His indifference and incompetence in the use of money was no doubt also a residue of his childhood, in which his strong, businesslike father had taken care of all such things for him. Possibly, his spontaneity in turning his fantasies into sounds, his feelings into music, and thus the richness of his musical imagination, was also a residue of childhood – and who would wish this spontaneity of an earlier phase to have been replaced by the lack of spontaneity normal in adults of his society?[1]

But in talking about Mozart's 'childish' traits it is easy to forget how grown-up he was in other respects. Evidence of this is the determination with which he carried through his personal revolt against his employer and ruler, and further evidence is the probably far more difficult revolt against his father. The crisis of this separation, the sign of Mozart's coming of age, may seem like a normal part of the human life cycle. But in view of the depth and length of the preceding bond, the break with the father is nothing less than astonishing. It demonstrates a strength of character which surprises us in view of his education.

Mozart was very anxious, as can be seen from his letters, to have his father on his side. The step he had taken gave a new direction to his whole future – of that he was well aware. And he had taken it without seeking his father's advice. That was something new in his life. He had acted impulsively, but at the same time he realised clearly that he had to act thus and not otherwise.

It is certain that Mozart was able to withstand the combined forces of his ruler and employer and his father only because he was strengthened by his knowledge of the value of his artistic work, and thus of his own worth. This knowledge had been consolidated during the prodigy's long years of travel and apprenticeship, and had clearly not lost one whit of its conviction through the setbacks he suffered in his search for a post.

One cannot avoid asking what would have become of Mozart if he had not been so deeply convinced at a relatively young age of the special nature of his musical gift, and of his duty to devote his life to it – a duty that gave meaning to his existence. Would he have been able to produce the musical works to which he owes his later classification as a genius if in the critical situation of 1781 he had not had the strength to resist the pressure of his ruler, his court superiors and his father – in short, the combined forces of Salzburg? Would we have operas like the *Seraglio*, *Don Giovanni* or *The Marriage of Figaro*, piano concertos like the admirable Vienna series, if he had gone back to serve in Salzburg – with all that meant in terms of instructions from the archbishop – and had not participated, or only sporadically, in the rich musical life of Vienna with its (comparatively) enlightened public? We cannot expect an incontrovertible answer to these questions. But it is very probable that if Mozart had decided, for the sake of earning a living, to obey the archbishop's command and use most of his working energy in the way his employer desired, he would have been more bound by the traditional forms of music-making and would have had less scope to develop the court tradition of music in the way that is characteristic of the works of his Vienna period and of his subsequent fame as a genius.

Mozart did not formulate it in general terms, but what he said and did in this critical period indicates how strongly he felt that he would not achieve fulfilment if he did not have the freedom to follow the musical fantasies that rose up in him – frequently without his bidding. He wanted to write music as his inner voices dictated, not as he was commanded by a person who offended his honour and lowered his sense of his own worth. That was the core of his dispute with the archbishop: a conflict over his personal and especially his artistic integrity and autonomy.

The conflict had been slowly brewing and burst out for the first time in the unequal struggle with his princely master and then in his emancipation from his father's guidance. From now on – with shorter and longer breaks – Mozart was pursued by it, just as in ancient mythology someone was pursued by the Furies. Only there it was the compulsion of a fate determined by the gods that drove people guiltlessly guilty into conflict. Here it was quite nakedly a compulsion arising from the co-existence of people and their unequal power-potentials – a social conflict – that was involved. It was fought out first between a ruling prince and an employee who possessed unusual talent and wished to follow his own voices, his own artistic conscience, his own sense of the immanent rightness of sequences of notes that arose in him as words do in others. But at the same time more was at stake than merely two people: two different conceptions of the social function of the musician, one of which was firmly established while the other had as yet no proper place. It was therefore also a conflict between two kinds of music, one of which, the craft music of the court, corresponded to the prevailing social order while the other, that of the freelance artist, was in contradiction to it.

The position of the musician in this society was basically that of a servant or official craftsman. It was not very different to that of a wood-carver, painter, cook or jeweller who, at the behest of fine ladies and gentlemen, had to produce tasteful, elegant or even mildly stimulating products for their edification and entertainment, to enhance the quality of their lives. Mozart undoubtedly knew that his art, as he saw it, would wither if he had to produce music to the orders of uncongenial, indeed hated people whom it would please, regardless of his own mood or his inner affinity to what was demanded. Despite his youth he felt very clearly that his energy as a composer would go to waste if it consumed itself in the narrow confines of the Salzburg court and the tasks it set, particularly as there was not even an opera house and only a mediocre orchestra. The archbishop for his part was doubtless aware that the young Mozart was uncommonly talented and that it would increase the prestige of his court to have such a man among his servants. He was also prepared to lend him to other courts if need be. But in the end he expected Mozart to fulfil his duties and, like any other artisan or servant, to deliver what he was paid for. In short, he wanted Mozart to produce divertimenti, marches, church sonatas, masses or any other fashionable piece of the time, whenever it was needed.

That, then, was the conflict – a conflict between two people, certainly, but two people whose relationship to each other was shaped to a very high degree by their difference in rank and thus in the means of power at their disposal. It was within this constellation tha Mozart took his decision. One must bear the inbuilt power difference in mind to appreciate how strong were the forces that drove him to take it.

To recall that Mozart once stood at such a crossroads, that he was forced to take a decision affecting the whole further course of his life – and not least to recall that he took it one way and not another – is to be made more clearly aware how mistaken is the conceptual severance of the 'artist' from the 'man'. We see here most clearly that Mozart's musical development, the special quality of his evolution as a composer, is inseparable from the development of other aspects of his person – in this case, for example, his ability to recognise which career, indeed which geographical location, would be most fruitful for the unfolding of his talents. The idea that 'artistic genius' can manifest itself in a social vacuum, regardless of how the 'genius' fares as a human being among others, may seem convincing as long as the discussion remains at a very general level. But if we examine exemplary cases with all the relevant detail, the notion of an artist developing autonomously within a human being loses much of its plausibility.

Mozart's revolt against prince and father is such an exemplary case. It is not difficult to imagine what the mood of the twenty-five-year-old would have been if he had prevailed upon himself to obey his master's command and return to his native city. Many musicians of his time and his age would probably have done so. Mozart would then, in all probability, have lived in Salzburg like a bird with clipped wings. The necessity of deciding thus would have affected him at the core of his courage to face life, and of his creative power. It would have robbed him of the feeling that he could have a fulfilling task, that his life could have a meaning.

All the same, in the social conditions of the time and for a musician of his rank it was a highly unusual decision that Mozart took. A generation earlier it would probably have been unthinkable for a court musician to give up a post without having found another. At that time practically no alternative was in sight within this social space. On his visit to Vienna Mozart had looked around, partly with the help of families he knew among the court aristocracy, for alternative means of earning. The hopes this had aroused played a major part in his decision to resign his post in Salzburg. He was able to entertain his desire for personal fulfilment and to settle as a kind of 'freelance artist' in Vienna because conditions in the Austrian capital had developed to a point where they offered him a slight chance of survival.

Whether his decision was realistic is a different question. Perhaps the older people were right who warned of the extreme insecurity of life in Vienna as a musician without a firm post and a fixed salary, and regarded his decision as a sign of his youthful folly, his ignorance of the world. At that time, and even today, it seldom happens that a person's striving for meaning and fulfilment, and the quest for a secure existence, point in the same direction. However, Mozart himself probably had little doubt as to how he should decide. In his eyes the return to Salzburg would have emptied his life of meaning; for him the plan of breaking with Salzburg and staying in Vienna made perfect sense. In Vienna he could breathe more freely, even if it cost him considerable effort to earn his living. Here he had no master with the right to order him about.

Of course, he was still dependent on other people. But it was a somewhat looser (and less secure) dependence. Even while he was living at the arch-bishop's residence and had had to bend himself to the servant's role along with a host of other house musicians, he had revived his earlier contacts with the Viennese court aristocracy. Countess Wilhelmine Thun, the court and state chancellor Count von Cobenzl, had invited the unusually gifted young man to visit them. He had started looking for piano pupils, apparently with some success. As early as May 1781, before the kick that sealed his departure from Salzburg, he had told his father about a 'subscription for six sonatas'.[2] He was referring to some pieces for piano and violin that he dedicated to a pupil, Josepha von Auernhammer, and which appeared in print at the end of November the same year. Vienna delighted and stimulated him. For a time after the break with the archbishop he was clearly in very good spirits. As always, he saw the possibility of a congenial post round the next corner; as always, it proved a castle in the air. However, there were as many piano pupils as he could have wanted. But he did not really like teaching and tried to limit it. He was counting on extra income from concerts in nobles' houses, from public subscription concerts and from subscriptions for the scores of his compositions.

And above all, a commission for an opera, with imperial backing, was in the offing. On 30 July 1781 a skilled and experienced author of opera texts, the younger G. Stephanie, gave Mozart the libretto for a German Singspiel with a Turkish subject, *Bellmont and Constance* or *The Abduction from the Seraglio*. Mozart worked on this project with great energy. Something of the joyful liberation of his first Viennese time is felt in the music he wrote for it. More than in his previous operas he took the liberty of developing the court music tradition in which he had grown up, and which had become second nature to him, in his personal way. To be able to do this, more than was permitted in Salzburg – to follow his own musical imagination, was one of his primordial desires. It was, as we have said, his way to fulfilment.

To this extent Mozart did indeed now resemble a freelance artist. But even this early attempt to give free rein to his musical imagination revealed something of the dilemma facing the 'free' artist. In giving latitude to his individual fantasm, and especially to his ability to synthesise previously separate elements in a way which breaches the existing canon of taste, he initially reduced his chances of finding resonance in the public. This need not be dangerous if the power relationships in his society are such that the art-loving public which pays to enjoy art is relatively uncertain in its taste, or at least is dependent in forming its taste on specialised art establishments to which the leading artists themselves belong. It is different in a society whose establishment regards good taste in the arts as in dress, furniture and houses as the natural prerogative of its own social group.[3] Here, the inclination of a 'freelance artist' to innovate beyond the existing canon can be extremely dangerous for him or her. Emperor Joseph II, who had involved himself somewhat in the planning of Mozart's opera *The Abduction from the Seraglio* as the prototype of a German Singspiel, was clearly not quite satisfied with the finished work. He told the composer after the Vienna *première*: 'Too many notes, my dear Mozart, too many notes.'

One of the singers, too, seems to have complained that her voice could not be heard above the orchestra. In this respect, too, without realising it, Mozart had inaugurated another shift in the balance of power. At the court opera houses of the old style the singers were in control. The instrumental music was subservient; it was there to accompany them. But in the *Seraglio* Mozart had changed this power balance somewhat; he sometimes liked to intertwine the human and instrumental voices in a kind of dialogue. He thereby undermined the privileged position of the singers. And at the same time he unsettled court society, which was used in an opera to empathising with the human voices and not with simultaneous orchestral voices. If Mozart gave the orchestra something to say, the public did not hear it. They only heard 'too many notes'.[4]

32

THE SYMBOL THEORY

As a young man Elias had lost his sight in one eye in a skiing accident. When he grew older, his other eye also deteriorated so that he became almost blind. Instead of writing his own texts he therefore now had to resort to dictating. During the last ten years of his life he always had assistants who would come in every day at 2.00 pm, and work with him till 10.00 pm or later. Because the work was quite strenuous, there were usually two assistants who came on alternate days; except for one, Rudolf Knijff, none of the assistants stayed on for much longer than a year.

The practice of dictating created special problems of composition for Elias. Being unable to read over his own text he had to have his assistant read aloud to him what he had been dictating. The lack of a clear overview made itself felt especially in the two most far-reaching monographs he completed towards the end of his life – *Time: An Essay* and *The Symbol Theory*. Both books dealt with the civilizing process of humanity at large. *The Symbol Theory* in particular was a magisterial combination of his sociological insights with current palaeoanthropological knowledge and evolutionary theory into one grand synthesis. It was in this book that he unfolded his theory of the five-dimensional universe in which humanity finds itself living: constituted by the three dimensions of space, plus time and consciousness.[1]

To conclude this reader we present the final pages of *The Symbol Theory* – written with an all-embracing grasp, and with some tongue-in-cheek asides.

It is sometimes argued that only since the coming of science in the sixteenth and seventeenth centuries of our era can humans be said to possess the means of acquiring true or valid knowledge of nature. They give the impression that scientific knowledge came into being as a result of the accidental appearance in Europe of a number of unusually gifted individuals. In actual fact the break-through to what we now call a scientific form of acquiring knowledge of nature would have been impossible and must remain quite incomprehensible without the antecedent advances in knowledge made in Antiquity and the Middle Ages. Even those of our ancestors who spent their lives as hunters and food gatherers or as early agriculturalists possessed a great deal of knowledge which, though one cannot call it scientific, certainly deserves to be called reality congruent. It deserves this characterization even though it was blended throughout with dominant fantasy knowledge.

At present the ability to perceive long-term processes encompassing thou-sands of years, such as the growth of humankind's knowledge of nature, is seriously impaired by the historical mode of perceiving and presenting the human past. This mode of perceiving the past not only suggests an often arti-ficial break between what is called prehistory and history, it also focuses attention to such an extent on details, that process structures which demand a long-term vision may be theoretically disregarded. If the development of humankind as a whole is used as a frame of reference, the growth of reality-congruent knowledge is indeed obvious. Although many details of that type of knowledge once possessed by members of simpler societies are now lost, humankind's overall fund of knowledge has grown over time at both the empirical and the integrating theoretical levels. With it has grown the rule of humans over their fellow creatures on earth. Orientation with the help of knowledge has given human beings a great advantage over almost all other species. Perhaps one can explain the constancy with which object-congruent knowledge increased as a sign of its high survival value.

This is not to say that the process of knowledge growth has uniformly gone in the same direction. A more detailed survey would show a rather complex pattern of advances in knowledge intermingling with blockages and regres-sions. I can briefly mention as an example four stages in the development of Middle-Eastern and European knowledge as a continuous process whose earliest known stage was the development of visual symbols, in other words writing, in addition to audible symbols, in other words spoken language, as means of communication in ancient Sumer. Once can distinguish two distinct phases of priest-dominated knowledge and two equally distinct phases domi-nated by secular groups:

First phase of priest-dominated knowledge (*c.* late fourth millennium–sixth century BC).
First phase of secular knowledge (*c.* sixth century BC–fourth century AD).
Second phase of priest-dominated knowledge (*c.* fourth century AD–fifteenth century AD).
Second phase of secular knowledge (*c.* fifteenth century AD —).

Comte's law of three stages comes to mind. However, the sequence briefly mentioned here is neither a law nor a model of a necessary and irreversible process. It is a purely fact-oriented model indicating one of the salient aspects of the continuity of knowledge transmission. It can be revised or abandoned if that is demanded in accordance with newly discovered knowledge of facts. The development of writing can serve as example of the continuity of knowledge development in spite of its transition from one people or one state to another. Whatever the descent of the Phoenician writing may have been, the Hellenic Greeks learned it from them. As far as we know it had no connection with the Mycenaean Greek alphabet which apparently was derived from an older form of writing developed in Crete. The Roman alphabet was one of the transformations of the Greek form of writing. The Roman writing transformed itself into the medieval writing and so into ours.

In Comte's time it was not unusual to include in the development of knowledge non-rational or religious knowledge as an early phase of knowledge development; he was not the only scholar of that age who suggested such a sequence as a quasi-natural necessity. At the end of the twentieth century one is in a better position to recognize that this was a fantasy. The scheme presented here indicates a close link between processes of knowledge and of state formation. The first flowering of priest-dominated knowledge was centred on the ancient Middle-Eastern monarchies of which those of ancient Sumer, ancient Egypt and Babylon are examples. In most of these states a priestly aristocracy headed by the chief priest and centred on the first large-scale social organization, the temple household on the one hand and a warrior aristocracy headed by the king and centred on the palace on the other hand, were bound to each other as fellow rulers of the state and as rivals in many power struggles. Though in Egypt, more protected from invasions than the Mesopotamian states during the earlier part of its history, the warrior aristocracy gave way very early to an aristocracy of state officials engaged in a fluctuating power struggle with groups of priests. Although the groups centred on the palace made contributions to the development of knowledge, at that stage by and large priests dominated the production and transmission of knowledge.

A striking feature of the knowledge process comes to light if one compares the priestly organization and the structure of knowledge of the first priest-dominated phase with those of the second phase. The latter did not simply represent a return to the former. The advances made during the first period of secular knowledge were not simply lost in the second period of priest-dominated knowledge. The latter represented a complex blend of regression and progression. Myth ruled again where proto-scientific enquiry had ruled before. But the priestly organization modelled itself on the state organization of the Roman Empire which had given birth to it. In the form of a church it became much more highly centralized and unified than religious beliefs and cults had in the first phase of priest-dominated knowledge. One of its most significant innovations was its reliance on the authority of a book. The concept formation of the church benefited greatly from the advances in concept formation to higher level of abstraction or synthesis made at the preceding secular stage. In this context these examples may be enough to indicate that the four-stages model had in no way the character of uniform progressions and regressions. But they may at least illuminate the complexity of the knowledge process. The model invites comparisons. That is one of the criteria of its reality-congruence. It led to the emergence of a scientific form of discovery.

The example also illuminates the nature and function of models of long-term processes, in this case of long processes of knowledge growth. The advances in the natural sciences may tempt people to regard process models as a kind of law or of law-like generalizations. Comte succumbed to this temptation. But sociological process models have in no way the character of general laws for numerous recurrent special cases. The process represented by the four-stages model was probably unique. It may never happen again. This model provides an articulation of what I have said before, that a continuous process of knowledge transmission and growth can bind to each other the knowledge traditions of different countries and peoples. One can trace back to ancient Sumer the process of continuous knowledge transmission and growth which in the Renaissance blossomed forth in the form of scientific knowledge in what we now conceive as European countries. In the course of this process specific secular groups succeeded twice in breaking the monopoly over the transmission and production of knowledge that priestly groups had acquired before, first in Graeco-Roman societies and later again in European societies. In all likelihood the first spurt of secular knowledge and the absorption of some of its aspects by the second phase of priest-dominated knowledge was one of the conditions of the second secular spurt. Why was it, this is the problem, that in the context of the Sumero-European tradition secular groups twice succeeded in creating a knowledge tradition of their own and in gaining for their secular type of knowledge dominance over the priest-controlled knowledge? The characteristics which distinguish scientific and non-scientific knowledge can hardly stand out clearly if attention and factual knowledge is concentrated on the latter. I am raising the question here as an example of the role that models representing high-level syntheses can play in the study of human societies.

It may be useful if at the end I briefly point out two aspects of this study which are implied but which have not been made explicit. In at least two respects the empirical field of vision underlying the symbol theory is wider and the level of theoretical synthesis correspondingly higher than they usually are in historical, sociological and other social science studies. *First*, the implied social frame of reference of such studies is usually the main survival unit of our age, the nation state. It is in traditional anthropological investigations the tribe. That the state is the main level of integration to which enquiries are geared may not be as obvious in the case of sociological investigations as it is in historical investigations, but if one examines what sociologists mean when they speak of society one usually finds that they rarely go beyond the integration level of the state though they may confine their field of vision to sub-divisions of a state. Moreover, they usually confine their efforts to state-internal relationships. Sociologists rarely include in their field of vision, and thus in their conception of society, relations between states and the changes these undergo. In other words, the developments of continental groups of states and ultimately of humankind are as a rule regarded as lying outside the problem fields of sociologists. They are not so regarded here.

As long as society is implicitly identified with state-internal relationships between human beings, relations between states and humankind as the unit of integration they form with each other are made to appear as existing outside society or perhaps as not existing at all. In point of fact relations between states are relations between people. They are only different from family relationships and others within a state society in so far as they represent a different level of integration. They are no less real than social relationships below or at the state level. If nothing else, the use of violence in inter-state relationships, in other words wars, makes that very clear. That family relations, industrial relations and inter-state relations as subject matter for research belong to different academic specialisms may contribute to the impression that state-internal relations are social relations and relations at the inter-state level are not. If nothing else, the very obvious interdependence of different levels of society and the constant interdependence of their development could correct the impression.

The problem one encounters here draws attention to a gap in the conceptual armoury of sociologists with which they are not very well equipped to deal. Human societies, as they are constituted today, have several interwoven levels of integration. The kin group level, the tribal level, the state level, the continental level, and finally the level of humanity, they all are steps on the ladder. Observers of the contemporary scene may notice a very pronounced difference in the power chances available to representatives of different levels of integration at different stages of humanity's development. Sociologists and indeed social scientists in general are not yet adequately equipped to deal with human relationships at different levels of integration and with the developmental changes these can undergo.

A striking example is the transition from the tribal to the state level of integration that one can at present observe in parts of Africa. I have vivid memories of these changes. In the early 1960s I was teaching sociology at a Ghanaian university. I was invited to one of the great local festivals, and remember the set-up. It took place in the open air. The guests were seated in a very wide circle. The hosts, local chiefs, were seated at one side of the circle.

At the opposite side was seated the guest of honour, the delegate of the state president. In their toga-like traditional costumes they looked like Roman senators, dignified and proud. The ceremony began with the chiefs getting up from their seats and walking with some of their followers slowly to the seats of the representatives of the state, presumably welcoming them to their festival. They returned to their seats. After a short interval the state representative and his staff got up and, walking through the whole circle, reciprocated the chiefs' visit, presumably thanking them for their invitation and expressing the good wishes of the head of state. What we saw was a symbolic representation of a certain equilibrium which had been reached in the long drawn-out tug-of-war between representatives of the two levels, of tribe and state. The president of the first African colony to become an independent state, while reserving more and more sources of real power for himself as head of state, wished to maintain as much as possible of the ceremonial power of tribal chiefs whom he regarded as a specifically African institution.

In details these processes of state formation may vary greatly. They can take the form of a hegemonic struggle for occupation of the state's governmental positions between different tribes or of a king's struggle with his powerful barons. Disintegration was usually the alternative to victorious integration at a state level. But many battles were usually fought before a final decision was reached. In Africa, too, the transition from the tribal to the state level often enough found its expression in war and destruction. The ceremony I witnessed indicated recognition of the supremacy of a state as well as recognition of the limited sovereignty of local chiefs. Analogous problems arise at the transition from the nation state to a continental federation of such states. They arise when superpowers put pressure on less powerful states. They arise too when superpowers in the name of humankind try to enforce rules to protect the individual against laws of his own state that they regard as inhumane. Struggles of this kind may well be the early stage of a long process in the course of which humankind as the highest level of integration may gain equality if not superiority of sovereignty compared with that of the state.

While in many parts of Africa the dominant integration struggle is still that between relationships at the tribal or village level and those at the state level, in other continents the dominant integration trend is the incipient movement from a nation state to a federation of such states. The transition from a multitude of European nation states to a union of European states is an example of this kind. Similar integration spurts in Latin America are still in the experimental stage. The nation state's supreme function as survival unit diminishes in an era of atomic weapons, supra-national economic markets and steadily shrinking travel time. Increasingly humankind as a whole emerges step-by-step as the most likely survival unit. This does not imply that the individual as a level of integration and unit of reference disappears. Just as in the

Renaissance a pronounced spurt of integration at the state level went hand in hand with a loosening of the individual's bonds with traditional groupings such as kin group or guild, so in our days a spurt of integration at the level of humankind goes hand in hand with a strengthening of an individual's rights within the nation state.

At different stages of development different levels of integration stand out as the most powerful and effective. But in order to perceive these differences one has to stand back and to distance oneself from a many-levelled society and from one's own position within it. In the field of human societies scientific observers have to place themselves as it were at a different level of the spiral staircase from that of the objects they study. If one speaks of the state in the singular one stands at the level of a multitude of states. If one observes the multitude of states one tacitly stands at the level of humankind. No higher level of integration is available. For the sake of comparison, therefore, one chooses in this case antecedent levels of evolutionary integration. One tries to perceive the distinguishing characteristics of humankind by comparison with those of animals. By extending one's field of vision in this manner one ascends from the state to the plurality of states and thus ultimately to humanity as the tacit reference unit of sociological enquiries. If that is done the singularity of languages as means of human communication and of funds of knowledge as means of human orientation stand out more clearly. It is not unusual to speak of language in the singular when one actually refers to languages in the plural. In the case of knowledge the use of the singular can be justified by the supra-national identity of natural science knowledge and of technology. Yet different knowledge traditions exist side by side with this identical knowledge in different nation states. It is one of many languages, one of many knowledge traditions which children receive as their own.

What one observes as a fact, humanity's drawing more closely together, may help to support the theoretical point. In sociologists' work humanity, from being a distant ideal becomes a level of integration and a social formation among others. Both the theory of civilizing processes and the symbol theory can serve as examples. Evidence for both can be found at all levels of social development. All are stages in the development of humanity. The unit of comparison is always the span between the least and the most developed social units at a given stage. Ice-age societies and thus ice-age humanity in all likelihood nowhere transcended the tribal stage. Differences in their stage of development may elude us because at first approach and seen from a distance what remains from them all over the globe seems so much alike. The stage during which tribal units still had a chance to conquer an earlier type of city states and territorial states usually run by groups of priests and of warriors, lasted a few thousand years. Now a relatively small number of states swallow the tribes wherever they still exist.

Multi-dimensional models of human societies are needed in order to come to grips with the empirical evidence. The difficulty is that social scientists and sociologists in particular are still captives of a philosophical science theory which started with Descartes and took its cue from physics at that early stage of development. At that stage there was no need for multi-dimensional theoretical models. All objects of physics, and thus according to many philosophers all objects, seemed to represent the same and the only level of integration. Theoretical models of the type we call universal laws or generalizations were sufficient, and sufficiently reality-congruent to serve the requirements of physicists at that stage. These models have not lost their usefulness. But for some time now they have been supplemented even in the physical sciences themselves by theoretical models which, unlike laws, are multi-dimensional and which make it possible to handle experimentally data about objects such as large molecules, genes and chromosomes with several levels of integration acting and reacting upon each other.

An introduction to the symbol theory cannot be the place to explore the great variety of avenues into which one is led by the human capacity for symbolic representation. But a word of caution may be useful. The relationship between symbols and the objects they represent is not necessarily identical in all cases. In the case of language symbolization this relationship is different from that which one encounters in the relationship between theoretical models and the objects they represent. In the latter some similarity of structure is essential. In the case of language representation no similarity need be expected. This excursion may help to explain the sociologists' aim. One of the major aims is the production of testable models which enable people to understand better how and why societies function as they do and thus also what one may regard as their defects. They help to explain and thus also make accessible to a public enquiry the malfunctioning of societies. Sociological models, theoretical or empirical, are a means of experimentation and planned discovery. Both can have unexpected results. Sociological models, therefore, can also give rise to unplanned discoveries. One may perhaps regard as an open question whether the strong trend towards individual discontinuity of the models built by sociological theorists is compatible with the complexity of their task. Co-operation is not made easier by the fact that political doctrine often prevails over reality-congruence as the yardstick of a model's cognitive value. This may also help to explain why representation of societies as many-levelled structures is rare in sociological theories. Political doctrine is apt to limit the field of vision to intra-state issues. In actual fact intra-state issues can hardly be separated from inter-state issues: theories of society have to embrace both. Here the field of vision has been extended from the level of intra-state relationships to that of humankind.

Present custom highlights what language and knowledge at all stages have in common. It fails to supplement their common function and structure by a testable model of the changes they undergo. One may expect a single person

– the 'great man' – to illuminate at one stroke in his work the great variety of problems which human societies present, but that is not a realistic expectation. This task cannot be performed single-handedly by one individual. It is a task which can only be performed by the co-operation of many individuals through a sequence of generations. It also requires, as I have already indicated, a widening of one's field of vision. One step in that direction has been taken here. A deep-rooted tradition which identifies society as society within a nation state has been challenged here. In the past the implied level of integration of the work of sociologists has often been neglected. Ultimately, in both cases, the frame of reference is humankind. This is one of the two extensions of the field of vision of which I have spoken. It implies above all, though by no means exclusively, a widening of one's vision of the contemporary scene. It accentuates the singularity of the only species of living beings who communicate with each other by means of languages and orientates itself as member of a specific knowledge tradition.

The *second* extension of the field vision underlying the symbol theory concerns above all the extension of its framework into the past. One of the main characteristics of scientific knowledge is the planned extension of reality-congruent knowledge. As I have already said, before people reached the stage in which they aimed at a planned discovery they did not lack reality-congruent knowledge, but its acquisition, by and large, was haphazard and coincidental. Galileo and his successors discovered planned discovery by means of continuous sequences of model-building and systematically testing experimentation. But they could not have made their breakthrough to the planned discovery of reality-congruent knowledge without a great fund of reality-congruent knowledge which resulted from unplanned discoveries. A great mass of reality-congruent knowledge acquired more haphazardly by accident or good fortune was the condition of planned discovery.

In this context too it is fitting to use humanity as the social frame of reference. Our animalic ancestors did not have the distinguishing characteristics of humans as long as their main mode of communication was not that of learned languages and their main mode of orientation not that of orientation by means of learned knowledge. From early days on discoveries of high survival value travelled from the originating society to other societies. This enquiry suggests that one can distinguish between two stages in the emergence and growth of living beings who mainly communicate by using languages and who mainly orientate themselves by using knowledge, first in the form of audible, and later also of visible symbols. Both stages are hypothetical. But hypothetical models are better than a void. They facilitate discovery. The first stage is the evolutionary metamorphosis of animal species who communicate and orientate themselves mainly by means of genetically predetermined activities into an order of living beings we call humans, who perform the same activities by means of learned symbols. They have a genetically predetermined disposition for the use of these symbols which requires patterning through learning. The second phase mainly concerns the non-biological, intergenerational growth of humanity's language and knowledge traditions. This is a social or developmental process which in the early phases may have run side by side and may have intermingled with the evolutionary metamorphosis of ape-like animals into hominids of the present type. The social process is better documented than the biological process. But even in its hypothetical form the picture of the evolutionary branch of the human-ization process articulates a problem which, answerable or not, social scientists cannot omit to raise if only as a means of clarifying the human image with which they work.

Two key questions are: how did humanity come into being? and what are its distinguishing characteristics compared with its more animalic forebears? If one speaks of the Palaeolithic or Neolithic age it is very much taken for granted that the social frame of reference is humankind as a whole. One often fails to see clearly that orientation with the help of a social fund of knowledge is one of the main characteristics which distinguishes humankind from other living beings. The search for properties which can help to explain differences in the make-up and behaviour of animals and those of humans are usually confined to differences in the properties of organisms seen alone as individ-uals and not yet also as societies. Bifocal vision and upright gait are examples. Best known and most popular are human distinguishing characteristics such as reason, mind, intellect or rationality. They all are concepts which support the ideal of the self-reliant individual, of an individual without group. They make one forget to observe as relevant differences in the manner in which animals and human beings live together, differences in their societies. And yet the latter, differences in their social life, are among the outstanding dis-tinguishing characteristics of animals and humans. As I have already observed, animal societies can undergo great changes only as part of a change in their genetic make-up. Human societies can undergo great changes without any such changes in genetic make-up. At the root of many of these differences is the heightened capacity of humans for acting upon learned knowledge. It is this human condition which makes communication by way of languages and advances or recessions to a different stage in the development of societies, possible. The natural constitution of human beings prepares them for learning from others, for living with others, for being cared for by others and for caring for others. It is difficult to imagine how social scientists can gain a clear under-standing of the fact that nature prepares human beings for life in society without including aspects of the evolutionary process and of the social development of humankind in their field of vision. This is the second extension of the field suggested here.

Extension with the accent on past and present times seems to demand supplementation by an extension of one's frame of reference into the future.

However, social scientists are no prophets. But there are aspects of the future of humankind about which one can speak with reasonable certainty. In this respect I can offer an observation. It concerns the implied assumptions about the position of the present age within the development of humankind. The usual scheme with which we work – represented by concepts such as prehistory and history, or Antiquity, Middle Ages and modern times – can easily give the impression that what we call modern times represents a relatively late stage in this development. Closely connected with it is the tendency to consider present times as a rather advanced stage in the development of human civilization. And if one considers the development of humankind in isolation this estimate is understandable. In this context it is not usual to extend one's field of vision to the development of the solar system. It is, however, not entirely without relevance for any estimate of the position of this age within the development of humankind. Life on earth and so the existence of humankind depends on the sun. Cosmologists inform us that the sun is at present at the middle of its foreseeable lifespan, as one might call it metaphorically, and that they expect the sun to continue its role as a life-supporting star for several thousand million years. If humankind does not destroy itself, if it is not destroyed by a meteor or another cosmic collision – which are certainly very real possibilities – the natural conditions of its existence will give humans the opportunity to tackle the problems of their life together on earth, or wherever, for a very long time to come. A future of 4000 million years should give humans the opportunity to muddle their way out of several blind alleys and to learn how to make their life together more pleasant, more meaningful and worthwhile. In the context of humanity's future, short-term perspectives are necessarily misleading. Today cosmologists appear to take it for granted that living creatures at the same level of development or even at a higher level exist elsewhere in the universe. I think one should not exclude from consideration the possibility that human beings owe their existence to a unique sequence of coincidences, that the development of human beings biologically equipped for the use of languages and knowledge is extremely rare, if not unique.

In the light of a future between the alternatives of self-destruction and a future of millions of years, the prevailing estimate which attributes to what we call modern times the character of a relatively late development demands correction. The fact that we have not yet learned how to curb wars, the reciprocal mass destructions of members of different states and other forms of behaviour that one cannot help calling barbarous, lends support to the assumption that in the overall context of the possible development of humankind what we call modern times represents a very early rather than a late stage of development. I like best the suggestion that our descendants, if humanity can survive the violence of our age, might consider us as late barbarians. I am not indulging in reproaches. Humans have to go through a long period of learning how to live with each other in peace. Our uncertainty, our inability to eliminate violence, are part of this learning process. No teachers are at hand. Outside help, evidently, is not forthcoming. Expressions of good will, exhortations to good behaviour, are welcome but hardly effective. The professing of antagonistic ideals inflames rather than tempers violence. People have to learn for themselves how to live with each other. In this case too planned discovery of explanations may be of help. As yet we do not know how to curb or how to eliminate violence effectively from human relations. We are trapped in a situation in which governments who are seriously concerned with eliminating wars also participate in and favour a flourishing arms trade which helps other nations to prepare themselves for war.

We have not yet learned to cope with the obvious contradictions of our age. We know already *that* human beings are able to live in a more civilized manner with each other, but we do not know *how* to bring it about in our life with each other, or at least only sporadically. We know already that much depends on achieving a better balance between self-restraint and self-fulfilment, but a stable social order that warrants such a balance still eludes us. It should not be beyond the reach of humanity in the thousands of years ahead of us.

NOTES

Notes to editorial and introductions
Page references to the four notes to the editorial introductions are given in brackets at the end of each note.

On Primitive Art
1   For substantial excerpts from the original transactions see Meja and Stehr 1990, pp. 86–106. [p. 9]

An Outline of The Civilizing Process
1   The translation of the first few lines has been amended slightly in order to convey the important point that Elias was not writing about man in the singular but about people in the plural. See on this issue Goudsblom 1977b, pp. 126–31. [p. 39]

Involvement and Detachment
1   The changes in Elias's reputation are clearly reflected in the acknowledgements made to him in the successive editions of *Human Societies*, a textbook in sociology written by a group of Leicester sociologists (Hurd 1973 and 1986). In the 1973 edition Elias was thanked briefly, after a long eulogy on Ilya Neustadt, because his 'introductory course in Sociology inspired his fellow teachers as well as his students' (p. viii). In the 1986 edition (p. ix) Neustadt received only one sentence of acknowledgement, while Elias was put on a par with Karl Marx, Max Weber, and Emile Durkheim, and praised extensively. [p. 84]

The Symbol Theory

1   That the notion of a five-dimensional universe is unfamiliar was demonstrated when the editor of the American review journal *Contemporary Sociology* changed the word 'five-dimensional' in the expression 'the five-dimensional universe of space, time, and symbols' into 'three-dimensional'. See *Contemporary Sociology* 22 (1993), p. 282. [p. 252]

Notes to the chapters

In citing sources, for most of his career Elias followed the older convention of giving only a book's author, title, date and place of publication, with no details of publishers. Only in his last publications in English did he conform to the current practice of providing the names of publishers too.

Court Society as a Sociological Problem

1   Cf. *'Tableau du siècle' par un auteur connu* (Saint-Cyr) Geneva, 1759, p. 132: 'La Ville est, dit-on, le singe de la Cour.'

2   'Court' has a meaning which changes with the period to which it is applied. In what follows, it refers to the princely court, in keeping with the usage of the time. However, if we were not concerned primarily with France, but also with Germany, a characteristic reservation would need to be made. For in Germany, above all in the western part, the households of more lowly members of the aristocracy, e.g. counts, had a court character in some respects: and as in Germany not all power was concentrated in *one* princely court, these petty court formations down to the households of the landed gentry had a very different social and cultural importance than did similar formations in France.

3   Franz Oppenheimer, *System der Soziologie*, Jena, 1924, vol. 3, 2, 1, p. 922.

4   At the time of the first Bourbons income from domanial possessions, as compared to that from other sources, above all taxes for the maintenance of the royal household, played only a very insignificant part. Substantial parts of the old domanial possessions had been disposed of by the kings in the wars and emergencies of the sixteenth and even the fifteenth centuries. Sully and after him Richelieu often complained about this. Both tried in vain to buy back the royal domain. Cf. Marion, *Dictionnaire des institutions au XVIIième et XVIIIième siècles* Paris, 1923, art. 'Domaine'.

5   Max Weber, *Wirtschaft und Gesellschaft*, Tübingen, 1922, p. 750. His way of posing the problem – and it is no more than this – went beyond that of Thorstein Veblen, who has the merit in his *Theory of the Leisure Class* (1899) of having dealt – no doubt for the first time – with problems of status-orientated consumption as sociological problems.

6   The index of *Economy and Society* contains only a reference to 'court justice' relating to a quite different period.

7   Werner Sombart, *Der moderne Kapitalismus*, 5th edn, Munich and Leipzig, 1922, vol. 1, 2, pp. 720–1.

The Expulsion of the Huguenots from France

1   Ernest Lavisse, *Louis XIV*, Paris, 1907, p. 41.

An Outline of The Civilizing Process

1   This expression should not be understood to mean that all the individual phases of society's history are reproduced in the history of the civilized individual. Nothing would be more absurd than to look for an 'agrarian feudal age' or a 'Renaissance' or a 'courtly-absolutist period' in the life of the individual. All concepts of this kind refer to the structure of whole social groups.

What must be pointed out here is the simple fact that even in civilized society no human being comes into the world civilized, and that the individual civilizing process that he compulsorily undergoes is a function of the social civilizing process. Therefore, the structure of the child's affects and consciousness no doubt bears a certain resemblance to that of 'uncivilized' peoples, and the same applies to the psychological stratum in grown-ups which, with the advance of civilization, is subjected to more or less heavy censorship and consequently finds an outlet in dreams, for example. But since in our society each human being is exposed from the first moment of life to the influence and the molding intervention of civilized grown-ups, he must indeed pass through a civilizing process in order to reach the standard attained by his society in the course of its history, but not through the individual historical phases of the social civilizing process.

Civilization and Rationalization

1   To understand this fact is not only of theoretical but also of practical significance. Differences in the extent to which thinking is charged with affects make themselves felt again and again in the relationships between states at different stages of social development. As a rule, however, the leading statesmen of highly differentiated societies devise their strategies on the assumption that the level of restraint, the code of conduct, represented by the foreign policy of all countries is the same. Without an understanding of the different stages of a civilizing process interstate policy must necessarily be somewhat unrealistic. However, to work out foreign policy based on the knowledge of these differentials in affectivity is far from easy. It will need to a good deal of experimenting – and of wisdom – before an effective political dialogue and co-operation between societies at different levels of development can be worked out. The same applies to those cases in which, under stress, the affectivity and the fantasy character of the foreign policy of one of the more developed countries increases again to a higher level than that regarded at present as normal in the interstate relations of the leading industrial nation state. Nor are these levels in the degree of affectivity entirely dependent on the differentials of the economic or industrial development of countries. Thus, in the political strategies of China, for instance, one can discover a level of self-restraint at least on a par with that of the most highly developed industrial nations. Although in terms of its own economic development China still lags behind, its state formation process in terms of duration and continuity surpasses that of most other existing state societies of our time. [*Author's note to the translation*]

2   The word figuration did not appear in the original German text of 1939 but was added by Elias in the English translation of 1982 [editor's note].

3   The waning supremacy of the Church, the changing balance of power between

religious and secular rulers – between priests and warriors – in favour of the latter opened the way to – or was, in other words, the *conditio sine qua non* of – the secularization of thought without which all that one means if one speaks of 'rationalization' could not have come into its own. The emergence not only of one but of a whole group of tightly organized and competing large territorial states ruled by secular princes, which is one of the major distinguishing characteristics of the European development, was one of its factors; the growth of large urban markets and long-distance trade and the growth of capital indispensable for it was another. A whole complex of social levers – levers of 'rationalization' – worked in the direction strengthening of less affective, less fantasy-oriented modes of thought and experience. The great intellectual pioneers, above all the philosophical pioneers of rational thought, thus worked from within a powerful process of social change which gave them direction, but they themselves were also active levers within this movement, not merely its passive objects. In fact one has to take into consideration the whole concourse of basic processes forming the core of the overall development of society – basic processes such as the long-term process of state formation, of capital formation, of differentiation and integration, of orientation, of civilization, and others. [*Author's note to the translation*]

The Naval Profession

1 Pepys, Tangier Papers, N.R.S., 1935, p. 121.
2 Page 7.
3 Page 22.

The Quest for Excitement in Leisure

1 John Stow, *A Survey of London*, first published in 1603 and reprinted in Oxford in 1908.
2 Ibid., pp. 96 ff.
3 Norbert Elias, *The Civilizing Process*, One volume edition, Oxford, Basil Blackwell, 1994, pp. 465ff. 'Feudalization' is an example of a spurt in the opposite direction.
4 Thus Geoffrey Green in his *History of the Football Association* (London, 1953, p. 7) takes the reference to 'the famous game of ball' (*ludum pilae celebrem*) by William Fitzstephen in his panegyric *Descriptio Nabilissimae Civitatis Londinae* (1175, quoted in Stow, *A Survey of London*), as evidence for the fact that football was played by the youth of London in the twelfth century, Though more cautious, Morris Marples in his *A History of Football* (London, 1954, pp. 19–21) concludes that 'there is a good reason to suppose that Fitzstephen is actually describing football.'
5 For an elaboration of this point, see Norbert Elias, *What is Sociology?*, London, 1978, pp. 75–6.
6 Not all games are 'sports' and not all sports are 'games'. The term 'sport-games' refers to those – football, rugby, tennis, cricket, golf, etc. – to which both terms apply.

Group Charisma and Group Disgrace

1   Max Weber, *The Religion of India*, translated and edited by D. Martindale and Hans H. Gerth. Glencoe, IL, Free Press, 1958, 1, 10, p. 49 (Caste and Sib).

2   Norbert Elias and John L. Scotson, *The Established and the Outsiders: A Sociological Enquiry into Community Problems.* London, Frank Cass, 1965. Second edition, with a substantial later Introduction, London, Sage, 1994.

3   I have consulted for this translation the German text which can be found in the *Gesammelte Aufsätze zur Religionssoziologie*, Bd II, *Hinduismus und Buddhismus*, Tübingen, Mohr (Siebeck), 1921, pp. 51 ff, as well as the English translation by Don Martindale and Hans H. Gerth (*The Religion of India*). This translation was evidently aimed in the first place at providing a readable English text. Without such a translation Max Weber's work might have remained buried in his native language. But in order to provide a readable English text, ideas which sounded alien in an English idiom had to be toned down or anglicized. In the present context, however, it was important to bring out in English as nearly as possible Max Weber's own concept, even if his phrasing sometimes sounds a bit un-English.

4   Max Weber's, 'Die Wirtschaftsethik der Weltreligionen', in *Gesammelte Aufsätze sur Religionssoziologie, op. cit.* (MS finished in 1920).

5   My own italics.

6   Max Weber, '*Wirtschaft und Gesellschaft*, Tübingen, Mohr (Siebeck), 1956, vol. I, p. 140 . . . 'eine als ausseralltäglich geltende Qualität einer Persönlichkeit . . . um derentwillen sie als mit übernatürlichen oder mindestens als spezifisch ausseralltäglichen nicht jedem andern zugänglichen Kräften oder Eigenschaften begabt . . . und deshalb als 'Führer' gewertet wird. Wie die betreffende Qualität von irgendeinem ethischen, ästhetischen oder sonstigen Standpunkt aus 'objektiv' richtig zu bewerten sein *würde*, ist natürlich dabei begrifflich völlig gleichgültig; darauf allein, wie sie tatsächlich von den charismatisch Beherrschten, den 'Anhängern', bewertet wird, kommt es an.'
    The translation of these passages in *The Theory of Social and Economic Organisation*, New York, 1947, pp. 358–9 is inaccurate ('The term "charisma" will be applied to a certain quality of an individual personality. . . .'). The clear distinction at which Max Weber finally arrived between a leader's 'objective' qualities (with which he was not concerned) and the collective beliefs of a group about his qualities is blurred, and with it one of the best examples of what 'understanding' meant for him.

7   Max Weber's italics.

8   The present standard translation of a large part of *Wirtschaft und Gesellschaft* under the title *The Theory of Social and Economic Organisation* (translated by A.M. Henderson and Talcott Parsons, New York, Oxford University Press, 1947) is often rather careless with regard to aspects of Weber's theories which the translators themselves regarded as not particularly significant. This is an example; apparently the translators attached no significance to the ambiguities in Max Weber's use of the word. One cannot follow Max Weber's efforts to distinguish between a leader's 'inherent individual qualities' (with which, as he sometimes – though not always – saw, the sociologist was not concerned) and the collective

belief about his qualities. For the time being anyone who wishes to probe into such problems will have to consult the German text. [These words were written before the publication of the excellent translation of *Wirtschaft und Gesellschaft*, edited by Guenther Roth and Claus Wittich: *Economy and Society: An Outline of Interpretative Sociology*. 3 vols, New York, Bedminster Press, 1968 – eds.]

9   Given the present state of Max Weber studies it is not easy to correlate the development of his concepts with the development and the experiences of Max Weber himself. As far as one can see he took over the concept of a charismatic rule from R. Sohm, and the mere theological connotation it had retained there during the 1914–18 war. His essays on the sociology of Hinduism with the references to the charisma of individuals and of groups, which have been quoted, were published first in 1916–17. The theoretical sections of *Wirtschaft und Gesellschaft*, which contain the more 'value-free', more detached versions of the concept charisma, were, according to Marianne Weber (*Max Weber: Ein Lebensbild*, Tübingen, Mohr (Siebeck), 1926, p. 679 [English translation by Harry Zohn, *Max Weber: A Biography*. New York, Wiley, 1975]), largely written 'in the last years of his life' – that is, probably between 1917 and 1920. It may be useful to remember that these years provided Max Weber with a number of practical experiences which had a bearing upon the concept of charisma. What we know of them indicates the strong personal significance which the concept of a charismatic leadership had for him. During these years of upheaval when it became increasingly clear that the old leading groups of Germany had signally failed and that new men would have to come to the fore, Max Weber felt very strongly that it was his task and his mission to give the nation – and particularly the younger generation – a lead. He was deeply convinced that the nation needed as leaders men like himself, non-aristocratic leaders amenable to adjustments and reforms, and at the same time able to steer the nation away from revolutionary innovations and to preserve the essential German traditions. But unlike some of the earlier sociologists – unlike, for instance, Comte, to whom in a comparable time of upheaval sociology itself, the scientific knowledge of society, appeared as the basis of his claim to a leading position in a period of social and political reconstruction – Max Weber, as far as one can see, kept his role as sociologist and his hoped-for role as political leader in separate compartments. It was as a potential charismatic leader that he saw himself, and a charismatic leader does not stand in need of sociology. He waited for a call; but the call of the nation never came.

However, he had during this period many practical experiences which may have contributed to his reflections on charismatic leadership. One of them was his vain attempt in 1918 at a student meeting in Heidelberg to rally around himself as leader the younger generation in order to resist to the death the occupation of German soil by Poles and other enemy troops. The attempt was received by the audience with 'icy silence'. His clear recognition, in the later versions of the concept, that the charisma of a leader fails if the followers do not believe in him and fail to respond to his mission, may owe something to this experience. His observations on the group charismatic claims of dynasties may have been influenced by the abdication of the Kaiser. He had urged that the Kaiser should abdicate of his own free will in order to preserve the imperial regime as such.

This proposal, too, remained without effect, as under the new German constitution he strongly advocated from about 1917–18 on that it should take the form of a 'plebiscitarian democracy' which might enable a charismatic leader to assert himself. Parliament should only function as a safeguard if the 'charisma' failed. His social ideals and his emotional involvements still obscured from his view the excesses of which a charismatic leader is capable, and the possibility that such a leader may not always give way to Parliament peacefully if the belief in his charismatic powers fades. However, in his own time this proposal did not materialize. Looking back at Max Weber's attainments as a teacher and scholar, one might think that it was in this field – in his role as a sociologist – that he found his greatest social fulfilment. In fact, particularly in the last years of his life when the end of the Imperial order appeared to give a man like himself his chance, he probably longed more than anything else for an opportunity to prove himself as a political – 'charismatic' – leader in the wider field.

It was in 1919 that his wife, as she reported (*Max Weber*, p. 723), hopefully said to him that in a few years when he would be older and healthier the nation might yet call him, to which he replied: 'I have the feeling that so far life has still denied something to me'.

An understanding of Weber's strong involvement in the ideal of charismatic leadership and of the personal significance it had for him is necessary if one is to appreciate the effort of detachment which enabled him in his scientific work to develop the concept into a tool of scientific analysis pure and simple. It is not surprising that he only partly succeeded.

The Breakdown of Civilization

1   See for example Dr. W.F. Könitzer and Hansgeorg Trurnit, eds., *Weltentscheidung in der Judenfrage: der Endkampf nach 3,000 Jahren Judengegnerschaft* [*World Verdict on the Jewish Question: the Final Struggle after 3,000 Years of Opposition to the Jews*]. Dresden, 1939.

2   The general problem of what sorts of beliefs can have this function and under what conditions lies beyond the framework of the present study. But even a limited study such as this may help people to see it in the right perspective and to appreciate its urgency.

The Civilizing Process Revisited

1   Talcott Parsons, *Essays in Sociological Theory* (Glencoe, 1953), pp. 359f.

2   Ibid., p. 359.

An Interview in Amsterdam

The interview took place on 23 December 1969.

1   Amitai Etzioni, *The Active Society*, New York: Free Press, 1968, p. 48.

2   See Norbert Elias, 'Problems of Involvement and Detachment,' *British Journal of Sociology*, VII (1956), pp. 226–52.

3   Maurice R. Stein, *The Eclipse of Community*, Princeton University Press, 1960, p. 329.

4   R. D. Laing, *The Politics of Experience*, Harmondsworth: Penguin Books, 1967,
     p. 50.

The Sciences

1   'At a constant temperature, the volume of a given quantity of any gas is inversely
     proportional to the pressure upon the gas.'
2   Whyte, L. L. (1965), 'Atomism, structure and form' in Kepes, G. (ed.), *Structure
     in Art and Structure in Science*, London: Studio Vista.

The Retreat of Sociologists into the Present

     I want to express by gratitude to Volker Meja for his great help in revising the
     original text for publication. I am also very grateful to my assistants Rudolf Knijff
     and Maarten van Bottenburg for helping me with the second part of this paper.

1   Since, viewed from the perspective of sociology, 'qualitative' is not the proper
     conceptual opposite of 'quantitative', one must search for a more appropriate
     term. Non-quantitative, or not exclusively quantitative, empirical sociological
     research is usually concerned with certain static and dynamic features of human
     groups. As an alternative to 'qualitative' I suggest 'figurational'.
2   The emphasis upon the reciprocity of economic and violence control functions
     (and of other vital functions as well) can perhaps appear as a purely theoretical
     advance in knowledge. In actual fact, it has far-reaching practical implications.
     To name only one of them: in the Soviet Union a monopolistic organization of
     violence control – and of knowledge control as well – has developed willy nilly in
     association with, one might even say in spite of, an officially sanctioned belief
     system which represents the development of the 'economic sphere' as the prin-
     cipal and often even as the sole driving force of social development. It represents
     the state organization merely as a superstructure in relation to the economic basis.
     In this case, the representation of the economic sphere as the basis of social devel-
     opment, and thus also of the social distribution of power, obviously conflicts with
     the observable course of events. It helps conceal the fact that control of the
     monopoly of physical violence can be as powerful a driving force of social devel-
     opment as the monopolistic control of the economy or, for that matter, of
     knowledge.
3   Perhaps we should also remember the walls around medieval castles and towns
     in order to better understand the degree of pacification of these societies. Garrelli,
     Le Proche-Orient Asiatique. Paris: Presses Universitaires de France, 1969.
4   It is not unlikely that priests, in the early stages of the growth of the temple organ-
     ization, combined with their priestly functions those of controllers of violence, of
     military protectors of the fields and the incipient irrigation systems. When in the
     course of time the balance of power between priestly and secular rulers shifted in
     favour of the latter, they – the leaders of troops, the military rulers – on their part
     often defunctionalized some of their priests and assumed priestly functions them-
     selves.

The Civilizing of Parents

1   N. Elias, *The Civilizing Process*. Oxford: Blackwell Publishers, 1994.
2   L. de Mause, 'The evolution of childhood' in L. de Mause (ed.), *The History of Childhood*. New York: Harper and Row, 1974: 25–6.
3   G. Kalow, *erdgaleere*. Munich, 1969: 38.
4   P. Ariès, *Centuries of Childhood*. Harmondsworth: Penguin, 1973: 396–7.
5   de Mause, *Childhood*, p. 5.
6   P. R. Gleichmann, 'Die Verhäuslichung körperlicher Verrichtungen' in P. R. Gleichmann, J. Goudsblom and H. Korte (eds) *Materialien zu Norbert Elias' Zivilisationstheorie*. Frankfurt a. M.: Suhrkamp, 1979, pp. 254–78.
7   Here we can note in this regard that in many societies we can observe both particular barriers between men and women and considerable distinctions between the standards of shame and embarrassment in both sexes, which stand in the closest relation to the unequal distribution of power potential between them.
8   The growing sensibility, the advancing thresholds of shame and embarrassment in relation to smells, particularly bodily odours, in the course of the civilizing process, perhaps requires closer examination. Today the sensitivity about *seeing* other people naked has reduced somewhat. But the sensitivity about other people's body odours has probably increased. Even talking about what one might experience here provokes feelings of embarrassment. Accordingly, industrial products to conceal or refine body odours flourish. On the other hand, adults' apparent discomfort in relation to children who cannot regulate their natural needs in time and space in the same way as adults often plays a not insignificant role in the relations between parents and children.
9   C. Wouters, 'Informalisation and the civilizing process' in P. R. Gleichmann, J. Goudsblom and H. Korte (eds) *Human Figurations*. Amsterdam: Amsterdams Sociologisch Tijdschrift, 1977, pp. 437–53.
10 *The United States Law Week*, Extra edition No. 1, *Supreme Court Opinions*, 47 (49) June 19, 1979. Here, then, we find the widespread legend that such a form of behaviour among parents is simultaneously an inborn instinct. The question is whether it is necessary for a higher court to call on traditions which contradict the current state of scientific knowledge.

Technization and Civilization

1   Elias, *Time: An Essay*, Oxford, Blackwell, 1992.
2   Robert Lacey, *Ford: The Man and the Machine*. London: Heinemann 1986.
3   O. Billian, *Beherrsche den Verkehr*. Zürich: Müller 1976.
4   Durkheim was probably the first to make use of statistical comparisons between different countries over a number of years to obtain a diagnostically precise definition of a social problem. He did this in an exemplary manner in his well-known book *Suicide* (1987). The comparative method is very promising, but its full potential can only be exploited to the full if it is utilized for recording development sequences, that is social processes. Table 28.2 is presented with this aim in mind. It indicates, to begin with, that the effectiveness of law-enforced regulation and of drivers' self-regulation for the prevention of injuries and deaths due to motor vehicle traffic differs between different European countries as well as

the United States and Japan. It shows this not only to be the case at any given time, but also that these differences vary relatively little over a developmental period of nearly thirty years. Table 28.3 shows comparable figures for some Asian and African countries, but in this case time-series data were not available for any significant period of time.

5   C.L. Mowat (ed.), *The Cambridge Modern History*, vol. 12, Cambridge: Cambridge University Press, 1960, p. 276.

6   Cf. Elias, *The Civilizing Process*, Oxford, Blackwell, 1994, pp. 3–41.

7   Or almost no one: in 1835 Alexis de Tocqueville, at the end of the first part of *Democracy in America* (vol. I, New York: Schocken, 1961, pp. 521–2) made his subsequently famous prediction that America and Russia would be the world powers of the future.

8   Elias, *The Civilizing Process*.

9   See N. Elias, 'Scientific Establishments', in N. Elias, H. G. Martins and R. Whitley (eds), *Scientific Establishments and Hierarchies*, Dordrecht: Reidel, 1982, pp. 3–70.

The Society of Individuals – III

1   One of the general features of a powerful philosophical tradition extending from classical epistemology to the metaphysical philosophies of recent times, whether they are more transcendentally, existentially or phenomenologically inclined, is that its exponents take the isolated individual as their starting point. The plurality of human beings appears in philosophy as, at most, a plurality of identical special cases of general laws or regularities. Classical physics was the godfather of this tradition. Its modes of thought, in combination with theological ones, are reflected in it. An attempt by Leibniz to introduce the plurality of human beings into philosophy failed. The notion of the windowless monad was invincible. Hegel's attempt to bring social processes into philosophy also failed.

2   Jean-Paul Sartre, *Nausea*, translated by Lloyd Alexander, London, 1962, p. 135.

3   J. P. Toussaint, *La Salle de bain*, Paris, 1985, p. 95.

Information and the Civilizing Process

1   N. Elias, *The Civilizing Process*, translated by Edmund Jephcott, Basil Blackwell, Oxford, 1994, p. 66. 'Thingis somtyme alowed is now repreuid', from Caxton's late fifteenth-century *Book of Curtesye*, p. 45v. 64.

2   Indeed, at first the problem of civilization appeared to me as a completely personal problem in connection with the great breakdown of civilized behaviour, the thrust towards barbarization, which was something totally unexpected, quite unimaginable, taking place under my own eyes in Germany. Under National Socialism, a latent tendency to let oneself go, to loosen the grip of one's own conscience, to roughness and brutality, which, as long as the external constraint of state control remained intact, could come out most informally in the private interstices of the network of state control, become formalized and, for established groups, elevated to a type of behaviour both demanded and supported by the state. Even as the question of the German spurt towards barbarization was becoming such an urgent issue for me, even as I was beginning to write my book on civi-

lization, it seemed to me to be totally inadequate to discuss this acute breakdown of civilizing controls simply as a problem for political scientists studying party doctrines – as a problem of fascism, as it would somewhat ashamedly be expressed today. That way, some of its central aspects could hardly be properly grasped. I was convinced that this could be done only if, as a social scientist, one could distance oneself sufficiently from the immediate situation, if one did not pose only such short-term questions as why the standard of civilized conscience broke down among a highly civilized people in the second quarter of the twentieth century.

First of all it seemed to me that we still knew absolutely nothing about how and why in the course of human development – and then, in closer focus, in European development – changes in behaviour and feeling took place in a civilizing direction. In a nutshell, one cannot understand the breakdown of civilized behaviour and feeling as long as one cannot understand and explain how civilized behaviour and feeling came to be constructed and developed in European societies in the first place. The ancient Greeks, for instance, who are so often held up to us as models of civilized behaviour, considered it quite a matter of course to commit acts of mass destruction, not quite identical to those of the National Socialists but, nevertheless, similar to them in certain respects. The Athenian popular assembly decided to wipe out the entire population of Melos, because the city did not want to join the Athenian colonial empire. There were dozens of other examples in antiquity of what we now call genocide.

The difference between this and the attempted genocide in the 1930s and 1940s is at first glance not easy to grasp. Nevertheless, it is quite clear. In the period of Greek antiquity, this warlike behaviour was considered normal. It conformed to the standard. People's conscience-formation, the structure of their personalities, was such that this sort of action seemed to them to be normal human behaviour. The way the conscience is formed in European societies – and, indeed, in large parts of humanity – in the twentieth century is different. It sets a standard for human behaviour against which the deeds of the National Socialists appear abhorrent, and are regarded with spontaneous feelings of horror. The problem I set myself to examine was, then, to explain and to make comprehensible the development of personality structures and especially of structures of conscience or self-control which represent a standard of humaneness going far beyond that of antiquity, and which accordingly make people react to behaviour like that of the National Socialists (or similar behaviour by other people) with spontaneous repugnance.

3   Andreae Capellani, *De amore libri tres*, ed. E. Trojel, Havniae, Copenhagen 1892, p. 235ff.

4   Cf. N. Elias, *The Civilizing Process*, 1994 edn p. 248, note 69; N. Elias, *The Court Society*, Oxford, Basil Blackwell, 1983, p. 48, note 15.

5   'Crass foxes' were in some ways equivalent to 'fags' in the British Public Schools. Each new member of a fraternity had to perform services for an older student (his *Leibbursche*) in return for which he was inducted by the latter into the fraternity, receiving also a degree of protection [translators' note].

6   *Time Magazine*, 27 November 1978, 'America's new manners', Letitia Baldridge, p. 47.

7　*The Amy Vanderbilt complete book of etiquette, a guide to contemporary living,* revised and expanded by Letitia Baldridge, New York, Doubleday 1978; quoted in *Time,* p. 48.

8　Cf. N. Elias, 'The changing balance of power between the sexes in the history of civilisation', in *Theory, Culture and Society* 4 (2–3) 1987: 287–316, especially pp. 287–90 [translators' note].

9　*Bielefelder Universitätszeitung,* no. 108, 12 December 1978.

10　Cas Wouters, 'Informalization and the civilizing process', in Peter Gleichmann, Johan Goudsblom and Hermann Korte, eds, *Human Figurations: Essays for/Aufsätze für Norbert Elias,* Amsterdam, Amsterdams Sociologisch Tijdschrift, 1977, pp. 437–53, p. 444. See also Wouters' essay, 'Developments in behavioural codes between the sexes: formalization and informalization in the Netherlands 1930–85', *Theory, Culture & Society,* 4 (2–3), 1987: 405–20. Compare also Christien Brinkgreve and Michel Korzec, *Margriet weet raad: Gevoel, gedrag, moraal in Nederland 1938–1978,* Utrecht/Antwerp, Het Spectrum, 1978 (summarized in English in 'Feelings, behaviour, morals in the Netherlands, 1938–78: analysis and interpretation of an advice column', *Netherlands Journal of Sociology,* 15 (2), 1979: 123–40). All three authors use their material both to test and to develop further my theory of civilization.
[Additional note by the translators: For further contributions to the discussion of informalizing processes and the so-called 'permissive society' see Christien Brinkgreve, 'On modern relationships: the commandments of the new freedom', *Netherlands Journal of Sociology,* 18 (1), 1982: 47–56, and the following essays by Cas Wouters: 'Formalization and informalization: changing tension balances in civilizing processes', *Theory, Culture & Society* 3 (1), 1986: 1–18; 'The sociology of emotions and flight attendants: Hochschild's *Managed Heart'*, *Theory, Culture & Society* 6 (1), 1989: 95–123; 'Social stratification and informalization in global perspective', *Theory, Culture & Society,* 7 (4), 1990: 69–90; 'On status competition and emotion management', *Journal of Social History,* 24 (4), 1991: 699–717.]

Mozart's Revolt

1　However, that his fantasies and feelings, and the passions that fed them, did not run away with him, that he was able to give their energy fresh and pristine expression in musical forms and thereby harness them, is an indication of adulthood – of successful sublimation.

2　Wilhelm A. Bauer and Otto E. Deutsch (eds), *Mozart, Briefe und Aufzeichnungen,* 7 vols, Kassel, 1962–75. Letter of 19 May 1781: III, p. 118.

3　In a letter of 4 November 1777 (*Mozart Briefe* II, p. 101) Mozart says he has written a concerto for the oboist of the Mannheim orchestra, who was 'mad with joy' about it. When he played the concerto on the piano in the room of the Mannheim conductor the listeners liked it very much. No one, Mozart adds ironically and not without bitterness, said that is was not well composed; but they ought to have asked the archbishop, he would soon have put them right.
This side of Mozart's relationship to his employer needs to be considered if one is to judge its outcome properly. To a member of the ruling class there was no question but that he had the necessary competence to judge on matters of music.

And if a servant was as proud of his ability as Mozart, he had to be shown that as a prince one always understood music better than a subject.

4   *Editor's note:* At this point there is a break in the original manuscript; the section which follows is headed Part 2 of 'Act IV' of the drama of Mozart's life ('Mozart in Vienna') and remains a fragment.

The Symbol Theory

1   Richard Kilminster has acted as editor of this paper. I am grateful to him. He has contributed much to whatever utility this paper may have. Obviously I alone am responsible for its weaknesses. The comments of Jan-Willem Gerritsen have been of great help to me and so has the continuous co-operation with my assistants Rudolf Knijff, Saskia Visser and Anne Gevers.

BIBLIOGRAPHY

Publications of Norbert Elias

In English (including translations from German)
1950a 'Studies in the Genesis of the Naval Profession.' *British Journal of Sociology* 1 (4): 291–309.
1950b 'Inquest On German Jewry.' (Review article of Eva G. Reichmann, *Hostages of Civilisation. A Study of the Social Causes of Antisemitism*). *Association of Jewish Refugees Information*, April, p. 5.
1956 'Problems of Involvement and Detachment.' *British Journal of Sociology* 7 (3): 226–52.
1964a 'The Break with Traditionalism: Report on the Discussion.' *Transactions of the Fifth World Congress of Sociology, Washington DC, September 1962* vol. 3, pp. 51–3. Leuven, International Sociological Association.
1964b 'Professions.' In: Julius Gould and William L. Kolb (eds), *A Dictionary of the Social Sciences*, p. 542, New York, Free Press.
1965 (with John L. Scotson) *The Established and the Outsiders. A Sociological Enquiry into Community Problems*. London, Frank Cass. [New edition, enlarged with an Introduction originally published in Dutch translation in 1976, London, Sage Publications, 1994.]
1966 (with Eric Dunning) 'Dynamics of Sport Groups with Special Reference to Football.' *British Journal of Sociology* 17 (4): 388–402. Reprinted in: Dunning, *The Sociology of Sport: A Selection of Readings* (London, Frank Cass, 1971), pp. 66–80 and in *Quest for Excitement* 1986, pp. 191–204.
1969a 'Sociology and Psychiatry', in S. H. Foulkes and G. Steward Prince (eds),

Psychiatry in a Changing Society, pp. 117–44. London, Tavistock.

1969b (with Eric Dunning) 'The Quest for Excitement in Leisure.' *Society and Leisure* 2, pp. 30–85. Reprinted in *Quest for Excitement*, 1986, pp. 63–90.

1970a *African Art from the Collection of Professor Norbert Elias, April 24th–June 14th 1970. Leicester Museum and Art Gallery*. Leicester, Leicester Museums.

1970b (with Eric Dunning) 'The Quest for Excitement in Unexciting Societies', in Günther Lüschen (ed.), *The Cross-Cultural Analysis of Sport and Games*, pp. 31–51. Champaign, Ill., University of Illinois Press.

1971a 'Foreword' to Eric Dunning (ed.), *The Sociology of Sport. A Selection of Readings*, pp. xi–xiii. London, Frank Cass.

1971b 'The Genesis of Sport as a Sociological Problem', ibid. pp. 88–115. Reprinted in *Quest for Excitement*, 1986, pp. 126–49.

1971c (with Eric Dunning) 'Folk Football in Medieval and Early Modern Britain', ibid., pp. 116–32. Reprinted in *Quest for Excitement*, 1986, pp. 175–90.

1971d (with Eric Dunning) 'Leisure in the Sparetime Spectrum', in Rolf Albonico and Katherina Pfister-Binz (eds), *Soziologie des Sports. Theoretische und methodische Grundlagen. Referate des 10. Magglinger Symposiums, 7. bis 13. September 1969 in Magglingen (Schweiz)*. Basel, Birkhäuser. Reprinted in *Quest for Excitement*, 1986, pp. 91–125.

1971e 'Sociology of Knowledge: New Perspectives.' *Sociology* 5 (2): 149–68 and (3): 355–70.

1972a 'Process of State Formation and Nation Building.' *Transactions of the Seventh World Congress of Sociology, Varna, September 1970*, vol. 3, pp. 274–84. Sofia, International Sociological Association.

1972b 'Theory of Science and History of Science: Comments on a Recent Discussion.' *Economy and Society* 1 (2): 117–33.

1973 'Dynamics of Consciousness within that of Societies.' *Transactions of the Seventh World Congress of Sociology, Varna, September 1970*, vol. 4, pp. 375–83. Sofia, International Sociological Association.

1974a 'The Sciences: Towards a Theory', in Richard Whitley (ed.), *Social Processes of Scientific Development*, pp. 21–42. London, Routledge and Kegan Paul.

1974b 'Towards a Theory of Communities', in Colin Bell and Howard Newby (eds), *The Sociology of Community. A Selection of Readings*, pp. ix–xli. London, Frank Cass.

1978a *The Civilizing Process*, Vol. 1, *The History of Manners*. Translation from German by Edmund Jephcott. New York, Urizen Books, and Oxford, Blackwell.

1978b *What is Sociology?* Translation from German by Stephen Mennell and Grace Morissey. London, Hutchinson.

1982a *The Civilizing Process*, vol. 2. Translation from German by Edmund Jephcott. Published under two different titles: *Power and Civility*, New York, Pantheon Books; and *State Formation and Civilization*, Oxford, Basil Blackwell [only the latter had Elias's approval].

1982b 'Civilization and Violence: On the State Monopoly of Physical Violence and Its Infringements.' Translation from German by David J. Parent. *Telos* 16, pp. 133–54.

1982c 'Scientific Establishments', in Norbert Elias, Herminio Martins and Richard

Whitley (eds), *Scientific Establishments and Hierarchies. Sociology of the Sciences Yearbook 1982*, pp. 3–70. Dordrecht, Reidel.

1982d (with Richard H. Whitley) 'Introduction', ibid., pp. vii–xi.

1982e 'What is the Role of Scientific and Literary Utopias for the Future?' In: *Limits to the Future. Prescriptions and Predictions in the Humanities and Social Sciences. Essays on the Occasion of the Second NIAS-Lustrum 1981*, Wassenaar, Netherlands Institute for Advanced Study.

1983a *The Court Society*. Translation from German by Edmund Jephcott. Oxford, Basil Blackwell, and New York, Pantheon Books.

1984a 'On the Sociogenesis of Sociology.' *Sociologisch Tijdschrift* 11 (1): 14–52.

1984b 'Some Remarks on the Problem of Work', in *Aktief, inaktief; de wederzijdse afhankelijkheid van aktieven en inaktieven in een verzorgingsstaat*, Noordwijkerhout, Centrum St. Bavo, pp. 5–8.

1985a *The Loneliness of the Dying*. Translation from German by Edmund Jephcott, with a new afterword by the author. Oxford, Basil Blackwell.

1986a (with Eric Dunning) *Quest for Excitement: Sport and Leisure in the Civilizing Process*. Oxford, Basil Blackwell.

1987a 'The Retreat of Sociologist into the Present.' Translation from German by Stephen Kalberg and Volker Meja, revised and enlarged by the author. *Theory, Culture and Society* 4 (2–3): 223–49.

1987b 'The Changing Balance of Power Between the Sexes – A Process-Sociological Study: The Example of the Ancient Roman State.' *Theory, Culture and Society*, 4 (2–3): 287–317.

1987c 'On Human Beings and Their Emotions: A Process-Sociological Essay.' *Theory, Culture and Society* 4 (2–3): 339–63. Reprinted in Mike Featherstone, Mike Hepworth and Bryan S. Turner (eds), *The Body: Social Process and Cultural Theory*, pp. 103–25. London, Sage, 1991.

1987d *Involvement and Detachment*. Oxford, Basil Blackwell.

1988a 'Violence and Civilization: The State Monopoly of Physical Violence and its infringements.' Translation from German, in J. Keane (ed.), *Civil Society and the State: New European Perspectives*. London, Verso.

1989a 'The Symbol Theory.' *Theory, Culture and Society* 6, pp. 169–217, 339–83 and 499–537.

1990 'Fear of Death', in Hans G. Kippenberg, Yme B. Kuiper and Andy F. Sanders (eds), *Concepts of Person in Religion and Thought*, pp. 159–71. Berlin, Mouton de Gruyter.

1991a *The Symbol Theory*. London, Sage.

1991b *The Society of Individuals*. Translation from German by Edmund Jephcott. Oxford, Basil Blackwell.

1992 *Time: An Essay*. Translation (in part) from German by Edmund Jephcott. Oxford, Blackwell.

1993 *Mozart: Portrait of a Genius*. Translation from German by Edmund Jephcott. Oxford, Polity Press.

1994a *The Civilizing Process*. One volume edition. Oxford, Basil Blackwell.

1994b *Reflections on a Life*. Translation (in part) from German by Edmund Jephcott. Oxford, Polity Press.

1995 'Technization and Civilization', *Theory, Culture and Society*, 12 (3): 7–42. Translation from German by Frank Pollock and Stephen Mennell, edited and with a foreword (pp. 1–5) by Stephen Mennell.

1996 *The Germans: Power Struggles and the Development of Habitus in the Nineteenth and Twentieth Centuries*. Translation from the German by Eric Dunning and Stephen Mennell, and with a preface by the translators. Oxford, Polity Press.

In German (not including translations from English)

1921 'Vom Sehen in der Natur.' *Blau-Weiß-Blätter: Führerzeitung* 2, pp. 133–44.

1924 (published under the name of Dr. Michael Elias) 'Anekdoten.' *Berliner Illustrierte Zeitung* 33, no. 29, 20 July 1924, p. 811–22.

1929 'Zur Soziologie des deutschen Antisemitismus.' *Israelitisches Gemeindeblatt* 7, no. 12, Mannheim, 13 December 1929, pp. 1–6.

1935a 'Kitschstil und Kitschzeitalter.' *Die Sammlung* 2 (5): 252–63.

1935b 'Die Vertreibung der Hugenotten aus Frankreich.' *Der Ausweg* 1 (12): 369–76.

1939 *Über den Prozeß der Zivilisation: Soziogenetische und psychogenetische Untersuchungen*. 2 vols. Basel, Haus zum Falken.

1960 'Die öffentliche Meinung in England', in *Vorträge gehalten anläßlich der Hessischen Hochschulwochen für staatswissenschaftliche Fortbildung, 18 bis 25. April 1959 in Bad Wildungen*, pp. 118–31. Bad Homburg, Max Gehlen.

1962 'Nationale Eigentümlichkeiten der englischen öffentlichen Meinung', in *Vorträge gehalten anläßlich der Hessischen Hochschulwochen für staatswissenschaftliche Fortbildung, 2. bis 8. Oktober 1960 in Bad Wildungen*, pp. 124–47. Bad Homburg, Max Gehlen.

1969c *Die höfische Gesellschaft: Untersuchungen zur Soziologie des Königstums und der höfischen Aristokratie, mit einer Einleitung: Soziologie und Geschichtswissenschaft*. Neuwied, Luchterhand.

1970c *Was ist Soziologie?* München, Juventa.

1977a 'Respekt und Kritik', in Norbert Elias and Wolf Lepenies, *Zwei Reden anläßlich der Verleihung des Theodor W. Adorno-Preises*, pp. 37–68. Frankfurt, Suhrkamp.

1977b 'Zur Grundlegung einer Theorie sozialer Prozesse.' Translation from English by Michael Schröter of the unpublished 'Towards a Theory of Social Processes', revised and enlarged by the author. *Zeitschrift für Soziologie* 6 (2): 127–49.

1978c 'Zum Begriff des Alltags.' In: Kurt Hammerich and Michael Klein (eds), *Materialien zur Soziologie des Alltags (Kölner Zeitschrift für Soziologie und Sozialpsychologie*, Sonderheft 20), pp. 22–9. Köln, Westdeutscher Verlag.

1978d 'Vorwort', in Renate Rubinstein, *Nichts zu verlieren und dennoch Angst. Notizen nach einer Trennung*. Translated from Dutch, pp 9–11. Frankfurt: Suhrkamp.

1980a 'Die Zivilisierung der Eltern', in Linde Burkhardt (ed.), *. . . und wie wohnst du?*, pp. 11–28, Berlin, Internationales Design Zentrum.

1980b 'Renate Rubinstein', in Elisabeth Borchers and Hans-Ulrich Müller-Schwefe (eds), *Im Jahrhundert der Frau*, pp. 169–70. Frankfurt, Suhrkamp.

1981 'Zivilisation und Gewalt. Über das Staatsmonopol der körperlichen Gewalt und seine Durchbrechungen', in Joachim Matthes (ed.), *Lebenswelt und soziale Probleme. Verhandlungen des 20. Deutschen Soziologentages zu Bremen 1980*, pp. 98–122. Frankfurt, Campus.

1982f 'Thomas Morus' Staatskritik. Mit Überlegungen zur Bestimmung des Begriffs "Utopie"', in Wilhelm Vosskamp (ed.), *Utopieforschung. Interdisziplinäre Studien zur neuzeitlichen Utopie*, vol. 2, pp. 101–50. Stuttgart, Metzlersche Verlagsbuchhandlung.

1982g *Über die Einsamkeit der Sterbenden in unseren Tagen*. Frankfurt, Suhrkamp.

'Soziologie in Gefahr. Plädoyer für die Neuorientierung einer Wissenschaft.' *Süddeutsche Zeitung*, 9 October 1982, p. 107.

1983b 'Über den Rückzug der Soziologen auf die Gegenwart.' *Kölner Zeitschrift für Soziologie und Sozialpsychologie* 35, pp. 29–40.

1983c 'L'espace privé – 'Privatraum' oder 'privater Raum'?', in *Séminaire 'À propos de l'histoire de l'espace privé'*, pp. 31–44. Berlin, Wissenschaftskolleg.

1983d 'Der Fußballsport im Prozeß der Zivilisation', in Modellversuch Journalistenweiterbildung an der FU Berlin (ed.), *Der Satz 'Der Ball ist rund' hat eine gewisse philosophische Tiefe. Sport, Kultur, Zivilisation*, pp. 12–21, Berlin.

1983e 'Zur Diagnose der gegenwärtigen Soziologie', in *Sozialwissenschaften und Berufspraxis*, pp. 6–19, Kiel.

1984c 'Nachwort', in Meike Behrman and Carmine Abate, *Die Germanesi*, pp. 197–202. Frankfurt, Campus.

1984d 'Notizen zum Lebenslauf', in Peter Gleichmann, Johan Goudsblom and Hermann Korte (eds), *Macht und Zivilisation. Materialien zu Norbert Elias' Zivilisationstheorie*, pp. 9–82. Frankfurt, Suhrkamp.

1984e 'Vorwort' to Horst-Volker Krumrey, *Entwicklungsstrukturen von Verhaltensstandarden*, pp. 11–15. Frankfurt, Suhrkamp.

1985b 'Das Credo eines Metaphysikers. Kommentare zur Popper's *Logik der Forschung*.' *Zeitschrift für Soziologie* 14 (2): 94–114.

1985c 'Gedanken über die Bundesrepublik.' *Merkur* 39 (9–10): 733–55.

1985d *Humana Conditio. Beobachtungen zur Entwicklung der Menschheit am 40. Jahrestag eines Kriegsendes (8. Mai 1985)*. Frankfurt, Suhrkamp.

1985e 'Vorwort' to Michael Schröter, *Wo zwei zusammenkommen in rechter Ehe*, pp. vii–xi. Frankfurt, Suhrkamp.

1985f 'Wissenschaft oder Wissenschaften? Beitrag zu einer Diskussion mit wirklichkeitsblinden Philosophen.' *Zeitschrift für Soziologie* 14 (4): 268–81.

1986b 'Figuration', 'Soziale Prozesse' and 'Zivilisation.' In: Bernhard Schäfers (ed.), *Grundbegriffe der Soziologie*, pp. 88–91, 234–41, 382–87. Opladen, Leske und Budrich.

1986c 'Über die Natur' *Merkur* 10, pp. 469–81.

1986d 'Wandlungen der Machtbalance zwischen den Geschlechtern. Eine prozeßsoziologische Untersuchung am Beispiel des antiken Römerstaats.' *Kölner Zeitschrift für Soziologie und Sozialpsychologie* 38, pp. 425–49.

1986e 'Hat die Hoffnung noch eine Zukunft?' *Die Zeit*, 26 December, p. 29.

1986f 'Conditio Humana: Beobachtungen über die Entwicklung der Menschheit', in Hartmut Krauß, Helmut Skowronek and Gerhard Trott (eds), *Bielefelder Universitätsgespräche 2*, pp. 4–10. Bielefeld, Universität Bielefeld.

1987e *Los der Menschen: Gedichte – Nachdichtungen*. Frankfurt, Suhrkamp.

1987f *Die Gesellschaft der Individuen*. Frankfurt, Suhrkamp.

1987g 'Thomas Morus und die Utopie', in Hans-Jürg Braun (ed.), *Utopien – Die*

Möglichkeit des Unmöglichen, pp. 173–84. Zürich, Verlag der Fachvereine.

1987h 'Das Schicksal der deutschen Barocklyrik zwischen höfischer und bürgerlicher Tradition.' *Merkur* 41, pp. 451–68.

1987i 'Vorwort' to Bram van Stolk and Cas Wouters, *Frauen im Zwiespalt: Beziehungsprobleme in Wohlfahrtsstaat* pp. 9–16. Frankfurt, Suhrkamp.

1988b 'Was ich unter Zivilisation verstehe. Antwort auf Hans Peter Duerr.' *Die Zeit*, 17 June 1988, pp 37–8.

1989b *Studien über die Deutschen: Machtkämpfe und Habitusentwicklung im 19. und 20. Jahrhundert.* Frankfurt, Suhrkamp.

1989c 'Als Assistent Karl Mannheims in der interdisziplinären Diskussion.' In: Bertram Schefold (ed.), *Wirtschafts- und Sozialwissenschaftler in Frankfurt am Main. Erinnerungen an die Wirtschafts- und Sozialwissenschaftliche Fakultät und an die Anfänge des Fachbereichs Wirtschaftswissenschaften der Johann Wolfgang Goethe-Universität*, pp. 96–9. Marburg, Metropolis.

1989d 'Der charismatische Herrscher.' *Der Spiegel*, no. 2, 1989, pp. 42–4.

1989e *Norbert Elias über sich selbst*. Frankfurt, Suhrkamp.

1991c *Mozart: Zur Soziologie eines Genies*. Frankfurt, Suhrkamp.

References cited in the Editors' Introductions

Brown, Richard, 'Norbert Elias in Leicester: Some Recollections'. *Theory, Culture and Society* 4 (1987), pp. 533–540.

Cohen, Percy S., *Modern Social Theory*, London: Heinemann 1968.

Eldridge, John, 'Sociology in Britain: A Going Concern'. In Christopher G. A. Bryant and Henk A. Becker (eds) *What Has Sociology Achieved?* London: Macmillan 1990, pp. 157–78.

Freud, Sigmund, *New Introductory Lectures on Psychoanalysis*, trans. James Strachey. New York: Norton [1933] 1964, p. 179.

Gleichmann, Peter R., Johan Goudsblom, and Hermann Korte (eds), *Human Figurations. Essays for / Aufsätze für Norbert Elias*. Amsterdam: Amsterdams Sociologisch Tijdschrift 1977.

Goudsblom, Johan 1977a, 'Responses to Norbert Elias's Work in England, Germany, the Netherlands and France'. In Gleichmann, Goudsblom and Korte, (eds). *Human Figurations*, 1977, pp. 37–98.

Goudsblom, Johan, *Sociology in the Balance. A Critical Essay*. Oxford: Basil Blackwell, 1977b.

Goudsblom, Johan, 'Introduction: Twenty Years of Figurational Sociology in the Netherlands'. In Kranendonk, 1990, pp. 13–27.

Hackeschmidt, Jörg, *Von Kurt Blumenfeld zu Norbert Elias oder Die Erfindung einer jüdischen Nation*. Hamburg: Europäische Verlagsanstalt 1997.

Hurd, Geoffrey, et al., *Human Society: An Introduction to Sociology*. London: Routledge and Kegan Paul 1973.

Hurd, Geoffrey, et al., *Human Society: An Introduction to Sociology*. 2nd edn, London: Routledge and Kegan Paul 1986.

Korte, Hermann, *Über Norbert Elias. Das Werden eines Menschenwissenschaftlers*. Opladen: Leske und Budrich [1988] 1997.

Kranendonk, Willem, *Society as Process: A Bibliography of Figurational Sociology in the*

Netherlands. Amsterdam: Publikatiereeks Sociologisch Instituut 1990.

Mannheim, Karl, 'Competition as a Cultural Phenomenon' (1928). In Meja and Stehr (eds) *Knowledge and Politics*. London 1990, pp. 53–85.

Meja, Volker, and Nico Stehr (eds), *Knowledge and Politics: The Sociology of Knowledge Dispute*. London: Routledge 1990.

Mennell, Stephen, *Norbert Elias, Civilization and the Human Self-Image*. Oxford: Basil Blackwell 1989.

Scheff, Thomas J., *Bloody Revenge: Emotions, Nationalism and War*. Boulder, CO: Westview Press 1994.

Stammer, Otto (ed.), *Max Weber and Sociology Today*. Oxford: Basil Blackwell 1971.

Wilson, Bryan, *The Noble Savages. The Primitive Origins of Charisma and its Contemporary Survival*. Berkeley: University of California Press 1975.

NAME
INDEX

SUBJECT INDEX